THE
FEMALE
POWER
WITHIN

A Guide to Living a Gentler,
More Meaningful Life

THE
FEMALE
POWER
WITHIN

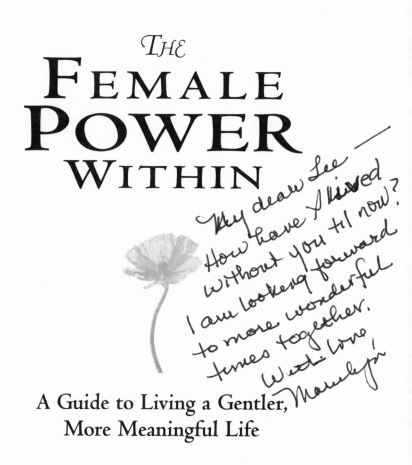

My dear Lee —
How have I lived
without you til now?
I am looking forward
to more wonderful
times together.
With love,
Marilyn

A Guide to Living a Gentler, More Meaningful Life

Marilyn Graman and Maureen Walsh

with Hillary Welles

L·IFE
WORKS
BOOKS

New York 2002

Life Works Books
55 Fifth Avenue – Penthouse
New York, NY 10003, U.S.A.
www.lifeworksbooks.com

This publication is designed to provide accurate and authoritative information in regard to the subject matter covered. It is sold with the understanding that the publisher is not engaged in rendering legal, accounting, or other professional service. If legal advice or other expert assistance is required, the services of a competent professional should be sought.—*From a Declaration of Principles Jointly Adopted by a Committee of the American Bar Association and a Committee of Publishers and Associations*

Names of persons used in stories and examples have been changed to protect the person's privacy. Any similarity to any known persons living or dead is purely coincidental.

Catalog-in-Publication Data

Graman, Marilyn.
    The female power within : a guide to living
    a gentler, more meaningful life /
    Marilyn Graman and Maureen Walsh ;
    with Hillary Welles.--1st ed.
    p. cm.
    Includes bibliographical references.
    ISBN 0-9718548-2-3

    1. Women--Psychology.   2. Self-actualization
    (Psychology)   3. Femininity (Philosophy)
    4. Success--Psychological aspects.
    I. Walsh, Maureen.   II. Title.

HQ1206.G73 2002   158.1'082
                    QB102-701383

LCCN 2002091283

Cover design by John Buse

Page design by Jason Gray

Printed on acid-free paper in the United States of America.

2 3 4 5 6 7 8 9 10   First Edition 2002

For all the women known and yet to come
who by their use of the information contained here
help uncover our collective female power.

Contents

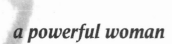

a powerful woman

knows that she can change
her world gracefully.

a powerful woman

opens her arms and embraces
what comes toward her.

Imagine a world where every woman has the opportunity and encouragement to be herself.

A world where success is not measured by how many deals you make or whether or not you have children, but by how authentically you are living.

A world where each woman is at peace with her power.

We envision the creation of this new world as each woman steps into the light of her power. Our world is hungry for tenderness, nurturing, communication, and cooperation. Without it, how can we end violence, disease, or world hunger? How can we save our ecosystem or help each individual to be the best person they can be?

We have the freedom to uncover our power and use it however it works best for us—for personal satisfaction, for mental health, for general well-being, to be able to enjoy the journey, to be able to experience creativity, to be an available mother, a patient friend, a generous coworker, a sharing wife, and a sensual woman. Coming into your power is not about getting stronger than someone else. Coming into your power means each of us getting as powerfully female and authentic as we can be.

How will you become that version of yourself?

In the pages that follow we will show you what has worked for thousands of women.

You have already begun.

a powerful woman

*knows that the resources she needs
are available to her.*

a powerful woman

*enjoys leaning back, allowing
a life of ease and grace.*

Introduction

Thanks to the work of countless extraordinary women, women today truly do have unlimited choices. We no longer have to live the lives designed for us by our mothers, fathers, teachers, ministers, magazine editors, or peers; we are free to look within and find what is true and right for us as individuals and to design our lives so they fit *us*. We are the first generations with this freedom and we have no role models. How, then, do we go about exercising our power of choice? How do we even begin to know what is authentic for us?

If, like us, you are a woman of the baby boom generation, you may have found yourself—back in the 1960s, 70s, and 80s—on the front lines of feminism, fighting passionately for your rights and your freedom. The anger we felt then fueled us well for the extraordinary revolution that needed to happen. We concentrated on changing what needed to be transformed externally in the culture because the external transformation had to happen first—not just for ourselves but for all future generations of women. It is through our efforts that women today have choices and possibilities we have never had before. There is no question that we brought about a radical culture shift.

The anger that fueled feminism no longer serves us. Being angry keeps us in reaction to what is happening or what we perceive is happening. It's time now to release that anger and relax into the understanding that we have accomplished much of what we set out to accomplish. And now we have the opportunity to use our energy to explore ourselves and allow ourselves to discover what is authentic for us as individuals.

If you are in your twenties and thirties, you may not identify with feminism because you were born into a world already changed by it. You are free to concentrate on finding your own path in life in ways your mother was not. But you may be afraid that you don't know how to do it—that if you don't do it right, you will not be powerful.

Our newfound freedom and opportunity brings new challenges and frustrations as we begin to look inward to what is authentic for each of us. Until now, we have looked to men as role models for how to be powerful. We saw that to succeed in a male-dominated culture we needed to use our male side—charging ahead, climbing the corporate ladder, and thrusting ourselves forward into the world. We needed to prove that we could succeed in the male culture, and now we know we can.

We suggest that comparing ourselves to men has become a glass ceiling for us. We have gotten distracted by looking at men's lives to see how our own lives are going, and this serves to limit our true self-expression. Looking to men for an indication of how we should live authentically simply does not work. To borrow a feminist slogan of the 1970s, comparing a woman to a man is like comparing a fish to a bicycle. Deep inside us we all know that being like men only goes so far for us as women. This knowingness opens us to a discussion of what a natural, authentic, powerful *female* life might look like.

Just what does success look like if it is neither living the lives our mothers led nor living lives based on men's lives? The answer is different for each woman. We have to be willing to move things around so that our lives work for us, and since there are few role models, we have to create the path ourselves. This book is here to help you find your unique path to your natural, female power.

What you will discover is that being authentic needn't involve blood, sweat, or tears. On the contrary, living your life in an authentic way can sometimes feel amazingly effortless and smooth. You are not trying to be someone else or live up to someone else's expectations of you; you are being *you.* You don't need to compare yourself to others, because you know you are making the best use of your talents and interests in a way that no one else could. What this involves, of course, is the willingness to discover *what has been in the way* of your authenticity.

One obstacle for so many of us is the old sense that being strong means being strident and forceful. That's a very male view of power. Yes, it used to be that to be heard in the male culture a woman had to be aggressive in a male way—but this didn't make her a strong *woman,* just a woman using her male side powerfully.

You probably already express yourself authentically in some areas of your life, but every one of us, simply because we are human, has had experiences that have closed off vital parts of ourselves. Those areas now need our nurturing, tenderness, and attention. Opening to those parts is what we'll be doing throughout this book.

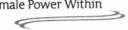

Revealing Our Power

As you begin this journey, we ask you to hold this thought: *You are already as powerful as you will ever be.* You may not have known your power, but that doesn't mean you don't have it. Everyone is endowed with power. It is not something you have to acquire. All the power you will ever need is already in you. The work here is to uncover it, allow it, accept it, honor it, move with it.

Michelangelo, one of the greatest sculptors of all time, said he could look at a block of marble and see the figures trapped inside it waiting to be released. In Michelangelo's famous series of partially completed statues, the figures seem to strain to emerge from unfinished blocks of marble. Unfinished faces look out of their prisons of stone and the fingers of unfinished hands reach out as if trying to pull themselves into existence. If you were standing in front of these works of art, you might imagine—as Michelangelo did—that completed figures truly exist inside the marble, waiting to be released.

Like Michelangelo's unfinished statues, each of us has incredible power already within us—and releasing it begins with clearing away what is obscuring it. Layers of cultural expectations, old beliefs, limiting ideas of who we are and what we can expect in life, lack of self-love, and psychological compensations and defenses stand in the way of being our authentic and powerful selves. When we identify and gently remove these layers, our selves can emerge whole and magnificent.

We each know, at some level, that we have something extraordinary within us that wants to be revealed. This book is here to help you remove the obstacles to that something, to help you see what keeps you from being boldly, beautifully, naturally yourself. Your sculpture will not look like anyone else's because you are one of a kind. You will bring your own magnificence to the discovery of your power as you become the best and truest version of yourself you can be—and only you know what that work of art looks like.

No one else but you can assess if you are having the life you are meant to have, or making your authentic contribution. Whether that means planting beautiful roses in your garden for all to enjoy or developing a cure for cancer, determining your authentic expression is up to you. There is no right or wrong way to do the Natural Power Work. There is only *your* way, and your way is perfect for you.

How to Use This Book

The insights in this book originated in a weekend workshop called the Natural Power of Being a Woman and weekly groups called The Gathering that began in 1988 in New York City. At one time we also offered workshops in Dallas and San Francisco. Since the first workshop we have been on a remarkable journey with many women who have uncovered how to live a fulfilling life as a strong, tender woman who can use her power gracefully and fully. We have seen so many women's lives transform from doing this work that we wanted to write a book to share the possibilities with you.

Being With This Book

Our approach is female, which means that it's nurturing, empowering, gentle, and supportive. We focus on the process rather than the result, and we hold the female belief that wherever you are is where you need to be and whatever is coming your way is for the good. We ask that you be open to this softer, female way, which allows you to relax into the work and let it wash over and through you.

As you read, we ask that you be willing to be nurturing and forgiving to yourself so that you can enjoy the process of learning, stretching, and finding out what is authentic for you. Often in life many different things are true at once, like "I want to have a child," "I want to have a full-time career," "I want time for myself," "I want to stay home with my child," and "I want an outlet for my creativity." One of our desires for the book is to help ease your anxiety about these conflicts by knowing that all things can be true, even if they seem contradictory, and to help you trust that eventually an authentic solution will emerge—often in ways you couldn't have imagined.

This kind of leaning back and allowing is a very female position, and we encourage you to take this wider view as you read the book. What will emerge is that you will see yourself as a unique light designed to interact in the world in your own authentic way—a way that includes the ability to be completely human, make mistakes, and learn from what other women are contributing. From your leaning-back position you will begin to have a different perspective on yourself and your life that will allow you to have more power in it.

As you read, expect that there may be times you will yawn, forget what you have read, feel a little sleepy. This is because our approach is intended to soothe, to allow you to have a relaxing, nurturing, tender, and accepting experience. The way we ask questions may seem new to you; they are designed to access your female side. The same is true for our use of language. At first you may find our passive phrasing a little awkward. A female way of expressing ourselves is often not efficient or *to the point.* Again, we are more interested in process than outcome, and we wrote the book to reflect that.

Throughout the book we will ask many questions designed to have you begin to see yourself differently. When you see a question in ***boldface italics***, we ask that you stop for a moment and consider the question before proceeding. You need not feel compelled to answer it; just spend a few moments letting it in.

At the end of many sections, you will find "uncoverings"—questions, statements, meditations—designed to have you bring the ideas we are working with into your own life. Sometimes the questions or statements are open-ended. That is deliberate; they are phrased to create an opening inside you, to help you look at something differently. Often a shift in perception is all that is needed to have your life be different. It works best to write down your responses and to record as many responses to each idea as you can—at least eight—without analyzing them or thinking too much. The first few responses are generally the ones you already know; the later responses will reveal deeper information. It is important to remember that this work is not about judging how you are doing. There are no right or wrong responses.

We have woven many women's stories into the fabric of this book (names have been changed to protect the women's privacy). These stories reflect the experiences of the women who have been doing the Natural Power Work at our Workshops and Gatherings. We hope that the stories will move, inspire, and support you as you do your own work.

Following are some suggestions for ways of being with the book.

Allow things to be easy

It is easy to go through life with your arms crossed in front of you, not even noticing what is right there. When you open your arms and invite change, you are far more likely to notice it when it appears. As you read this book, imagine yourself standing with arms spread wide at the bottom of a slide, knowing that what you want will come to you.

Change doesn't have to be hard work. We ask that you be open to having something shift easily and gracefully. When it does, allowing yourself to feel delighted will get you comfortable with the ability to transform the texture and outcome of your life.

You may find some of the "uncoverings" in the book easier to do than others. You won't always be able to complete each one. You may find that you want to skip over certain questions or return to them later. That's fine. This isn't a contest. What we suggest is that you lean back, take a few deep breaths, and just allow the material in. What you choose to do with it is up to you.

You may find yourself disagreeing with some of the things we say. Approaching the work in a female way means opening your arms and embracing all of it, even if you don't necessarily agree with it. Sometimes discomfort is a good thing because it means change is taking place, and changing can be uncomfortable. Allowing yourself to sit with the material, letting yourself be with unanswered questions, and allowing yourself to notice your level of ease encourages an environment for change.

Be open to subtle shifts

The Female Power Work is subtle. Change probably won't hit you like a tidal wave, but rather might gently stream into your life. Like an underground spring, it may be happening under the surface, and only a little trickles into daylight. As you continue adopting and practicing this way of being naturally yourself, the trickle may continue until one day you might notice it has created a river.

This approach may be different than any you have experienced before. It is designed to have you shift your perception, as if you were tilting your head slightly to look at something from a different angle. This is how change happens; it begins with something as subtle as a shift in how you see. Changing your perception allows you to have different thoughts. And having different thoughts allows for different feelings. Different feelings will often lead to different action. And taking a different action produces a different result.

Begin a practice

With this Female Power Work we are asking you to begin a practice. A practice is something that you decide to take on because you sense that it will be good for you. It is something you agree with yourself to do. A practice has a wavelike motion because its course may not always be steady. It may be that you do it, and do it, and do it—then you don't do it. When you notice you are not doing it, you start doing it again. You do it, and do it, and do it—and then you don't do it. Eventually you notice once again that you are not doing it. You notice, and you notice, and you don't do it—and then you begin doing it again.

A female view of practice is that the *not* doing it is part of the ebb and flow of it. Knowing this allows you to be gentle with yourself when you notice you're not doing it. This forgiving way to bring change recognizes that you are human and won't do things perfectly. If you expect you will do it every day for the rest of your life without fail, you are much more likely to quit the minute you notice you've stopped. Expecting that you will stop doing the practice and then start again prevents you from giving up entirely the first time you stop.

Giving up when you notice you've stopped is like giving up a diet the first time you eat a cookie. A diet that really works has the cookie built in from the beginning. It doesn't mean that now it's OK to eat a whole chocolate cake, but it does mean accepting eating the cookie as a part of the practice of designing a new eating plan. This is a female way: gentle, caring, and supportive of yourself.

Be gentle with yourself as you go through the hard parts

As you do this work, it will benefit you to expect resistances. You may not know exactly what they'll be, but when they come you can say, "Here are the resistances I expected." You *will* move through them—perhaps a great deal more easily than you thought you would. You are worth going through the hard parts. Be gentle and tender with yourself.

It's easy to have a positive relationship with yourself when things are going your way. It's when things get hard that we often break our loving relationship with ourselves. Tragically, our tendency as human beings is to stop at the hard part as if we are not worth living through the difficulty—even though it is that very passage through difficulty that will get us where we want to go. Look back on your life so far and you will probably see that some of the most difficult times were actually very powerful because they demanded that you grow and change.

Often the way to help yourself is to look at a situation in retrospect so you can see what you could have done. Then next time you get to the same place you may have something new to try. Imagine being a good mother to yourself and giving yourself the nurturing and support you needed as a child. You deserve the time and attention it takes to have your life be the way you want it.

Find support

The 80s icon of Superwoman doing it all on her own made us feel we needed to be fiercely independent, perfect at everything, have it all, and do it ourselves without help. Coming from a more female consciousness, we can see that a powerful woman allows support in. She knows she is strong while someone else is helping her, and accepting support doesn't in any way diminish her power. Finding others who will support you will relieve and bolster you as you do the Female Power Work and become more yourself.

What you need for support may look different from what your best friend needs. Everyone feels supported in different ways. You may find that you want to share parts of your experience with others. It will support you to select people who listen in ways that give you room to grow. You may notice that in the presence of certain people you feel powerful, and in the presence of others you feel self-conscious. If you feel self-conscious in someone's presence, that person is probably listening to you critically. If you feel intelligent when you are talking to someone, that person is likely expecting the best of you.

Women in our Gatherings find support in seeing each other grow and change. As part of each Gathering the women all get an opportunity to sit in a thronelike chair we call the Magnificence Chair. When a woman is in the Magnificence Chair, she can share her experience with the other women in the Gathering, knowing she is being fully listened to and supported to be magnificent.

You may find other ways of supporting yourself, like attending uplifting events, meeting with friends, taking walks in the woods, getting plenty of sleep, eating healthfully, having fun, or trying something adventurous. You deserve all the support you can find during your process, and part of getting support is knowing what will be good and right for you as you proceed. You may try something and discover it is not good and right for you, and then you can simply turn around and try something else. You are already supporting yourself by taking the time to read this book and do the uncoverings; this is supporting you becoming more you.

Supporting yourself

There are a few things we want you to do in preparation:

Find or purchase a notebook. Your notebook will serve as your companion as you work through this book. It will be the place where you will record your answers to the questions and uncoverings. Choose a notebook that you feel comfortable writing in. You will undoubtedly find it useful to have a written record of your process. Since the female way is subtle, often the process of uncovering is a series of small yet powerful shifts. It is important to be noticing how the texture of your life is changing—whether you have more ease, contentment, satisfaction, tenderness, grace, liveliness, and whether you are moving in your own direction. Looking back on your notebook entries will show you how far you have come.

Find pictures of yourself as a little girl at different ages. See what you discover about yourself. We will be using these pictures in specific uncoverings.

Find pictures or images of women who exemplify womanliness for you. They may be pictures of women in magazines, famous women who are strong and womanly, personal role models, pictures in a book, or pictures of friends or family members. As we explore the nature of women's power and what it means to be a strong womanly woman, it will be supportive to refer to examples.

What Lies Ahead

Coming into your natural power means healing your past, making available to yourself all the energy you use trying to live a life designed by others, and beginning to create the future you want—one that may end up being different from anything you've known so far. As you read this book you will journey through all the days of your life and into the future.

In Part One, you will begin to understand the true nature of your female power and your authentic self. In Part Two, you will see the forces of history and personal experience that helped you form the experience of power you now hold. All of these chapters will ground you in the concepts you will bring into your Natural Power practice in Part Three. In Part Three, you will go deeply into yourself, discovering your power centers and all the parts of yourself that make you who you are. Then, as you begin to live authentically in the present, the chapters in Part Four will help you create the future you want and deserve as the tender, powerful woman you truly are.

Welcome to the Gathering.

Part One

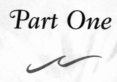

The Present:

Understanding Your Power

a powerful woman

*knows that she is powerful when
she is tender, nurturing,
and empowering.*

a powerful woman

*knows that no one is like her and
knows she is a unique
contribution.*

1

Enjoying What Comes Naturally

Your Female Nature

What would life be like if...
you knew that your female nature is extraordinarily powerful?

Just what *is* our female nature? It is an energy that is soft, tender, and nurturing—a quiet energy that doesn't thrust itself forward. Because it is quiet and tender, it is easily lost amid the forcefulness and loudness of male energy. Male power, male energy, crackles and makes itself heard—it pushes forward, seizes opportunities, climbs the corporate ladder, wages war, makes a killing in the stock market, and plays football. Male power establishes hierarchies and encourages competition. The military, the corporate structure, and sports teams are all examples of male power.

Female power is like a soft and gentle light, and because it is subtle it can be easy to miss. It can accomplish many tasks simultaneously, see who needs help and offer it freely, and create a home to be a place of rest. Female power knows how to follow when dancing and knows how to soothe scraped knees and bruised egos. It works to include everyone and can be genuinely happy for a coworker's success. Female power can bring people together over good food and conversation, plan projects in cooperation with others, talk things over, stimulate new ideas, help others realize their potential, soothe a hurt, accomplish many tasks at once, attend to details, meet deadlines, include everyone, and create a nurturing environment.

When you are being tender with someone, you are being powerful because you are letting the soft light of your female nature shine. The trouble is, female power is often not experienced as power at all because it doesn't feel, look, or sound the way we, until now, expect power to feel, look, or sound. There is no force to your female power, and it makes no sound. It doesn't have the crackling energy of male power. Its soft light cannot be forced to appear but can only be revealed through the process of getting to know your self.

Your power as a woman doesn't lie outside you, in what you *do*, but within you, in your true nature—the authentic you who was there the moment you were born. You might call it your spirit or your soul. In the Natural Power Work we think of our true nature as a light that has always been inside us and will always be there until we pass out of our bodies. The process of living as a human being tends to have us stifle or hide our light. Natural Power Work is about finding it again.

Being powerfully female doesn't mean that you give up the male aspects of you that work in your life, but to the extent you are repressing or denying your female nature you might notice you are missing some of your natural self-expression. Coming to your female nature will allow you to experience it with more awareness.

Make no mistake. Your female nature is extraordinarily powerful. While we're often told otherwise, there is power in our natural desire to nurture ourselves and others. There is power in expressing tenderness and in allowing ourselves to be soft and gentle in our approach. There is power in our natural ability to facilitate communication and stimulate cooperation. There is power in our natural healing ability and in our capacity to empower others. There is power in attracting to ourselves what is good for us. There is power in the creativity that stems from our ability to create new life. There is power in envisioning and there is power in our intuition.

Imagine that you're watching a board meeting for an arts organization. The middle-aged, mostly male board members engage in heated debate over an important issue. Frances, an older woman, also on the board, sits quietly knitting as the argument rages on. The others ignore her, assuming that she is preoccupied. Suddenly she looks up, speaks a quiet sentence, and in doing so changes the entire course of the conversation before going back to her handiwork. In an unselfish act of empowerment, she has facilitated cooperation and communication among the members of the board. This is an example of female power. It is quiet, to the point, and often not noticed—and it changes the course of events in a subtle way.

Think of a time...
when you needed nurturing and no one was there to care for you, and you will see how powerful nurturing is.

Think of a time...
when two people needed to make themselves understood and they weren't listening to each other, and you will see how powerful communication is.

Think of a situation...
that needed a soft, gentle approach and no one was being tender, and you can see how powerful tenderness is.

When you remember situations that needed the female qualities of nurturing, communication, or tenderness, you can feel the sadness of them—and yet if nurturing, communication, and tenderness had been there you might not have noticed because the situation was working well. That's the way female power often works. It just quietly allows the world to work by having it be gentler, more understanding, more cooperative, and more nurturing. It doesn't force itself or demand to be noticed, but adds to the quality and texture of our lives.

Looking at lovemaking between a man and a woman is another way to understand the nature of your female power. During sex, a man's power is in moving forward, thrusting, and using force. A woman's power is in leaning back, opening, and allowing. Women can't do without men being the way they are, and men can't do without women being the way we are. For a successful outcome in lovemaking, it is as powerful for you to lean back and allow yourself to be vulnerable as it is for the man to thrust forward. There is power in leaning back, there is power in opening, and there is power in receiving.

Seeing the power in leaning back, opening, and receiving gives you a different way to think about your life. Instead of feeling the pressure to rush out and grab what you want, you can envision what you want and then open your arms and invite life in. Rather than trying to be someone who *makes* things happen or forces things to happen, you can simply be open and available for the best possible things to happen. Our power comes from experiencing its unfolding and enjoying the journey rather than only focusing on results.

Women enjoy being in the richness of experience—think about how you interact with your women friends. We enjoy talking about something, trying it out, discussing how it worked or didn't work, trying it again, and discussing it again. Often, this experience alone is satisfying and we don't need to have a certain result to feel "successful." We know that somehow in the future we will use what we just discovered or uncovered, and that we can sit with it patiently for a while before using it.

Men are more result-oriented. If eleven women were together on a Sunday afternoon with nothing to do, we would never think up football. Football requires the same skills men historically used as hunters and protectors. It is the modern version of "survival of the fittest." Football emphasizes the male qualities of quick strategizing and the use of strength and force. It involves getting there as fast as possible, understanding that some will be flattened along the way.

Because male power is based on survival of the fittest, it creates hierarchies. When men were protecting the caves, there had to be one person clearly in charge. If quick action needed to be taken, there was no time for everyone to discuss their individual opinions. The military is a modern example of a male hierarchy. It is based on a rigid power structure where everyone knows their place, from new recruits up to the level of general—and everyone knows that some people are more important than others.

Women by nature are inclusive rather than hierarchical. We function in a more circular manner, where everyone in the circle has her place and everyone's contribution is valued. Mediating labor contracts, organizing a bake sale or car wash for fundraising, getting out the vote, creating peace conferences, attracting a supportive staff, talking over a child's well-being with a doctor or a teacher, encouraging communication with business partners, running food cooperatives, and maintaining support groups and lifelong friendships are all female, circular ways of being. And they are powerful.

What would life be like if…
you looked at power as not something to go out and
get, but something that is already inside you?

We are accustomed to looking at power as having to do with force or aggressiveness. In football or in the military, power is gained by being stronger, more forceful, and faster than the other person. We think that having power means going out there and getting it. You can begin to see now that you don't need to go out and get it because your female power is already inside you. You may not have known it was there, but it is. It may have been obscured by your need to survive in a male world, but it is there. Coming into your own power doesn't mean getting power from someone else or taking power away from someone else. It means exploring the rich depths of your own being.

The Natural Power Work will first help you identify and explore *what is in the way* of experiencing your female power. This is the first step of returning your power to yourself. We all have things that stop our power. Being caught up in nagging, complaining, upsets, disturbance, drama, or chronic dissatisfaction siphons off your power. Fear, anger, and procrastination can also get in the way of your powerful self-expression. As you read and do the uncoverings, you will be gently removing the layers of defense mechanisms, misunderstandings, pain, trauma, and misuse that have formed over the tender pulse that is your authenticity.

Coming further into your power, you will discover the reasons you may have hidden your power from yourself and explore the history that could be holding you back from expressing yourself. It means developing a supportive, nonjudgmental, and loving relationship with yourself.

Uncoverings

Write what crosses your mind as soon as you ask yourself:

> *Think of a time I was with a woman who was being powerful in a female way. What was that like for me?*

> *Think of a time I was being powerful in a female way. What was that like for me?*

Meditate on the nature of one of the following each day for two weeks. What do you notice? Take notes.

> *Gentleness*
> *Tenderness*
> *Softness*

Nurturing

Empowering

Envisioning

Healing

Communicating

Intuiting

Cooperating

Opening

Allowing

Inviting

Receiving

Falling in Love With Yourself

At the core of having a life that will make you feel content and happy is learning to love yourself. If you are stuck in the past, repeating old patterns, and feeling unhappy and unsatisfied, it is difficult to reflect positively out into the world. Healing your past will have you move beyond old hurts and be able to more fully love and accept yourself.

The process is an organic one: The more you are living a life that is authentic for you, the more you will fall in love with yourself. The more you love yourself, the more you will be open to the expression of who you are. You will be free to share your matchless gifts with the world, gifts that no one else can offer because they are the true and real expression of your self. The more open you are to the expression of who you are, the more your world will work for you.

You may be here to express something others are also expressing—and you will do it in your own way. Whether you are writing a book, planting a garden, teaching a class, raising a family, painting portraits, helping people heal, listening to friends, hiring just the right person, drawing floor plans, speaking opening remarks at a trial, coordinating projects—how you do it will be unique because you do it from your own point of view. There is no one else with your background, experience, talent, and knowledge.

Your authentic expression is what you can offer that comes easily and naturally to you—whether it means you are soothing a hurt child, raising money to feed the hungry, balancing your company's budget, helping your friend move into her new house, entertaining guests, giving lectures, organizing a recycling program in your neighborhood, spending time alone, or negotiating contracts.

When you are expressing yourself authentically, you will feel good about yourself. You won't feel defensive about what you are doing or not doing. You will want to wake up in the morning because your life will be distinctively, wonderfully your own. You will be more patient with yourself and with others because you will be less stressed. You will have compassion for yourself and others because you will not be used up in ways that don't feel right or comfortable. By finding comfort with yourself and coming into your own power, you will influence everyone around you. If you have a smile on your face, everyone can have a better day.

Knowing Your Authenticity

What do people come to you for?

What do you do easily and naturally?

As you begin exploring your authenticity, it can help to begin seeing what people come to you for. It may be that people come to you for information, or maybe they come to you for inspiration to start a project. It could be that you are fun to be with, that you are nurturing, that you are a good listener, or that you can run a project with ease. You may be a place some people come to relax. Perhaps you are good at showing people what to do, showing them what not to do, or helping them see what is missing.

Seeing what people come to you for can point out what it is you are good at that you may not even recognize. Martha had a well-paying job as a corporate banker that provided her with status, money, and respect. But after a few years in the business she realized she was waking up every morning tired and depressed, wanting only to get through her workday as quickly as possible. She felt as if her real life happened during the evenings and weekends because that was when she would get together with her large and diverse group of friends. Her friends often came to her with their problems, especially when someone close to them was sick or had passed away. Martha attended funerals and kept vigil at hospitals, spending hours consoling and supporting her friends.

Grateful for her sympathy and support, they started referring others to Martha when they were in trouble.

One day Martha found she couldn't make herself go to the bank at all. She called in sick and paid a visit to her pastor, explaining to him that she felt fulfilled when helping people in their times of grief and hardship and that her corporate job now seemed stale and lacking in creativity. Her pastor suggested she go to divinity school and become a pastor herself. Astonished, Martha realized she had been filling the role of pastor and guide to her friends and acquaintances simply by doing what came easily and naturally to her. She quit her job, went to divinity school, and is now a pastor with her own parish where her supportive and counseling talents are well used.

Sometimes we don't recognize our own strengths because they require so little effort. It's easy to take them for granted and not even notice that others can't do them well. Perhaps you find it effortless to throw a dinner for forty guests. Because it comes so easily to you, you may not realize that other friends are overwhelmed at the prospect of having a dinner for two. Or perhaps you are excellent at listening to your friends and offering heartfelt and discreet advice. It would never occur to you that other people might get thrown off base by being put in the position of listener and advisor. These things that come easily and naturally to us can point us toward our authenticity.

Living Authentically

What did you do in childhood through young adulthood that you loved and do not do anymore?

What do you enjoy?

What do you do that you really look forward to?

It is powerful to come to a place of being matter-of-fact about who you are. As children, most of us had, at some point, a sense of who we were. Without thinking, we would naturally find things that were fun and interesting for us—whether it meant following a butterfly or making a mud pie. We knew what we liked and what we didn't like, what was fun and what wasn't—and it was different for each of us. Mothers know that every child plays and interacts differently from the start, and this is because children are being their natural, authentic selves. Today, you can get a sense of who you are by looking back at moments in your childhood when you felt absolutely caught up in the moment and were enjoying yourself fully.

People who are living authentically don't apologize for who they are or what they're doing. They are naturally expressing themselves, so they don't need to apologize or to change just because someone else doesn't feel comfortable with what they are doing. This is not the same as being stubborn or not listening to others. It's being aware of who they are and confident in their own lives.

When a woman is being authentic she can be around many different kinds of people without a struggle because she is not thrown off-center by others and doesn't get defensive. She has a matter-of-fact attitude about her own strengths, knowing what she is good at, not needing to be good at everything. She is not envious of others because she is sure of her life choices. She doesn't need to make sure others know what she's good at because she is content in her knowledge of herself.

What do you do that has you lose your sense of time and self-consciousness?

One way to identify what's natural for you is to think of the things you look forward to at the beginning of the day and that at the end of the day you are glad to have done. Martha knew her job at the bank was not natural for her because she began to dread it as soon as her alarm woke her in the morning. At five o'-clock she would leave the bank as quickly as possible, already dreading going back the next morning. What kept her going throughout the day was looking forward to spending time with her friends in the evening. When she lay in bed at night and reviewed her day, the high point was always the evening with friends. Martha used these signals to find what was authentic for her and to make changes so she could live more authentically.

Children can be authentic because they're doing what is natural for them. Think of the things you do that are so natural for you that you get lost in them, you have extraordinary energy, and consciousness of time or place disappears. Perhaps this happens when you are starting up a new project at work and become so absorbed that the time passes quickly. You are totally involved in your creative process and have no sense of time or self-consciousness. Afterward, you can see that the project was just right for you because it had you totally involved and expressing yourself naturally.

What is working in your life?

What do you do that feels fulfilling?

What do you have to be grateful for?

It is human to focus on what isn't working in our lives, taking for granted what is already working well for us. You could do yourself a great favor by looking at what *is* working and honor it. This will allow space for more of it to come into your life. It will give you the opportunity to fill up your life with what you love to do and with what comes easily and naturally for you. When you are living an authentic life, you will have a lot of yourself present and you will be in your life in a different way. You will be more awake and alert, able to be present in the moment and alive to new possibilities.

What do people acknowledge you for?

What are the positive things people say and think about you?

If you are alert and awake, you can start to notice positive things people say and think about you. Paying attention to the good things people notice about you can help you identify your natural strengths and talents. When people consistently speak about an aspect of you, you can see that it is something that's evident to others—whether you have been aware of it or not.

Deena loved to entertain friends, and she often gave elaborate dinner parties with ethnic themes and décor. She enjoyed the weeks of preparation—gathering and sampling recipes, scouring flea markets for decorations, and arranging for games or live entertainment. When the day finally came it was always a roaring success and Deena would bask happily in the glow of her achievement as her guests downed chicken tikka or chocolate soufflé.

Deena's happiness would always end abruptly a week or two after her party when she realized that not one of her guests had reciprocated by inviting her to dinner at their own homes. Sometimes they would take her to restaurants, but she felt hurt and left out that she never got to experience the hospitality of their homes. She started to wonder if people thought she was showing off when she entertained, or if they secretly laughed at her for her efforts. She told herself that maybe she should stop having her parties. One day, unable to stand it anymore, she screwed up enough courage to approach her friend Liz about the problem. Liz's response startled her.

"Deena, I could never invite you over to my place after having the gourmet, gorgeous meals and entertainment you give at your house," Liz said candidly. "I'm not the greatest cook, and frankly I'd be embarrassed to have you over for spaghetti and meatballs after one of your amazing shindigs. You're such a fabulous cook and hostess that I could never measure up."

Liz's response gave Deena a new way to think about her parties. Entertaining came so naturally to her that she had never stopped to think it was a talent she possessed that others might not have. As she shifted her perspective, she realized she could use her talent to create a fulfilling career for herself. She enrolled in catering school, quickly established herself as the star student, and after graduating she started her own catering business. Now she has a staff that assists her in producing lavish parties for people in their own homes. She will be forever grateful to Liz for pointing out her not-so-hidden talent and thankful that she didn't bury it just because others couldn't respond in kind. She no longer feels bad about not being invited to others' homes and realizes she can take it as a compliment.

Listening to Liz changed Deena's perspective on herself and changed her life. It would be powerful for you to listen to what your friends, family, and colleagues have to say about your unique talents and abilities. You might have strengths that you never realized you had, and recognizing them could lead you to discover what it is you would like to wake up to every morning.

What do you yearn for?

It may be that you long for things that are not yet in your life, and the things you crave but don't yet have can be an indication of what really matters to you. If you look at what you desire as a statement of what is authentic, you can use your yearnings to have more of what you want. Not everyone yearns for the same thing, so what you long for says something special about you and deserves your attention.

Your yearnings can sometimes be easily dissuaded by people around you, by fear, or by practical matters that seem to stand in the way. Martha yearned to console and counsel people full time, and she paid attention to her yearning and followed its path even though it looked like there were obstacles in her way. She had to figure out a way to have her yearning work in the real world by arranging to work part time while she went to divinity school, selling her second car, and finding a less expensive place to live. Martha knew she deserved to help herself go through the hard part, and the people she helps every day are grateful she did not give up on herself. You are worth going through the confusion and disorientation that may come when you rearrange things so you can fulfill your yearnings. It is good to follow your yearnings and to find a way to have them work in the real world, as Martha did.

If you can't think of anything you long for that is not already in your life, that is perfectly natural too. As you do the work of this book your heart will open and you will probably discover yearnings you didn't know you had. If your yearnings are not present now, they are probably on their way—so it would be good to be open to them. It takes getting to know yourself to see what is next, and paying attention to what you long for is a powerful way to get direction.

Life Changes as You Change

It is important to bear in mind that what is authentic for you can change as you change. It's easy to judge ourselves for past choices, but those may have been just right at the time. It may be that at one point in your life being alone and having an independent life was authentic, but that now is the right time for you to share your life with someone else. The fact that it shifted doesn't make the first part wrong; it just means that you have done that, learned from it, and can now shift to a different way of living.

As a young woman, Brenda ran her own business as a clothing designer and manufacturer. She enjoyed her business but it wasn't terribly successful financially, so when she married a man who made a significant income, she became a full-time homemaker. Being a homemaker suited her, and once her son Cody was born she found herself busy and happy as a full-time mom.

It soon became evident that Cody suffered from multiple learning disabilities, and Brenda worried about what would happen to him when he entered school. She was determined that he would be part of the public school system, so she started educating herself about his disabilities in order to be able to communicate his needs to his teachers. When Cody was old enough to go to school, Brenda was grateful for her foresight because she soon found she had to be proactive in getting the attention for Cody that he needed. Advocating for his needs brought her into contact with other mothers of children with disabilities, and they soon began to rely on Brenda's ability to communicate their concerns and frustrations.

Soon Brenda was established as an expert on learning disabilities among her peers, and her active voice in the school district brought her to the attention of the supervisor. The district offered her a job as an advocate for learning disabilities in the schools, and Brenda happily accepted the offer. Now she is thrilled to be earning money doing what she had been doing for free. She stepped naturally into a career that is authentic for her, and she feels good about herself, knowing she is doing what she is meant to be doing in her life. She knows that her clothing business was right for her at one point, and being a homemaker was right for her at another point—and that what she is doing today, being an education consultant, is right for her now.

Some people have trouble accepting what is authentic for them. When they are praised for a contribution they've made, they might shrug it off or make a self-deprecatory comment. If you find yourself making excuses when complimented or being unable to accept acknowledgment or praise, it may be that you haven't accepted that aspect of your authenticity yet. Brenda was able to take the praise and encouragement of the other mothers, and eventually of the school district, as deserved and earned. Because she could accept it, she was able to ease into the next phase of an authentic life.

Uncoverings

Write what crosses your mind as soon as you ask yourself:

What do people come to me for?

What do I do easily and naturally?

What did I do in childhood through young adulthood that I loved and do not do anymore?

What do I enjoy?

What do I do that I really look forward to?

What do I do that has me lose my sense of time and self-consciousness?

What is working in my life?

What do I do that feels fulfilling?

What am I grateful for?

What do people acknowledge me for?

What are positive things that people say and think about me?

What do I yearn for?

Do something you love to do that you have not done for a long time.

a powerful woman
is aware of her strengths and talents,
and lives with them as
a matter of fact.

a powerful woman
uses all her experiences for
her well-being.

2

✐

Using Your Energy for Yourself

Creating Your Road Map

How do you know you're getting where you want to go?

Like Martha, Deena, and Brenda, every woman who is living authentically has to create her own route to her authenticity. There are no road maps for us because our mothers and grandmothers were living in a culture where their options for authentic living were limited. Life has not just happened to us the way it might have just happened to our mothers or grandmothers. We are among the first women who have the opportunity to live a *considered* life rather than one that happens to us. It is important to realize we have made choices in our lives that have led us to be part of this transitional experience of being women.

Having a myriad of choices can sometimes seem overwhelming and burdensome, and navigating without a map may cause us to feel uncertain, confused, angry, or disappointed. With a shift in perspective, however, we can see our choices not as burdens but as containing infinite possibilities. Some women, for example, have already begun to make the choice to redesign their lives in ways that work. We can learn a lot by watching other women engaging in trial and error as they invent their lives.

Celia, a journalist, was very busy and left much of the care of her two children to a nanny. When she discovered she was pregnant with a third child, she and her husband decided she should quit her job and start parenting full time. As she learned to negotiate the process of parenting, she found it difficult to know where to find educational programs, where to find a clothing exchange, and where to find child-friendly restaurants and shops. When she went to a bookstore to find a guidebook to children's supplies and services in her community, she was surprised to discover that no such book existed. She decided to take notes on her own discovery process, then write a guidebook for parents on where to find everything from good toy stores to violin lessons. Based on the success of the book, Celia started a monthly newsletter for parents.

Elena, an architect, was tired of trying to sandwich motherhood between her long work hours. She wanted to have more time to spend with her two-year-old, but she couldn't afford to quit her job. She couldn't see a way out of her dilemma until one day when her friend Stacy came over and saw her son Sam's bedroom.

"Oh my gosh, it's the inside of a rocket ship!" Stacy gasped.

Elena shrugged. "I designed it for fun in my spare time. Sam loves it."

"You have got to design my daughter's bedroom for me," Stacy gushed. "Can you do an aquarium theme?"

Stacy's enthusiasm sparked Elena's creativity. When the aquarium room she designed for Stacy's daughter was met with glee, she quit her job at the architecture firm and started up her own company specializing in custom bedroom design for children. Working from home, she had time for both her job and her son—and in fact, she often took Sam with her on the initial visit to clients for his input on what would be fun and exciting for children's rooms.

Karen adored her job as a professional chef, but after ten years she began to tire of her restaurant's grueling schedule. She wanted to have time to have a social life, but in the restaurant business there seemed no way to avoid working nights. She realized she would have to go into business for herself if she wanted to be in charge of her schedule, so she contacted everyone she knew and offered to cook them healthy gourmet meals to stock their freezers with. Most people, too busy and stressed out to cook for themselves, loved the idea—and Karen quit the restaurant to work from her own kitchen.

These women, and many others like them, realized that working for themselves was more authentic and more fun. With the immense creativity all women possess, they reconceived their lives. But working for ourselves isn't the only option. Increasing numbers of corporations are experimenting with a female approach, in large part because they have found that employees work better in an environment that is more nurturing and where their ideas and needs are listened to. Many women are finding ways to express their authenticity in a corporate environment.

Clarissa, a computer technician for a large corporation, often found herself providing technical assistance to friends in her spare time. As a woman, she could sympathize with the anxiety many women felt when faced with new technology. Her gentle, caring approach soon earned her the nickname "the computer goddess." Realizing she had a unique combination of compassion, technical expertise, and a desire for change in her work life, Clarissa was inspired to request that her company loan her to a national woman's nonprofit organization to install a new computer network in their Washington, D.C., headquarters. She enjoyed being in the capital for six months and enjoyed returning to her company, feeling that she and her company had made a major contribution.

Some corporations are shifting toward a more female approach by introducing family-friendly options such as flex time and job sharing, offering on-site child care, memberships to health clubs, better maternity- and paternity-leave programs, and leaves of absence for elder care. Such changes in the corporate culture have created an opening for women *and* men who want a more humane work environment.

So how do you choose what's right for you? That's where we come in. We are here to coach you through the uncoverings, help you heal the past, discover your authenticity, use your energy for yourself in the present, and create the future you want.

Getting to Know Your Internal Committee

As you go about discovering what is authentic for you, you may also discover you have conflicting voices. Like everyone, you have many aspects, and these aspects don't always reflect the same needs, wants, and desires. You may have a voice that says, "I want to live in the country, have a family, and be self-sufficient," and you may also have a voice that says, "I want to have an important job in a big city." Another voice may tell you, "Just forget it. It's too hard to design your own life, so you might as well just coast along like everyone else seems to." We call these aspects your *committee members*.

If you imagine your conflicting voices as members of a committee engaging in dialogue about your life, you can begin to identify which committee members serve you and which ones you need to heal. Some committee members may be disempowering you. Some committee members may be vestiges of childhood wounds that will heal as you do the work of this book. As you continue to uncover the layers obscuring the essence of your power, you will come to understand your committee members better.

Uncoverings

Write what crosses your mind:

What am I doing now that feels really right for me?

What am I growing toward that is authentic for me?

What in my life feels like a misfit?

What do I want to have be different than it is (even if I don't know what I would put in its place)?

What am I confused about that is in my life?

What do I desire?

Using Your Power

What would life be like if...
you knew you had all the power you need?

As you begin to uncover what is real and true for you, you will begin to see that *you are already as powerful as you will ever be.* Why, then, might you not *feel* powerful? Perhaps you don't feel powerful because you're using your power *against* yourself as well as *for* yourself. Instead of using your power to be gloriously, authentically yourself, you may be using it in ways that keep you limited. Most of us learn early in life that it is not okay to fully express our power, so we start turning our power against ourselves. This means that sometimes we use our power to powerfully restrict ourselves— we powerfully criticize ourselves, limit ourselves, scare ourselves, worry about what others think, repeat patterns of the past, sabotage ourselves, and compare ourselves to others.

Comparing ourselves to others, in fact, is one of the most destructive ways we use our power. It is as if we were at a dinner table, busy looking at what everyone else has on their plates so we can reassure ourselves that we are doing the right thing, that we fit in, and that we don't have to feel vulnerable or humiliated.

Looking at someone else's plate, though, often gives us the feeling that our own lives don't measure up. If we could look at what is underneath the surface, we would probably be grateful not to have someone else's life—no matter how perfect they look at first glance.

"Somehow I always thought I wasn't good enough because I wasn't the best at everything," admits Ursula, a forty-six-year-old lawyer. "I was always looking over my shoulder at someone else, wondering why I didn't have what they had. If someone else was richer, smarter, better dressed, more successful—I couldn't be happy for them because I was always secretly comparing myself to them. And I always came up short. Then I realized I was spending so much of my power on comparing myself to others that I didn't have a chance to really be myself." When Ursula stopped comparing herself to others, she found she could use the same energy to help herself by joining a health club, finding an investment counselor, and working with a personal shopper.

When you begin consciously using your power for yourself instead of against yourself, you will be amazed at how much energy you have for choosing well, allowing yourself to receive, drawing good people toward you, and having fun.

Uncoverings

Write what crosses your mind:

How do I use my power for myself?

How do I use my power for others?

How do I use my power against myself?

How do I use my power against others?

Using Your Energy

Think of a time...
when you restricted your playful self-expression.

A lot of women feel that they simply don't have the energy to create the lives they want. Believe it or not, every one of us possesses *extraordinary* energy. Many of us just don't realize it because we use so much of our energy against ourselves. If you wake up exhausted in the morning, drag through your day, and fall into bed exhausted at night, it may be because all day long you are using your energy against yourself.

It takes a lot of energy not to be the divine, extraordinary, magnificent person you are. Criticizing yourself, ignoring your needs, and limiting yourself—these activities end up depleting you. Remember the one who danced for everyone unselfconsciously as a child, the one who would laugh loudly or shriek in delight even though she was in a public place? She is the one who is truly you. The curious, amusing, delighted child you were before you were shushed, squashed, humiliated—she is truly you. She is the essential energy of who you are. You may have forgotten that you are that essence because when life traumatized you, you needed to adapt to what was going on around you and defend yourself from it—but you still have that essence in you.

What would life be like if...
you didn't have to use so much of your essential energy expecting perfection from yourself?

Being human means making mistakes and not doing everything perfectly the first time. Like everyone else, though, you probably spend a lot of your energy trying *not* to be human. Somehow we all get the idea that we are supposed to be perfect and have it all figured out the first time—and when we don't do things perfectly, we beat ourselves up. Where did we get this idea of being perfect? Wherever it came from, it ends up ruling our lives. This is a trial-and-error universe, and there is no such thing as perfect.

Think about Nadia Comenici getting seven perfect scores in gymnastics at the 1976 Olympics. She certainly did not do her routines perfectly every time she practiced them in preparation for the games. She had to make many mistakes in order to attain a level of excellence that was labeled perfection. And today, her performance would not have gotten a perfect "10" because standards have become higher as athletes strive to improve. What Olympic athletes really work for is not perfection, but excellence. They don't do it perfectly the first time, so they demand a little more of themselves when they try again. If gymnasts couldn't fall because it meant they weren't doing it perfectly, they would never make it to the Olympic games. It takes a lot of falls to achieve a "perfect 10."

What would life be like if...
you could allow yourself to make mistakes, try things
out, or do it wrong—without harming yourself with
negative self-talk?

When Thomas Edison was developing the filament that would produce electric light, he didn't get it right until the 158th filament. The first 157 didn't work. What if he had given up after the first one, or the first ten, or the first hundred filaments? When Marie Curie was working to find the source of radioactivity, she undoubtedly took many wrong turns before the discovery of two new radioactive elements that earned her and her husband the 1903 Nobel Prize for physics. She went on to isolate radium and study its chemical properties, earning her own Nobel Prize for chemistry eight years later. What if she had listened to the voices in her head that told her she would never do it? Babe Ruth held the record for the most home runs for many years—and also for the most strikeouts. He didn't achieve his home run record by expecting perfection of himself, but by getting up to bat more frequently than anyone else. What if he hadn't allowed himself not to do well in order to do well?

Nadia Comenici, Thomas Edison, Marie Curie, and Babe Ruth all had to accept that they were human, not perfect, and would make mistakes in order to allow themselves to succeed eventually. Most of us try to avoid being human in many ways that keep us using our precious energy to run away from ourselves. We desire to be perfect, so we try to keep out everything that feels uncomfortable or vulnerable.

Becky, a twenty-seven-year-old retail buyer, is naturally high-spirited and expressive. During her childhood, her father worked nights and was usually home sleeping when Becky got home from school. Becky would often burst into the house exuberant about a good grade she received or a funny thing that happened in the classroom. Her mother would quickly silence her by saying, "Becky, your father is sleeping. You're being too loud. You must learn to contain your excitement."

Becky grew up trying to contain her energy, constantly chastising herself for being too enthusiastic. Containing her energy took up a lot more energy than expressing herself, and she often found herself exhausted and depressed. After two years in the Gathering, Becky has learned to accept who she is instead of trying to repress it.

"If you own who you are, a lot of the pushing up against it just relaxes and you can be more yourself," she explains. "I learned to relax into myself, and my enthusiasm just isn't much of a problem anymore. Also, I have a lot more energy to do projects that are healthy for me—exercising and eating better, looking for a new job, dating. I never would have thought I'd have the energy to do all these things and not feel exhausted."

What would life be like if...
you could use your creative energy for yourself instead of against yourself?

If you could accept that you are human, you are not perfect, and you will make mistakes, think of all the energy you might have left over to create, to love, to feel gratitude, to enjoy your life. In doing the Natural Power Work, we acknowledge that being human is here to stay. We can't change the fact that we are large spirits stuffed into human bodies destined to go through all the vulnerable, humiliating, imperfect experience of being alive. What we can do is incorporate our human condition in the best way possible so our lives can unfold and we can each become what it is we are designed to be. Embracing the full range of human experience allows us to express what we are here to express, and fulfill what we are here to fulfill.

Where Is Your Energy Going Now?

Doing the following uncoverings will help you identify where your energy is going in your life right now. Identifying where it is going allows you to see it differently than you have in the past, and this change in perception begins to make room for change. If you can see where you are putting your energy, and where you would like to be putting your energy, you start taking your power back.

Uncoverings

Write what crosses your mind:

What does not work about how I use my energy?

How do I sabotage my self-expression?

How do I use my energy that works?

How would I like to use my essential energy?
To use my essential energy best, it works to remind myself…

Becoming Matter-of-Fact About Yourself

What is just plain terrific about you?

Your power is in your essential energy, in the essence of who you are. You are beginning to come into your natural power simply by clearing out what is in the way of it. But most of us are so taken up with the dramas of everyday life that our energy is directed outward, or it is directed against ourselves. Much of the work of this book involves uncovering your essential energy and using that energy to help yourself.

Think of someone…
who loves you and chooses to spend time with you— your best friend, for instance.

Sometimes other people see us more clearly than we see ourselves. Your best friend may see you differently than you see yourself because she recognizes something about your essential energy. She sees something in you that is incredibly unique and valuable. It is powerful to start seeing yourself as your best friend sees you.

You can probably think of a dozen negative things about yourself, but if asked to list positive things about yourself, you might start feeling uncomfortable. In fact, you might even list things that weren't really positive, such as "I am a perfectionist." It may be uncomfortable to say positive things about yourself because as a child you may have been discouraged from praising yourself when you did a good job. Pointing out something good about yourself may have been quickly nipped in the bud. "Who do you think you are?", "You're so full of yourself!", and "Don't be so conceited!" are ways many parents, teachers, and friends have of discouraging children from speaking well of themselves. Becoming matter-of-fact about yourself means acknowledging you are good at something—as a fact. It means being able to take an objective inventory of your strengths, talents, and graces.

When Samantha visited Greece in her teens, she often received compliments from young Greek men. She would always thank them for complimenting her, but this response was confusing to them. "Why thank me?" they would respond. "I'm just stating a fact." If you could state positive facts about yourself, it would encourage you to look at the good things others see in you.

Being matter-of-fact with yourself allows your energy to shift away from perfectionism or trying to fulfill unrealistic standards, and it allows you to begin to love yourself. It helps to start by acknowledging the good things people notice about you.

Uncoverings

Write what crosses your mind:

The positive things people say and think about me are...

Go to a mirror and look into your own eyes. Read the list out loud in a matter-of-fact manner.

Celebrate yourself by doing something authentically joyful.

Freeing Your Power

How do you measure how your life is going?

You have begun to identify ways in which you have been using your energy against yourself, and to see what an abundance of energy you *could* have to use *for* yourself once you free it up. Perhaps without knowing it, you have also been using a lot of your essential energy to gauge how you are doing in life—and this way of measuring your success may be working against you. Once you understand how you may be using your energy to keep yourself in a cycle of frustration and limitation, you can start returning more of that energy to yourself.

Nancy, a small business owner, came to see how she was using her energy against herself on a trip to Italy. She planned her trip to include a ferry ride to Greece. The ferry was scheduled to leave at 7:30 a.m., so she and her husband arrived in Bari the night before. They got up at 6:30 a.m. in order to be at the ferry dock by 7 o'clock. Yawning, they dragged their bags to the dock—only to discover there was no ferry in sight and no ticket agent in the locked booth. They sank onto a bench to wait, watching as more and more Italian families wandered slowly onto the dock, laughing and talking in groups.

Nancy kept checking her watch, reassuring her husband that the ferry must be coming any minute. Finally, nearly an hour later, a man in a dark blue uniform sauntered down the dock toward the ticket booth. She ran to him, gesturing in frustration, as she demanded to know what time the ferry would arrive.

"I don't know," he answered, unlocking the door of the booth.

"What do you mean you don't know?" Nancy asked in frustration. "It was scheduled to leave at 7:30! When do you think it will come?"

The official shrugged. "She comes when she comes," he replied calmly.

Nancy, used to having things happen when she expected them to happen, was floored. She and her husband had wanted to make the most of every minute of their vacation, and now they were wasting their entire morning sitting on a dock! They sat fuming in silence until the ferry finally arrived.

In Nancy's experience waiting for the ferry in Bari, we can see that her extreme frustration at sitting on the dock was not solely due to the fact that she came to it with the expectations of a culture where things happened on schedule. We can look deeper to see that she suffered partly because she had a way of judging her experience that differed from how the Italians judged their experience. Nancy's judgment came from the question, "How much am I accomplishing?" Since she didn't appear to be accomplishing much while sitting on a bench on the dock, she judged she was having a terrible experience that was a waste of time. The Italians laughing and joking around her had a judgment that asked the question, "Am I enjoying myself in the moment?" Because they were enjoying themselves in their eyes, they were having a great time.

Scorecards

On an episode of the popular sitcom *Friends*, Rachel was sitting in front of her cake at her thirtieth birthday party. Was she enjoying the party her friends had thrown for her? No, because she was busy calculating how much time she had left to meet the man she would marry. She had always planned to have children by age thirty-three, so she figured she still had some time left to meet her man. As she continued her calculations, however, she realized she needed a certain amount of time to go out with him before they got engaged, then a certain amount of time to plan her wedding. Then she wanted to be married for a certain number of years before having kids. Then, of course, it would take nine months to have a child. Suddenly she realized that according to her plan for her life, she should already have met her future husband. Since she hadn't, she figured she was a failure.

Rachel set herself up for feeling badly by imposing arbitrary rules on when and how things should be happening for her in life. We all do this in our own way because we need some method for judging and evaluating how our lives are going. Otherwise how would we know whether or not we are happy?

In the Natural Power Work we refer to these personal measurements as *scorecards*. Our scorecards are filters that have us see our lives in limited ways. Because they only ask certain questions, we may not realize that there are other ways to look at how we are doing. If, for example, Nancy had a scorecard that asked, as the Italians' scorecards did, "Am I enjoying myself in the moment?" she could have relaxed into the experience instead of looking at it as a failure because she wasn't getting to Greece on schedule.

Scorecards can be based on many factors including family history, comparison with friends or colleagues, role models you want to emulate, a need to be popular and accepted, expectations of parents, teachers, and mentors, and your own picture of how your life should be.

Melissa, a twenty-eight-year-old advertising rep, has a scorecard that asks, "Am I pleasing a male authority figure?" If her boss drops by her desk to tell her she's doing well, she feels happy—for a while. She has gotten a "10" on that scorecard for the day. Unfortunately, the happiness doesn't last long because it is based on outside approval. Melissa also has dozens—perhaps hundreds—of other scorecards. When she gets home to find that there isn't a message on her answering machine from the man she's dating, her happiness dissipates. Her "Do I have a man who is romantically interested in me?" scorecard is a zero, and suddenly she is plunged into a negative conversation with herself about how she is "always a bridesmaid and never a bride."

You, too, keep scorecards on yourself. The first step toward having scorecards that support you is to identify them. Some of them may work well for you, and obviously those would be good ones to keep. But you undoubtedly also have some that keep you stuck, limited, or feeling badly about yourself. It is powerful for you to recognize that you are the one who made up the measurements (of course adopting some from the world around you) that you use to check how you are doing in life—and that you can change them if they are not supporting you.

Everyone bases their scorecards on different criteria. Your scorecard reflects the history and expectations you have. All scorecards are usually based on what we think we should be doing, or on what people who influence us think we should be doing, rather than on what is authentic for us to be doing.

You may be very successful in your life, but you may not experience yourself as successful because your scorecards are in the way. You may have scorecards that are judging you only in places where you don't feel successful, and there is a good chance that they keep you looking outward for indications of your success rather than focusing inward on what is soul-satisfying for you.

Your mind will set up scorecards no matter what. Doesn't your ego want you to be the best human being on the planet? Isn't there a part of you that feels you are a failure if you aren't the "mostest" of everything? And of course you can't be that—but your mind is not always logical.

A scorecard women often use is, "How am I doing compared to others?" We compare ourselves to family members, colleagues, friends, and even celebrities and characters on television. Melissa got a "10" when her boss praised her, and her coworker Emily, who was ignored by the boss, got a zero. If Melissa compared herself to Emily on the "Am I pleasing a male authority figure?" scorecard, Melissa was doing well in comparison—but it is a false way to judge. It could be that Emily doesn't feel bad that Melissa did well on that particular scorecard because Emily might have scorecards that ask different questions such as, "How much work did I get done?" and "Who makes the most money?"

If you have a scorecard that asks, "How am I doing compared to my brother or sister?" it keeps you looking at their lives for judgment rather than at your life to see what you may really want. If your sister is a successful urban businesswoman with a fancy car and a great house, how can you live modestly in a rental apartment and still feel successful? Because you are absolutely unique and there is no one like you, comparing your life to other people's lives only keeps you trapped. How can you compare yourself to someone else if you are the only one of you on the planet?

Your scorecards are partly based on your family expectations and your history, and they reflect your perception of what your family expects of you. Your perception may be accurate or it may be partially invented by you. Chloe had a scorecard that said, "How am I doing compared to my father's expectations of me?" That scorecard kept her in a marriage that was unhealthy for her because her father was religious and she thought he wouldn't approve of a divorce. When she finally had to get out after ten years, she tearfully confessed her failure to her father. "Oh, honey, don't worry about what I think," he said with concern. "All I've ever wanted was for you to be happy." Chloe was shocked to realize that she had stayed in an abusive marriage partly because of a parental expectation that didn't even exist except on a scorecard in her mind.

Scorecards are often unsupportive because they tend to point out what is missing or what is not done yet, rather than what has already happened or how rich the quality of your life is. They generally attend to problems rather than acknowledgments. If everyone in your family has always been successful in business and you are not successful in business, then your scorecard probably says you are not doing well even if you are doing something that satisfies you. If everyone in your family believes that women should have children by age twenty-five and you don't have children by age twenty-five, then your scorecard says you aren't doing well. You might also have a scorecard that gauges your level of rebellion, asking, "How am I doing compared to my vow that I'll never be like my family?" This scorecard may seem like it is freeing you, but it also limits you by keeping you in reaction to your family rather than living what is real and true on your own terms.

Your mind needs scorecards, and it is impossible to avoid having them—but now that you know you have them, you have the power to create scorecards that will support you rather than limit you. You can keep doing exactly the same thing you are already doing, but if you start seeing your life through a different lens you might like it more. So the first step toward having supportive scorecards is to identify the ones that aren't. Later in the book we will help you create new scorecards. For now it would be powerful for you to make a list of your scorecards that don't work—then burn the list.

To help you get started, there are some sample scorecard questions in the following uncovering. You may have some of these scorecards, and you probably have many others as well.

Uncoverings

Check to see if you have the following scorecards:

How am I doing compared to others? Am I first, last, quickest, smartest?

How am I doing along a time frame? Have I accomplished all I should have by now?

Am I making enough money?

Am I liked, popular, current, and fashionable?

Do people agree with how I'm living?

How may degrees, awards, promotions do I have?

How am I doing compared to my parents' scorecards?

How am I doing compared to my siblings'/cousins'/friends' scorecards?

Am I making sure I do the opposite of what my family wants?

Am I taking enough risks?

Does everybody like me?

Is anyone upset with me?

What other scorecards do you have?

Five Ways to Support Yourself

Getting rid of unsupportive scorecards is all about changing how you judge yourself. As you shed the harsh judgments and begin to treat yourself gently, you open up the space for change to happen. What follows are five additional ways you can support yourself as you continue to uncover your Natural Power.

1. Quiet the Mind

What would life be like if...
you could observe what is happening with a quiet mind?

Quieting the mind is one of the best ways to support yourself. It starts with nonjudgmental noticing, with being able to experience, perceive, and state the fact of what is happening without having any commentary about it. Jack Webb, who women of a certain age will remember from the television show *Dragnet*, was fond of saying, "Just the facts, ma'am. Just the facts." As you do the Natural Power Work, you may notice your mind wanting to have judgments about how you are doing, or what is changing or not changing. If you are caught in self-criticism, feeling badly about what you are doing, or experiencing self-doubt, you don't have an objective view of the situation and you have much less power to change it. Cultivating a practice of nonjudgmental noticing in your everyday life allows you to experience what is happening without jumping to conclusions about it.

In a heated argument with a friend, nonjudgmental noticing would mean commenting *only* on what is happening—not on whether you are doing it right, who is right or wrong, or what it means about you, them, and life. A running nonjudgmental commentary would go something like this: "Now I'm raising my voice, now my heart is starting to pound and veins are starting to throb in my temples. Oh—I'm angry. Now I'm having the thought 'how dare she.' Now I want to say something to harm her. Oops—it just slipped out of my mouth..."

Nonjudgmental noticing takes away the sting of self-blame and self-judgment, and it keeps you from perceiving false meaning in a situation. The more you can watch what is going on without judgment, the more you can have power with changing, rearranging, releasing, and transforming it.

At this point, or others, you may notice yourself becoming sleepy or restless. That's to be expected. What we are working with here is a calming of the central nervous system, a letting go of the adrenaline that keeps a lot of us running, and this gentle downshifting can be uncomfortable at first. Restlessness and sleepiness can be powerful signs that you have shut down about something important. Just pay attention and trust that this work is creating an opening within you, allowing you to discover things about yourself and your desires that you may have been pushing away for years.

Uncoverings

Write what crosses your mind:

Think of something that happened today that was a little disturbing.

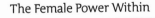

Just state the facts of what happened.

What happens when I just state the facts?

2. Do the Best You Can

Imagine the relief of knowing you are already doing the best you can.

Being human means that we will make mistakes and also that we may judge ourselves for making them. You can do most things perfectly in hindsight because you have the wisdom you've gained from having that experience, but you wouldn't have that wisdom if you hadn't had that experience exactly the way you had it. And if you had that wisdom you would have used it then, wouldn't you?

As you cultivate nonjudgmental noticing, you can choose to adopt the female viewpoint that at any given moment we are all doing the best we can, because if we could do better we really would. Your parents, your friends, and your coworkers are all making decisions and taking action from the place they are in, and they are making the best decisions they know how to make in that moment. Remember that you, too, are doing the very best you can at any given moment.

Having such a forgiving, accepting view of your own and others' humanity allows you to stop spending energy wondering, "How could I have done that?" or "How could she have said that?" Even if it's hard to believe that someone is really doing the best they can, simply assuming they are allows you to return your energy to yourself. You can't change what anyone else is doing, so spending time trying to figure out how they could possibly be doing it ends up depleting you of precious energy you could be using to have more of what you want in your life. Accepting that we are all doing the best we can allows for a fuller range of motion in life, one that includes making mistakes.

Uncoverings

Write what crosses your mind:

Think of a time you did something you wish you had done differently.

Acknowledge that you did the best you could.

What happens?

3. Be Gentle With Yourself

Think of a time...
someone was gentle with you when you made a
mistake.

You are in constant dialogue with yourself as you go through the everyday of your life—and unfortunately, like the scorecards you use that measure you falsely, much of what you say is not supportive of the amazing job you are doing at negotiating this challenging adventure called your life. It would be powerful to start tuning in to the conversations you have with yourself and nonjudgmentally noticing how much of what you tell yourself is negative. Once you can notice what you are telling yourself, you will have the power to start having a more supportive, positive internal conversation.

How you speak to and about yourself is important because it sets the tone for what you draw into your life. You would never tell a toddler who was first learning to walk, "No, that's not the way to do it. Will you ever learn? I can't believe you haven't mastered it already." But you may speak very harshly to yourself, criticizing and blaming yourself for not doing something right. If you are constantly having a conversation involving fear and worry, you cannot notice what is going well because you cannot be present and open to the situation you are in.

The good news is you don't have to live with your negative dialogue anymore. You have already begun to change it by telling yourself positive things people say and think about you, by starting to see how you are using your power and energy, and by throwing out the scorecards that judge you negatively. Continuing to nonjudgmentally notice your internal conversation can help you change the way you talk to yourself, having you choose positive conversation over critical self-talk. Positive conversation, in turn, helps you attract what you want into your life because it always has you doing more and better even if it is difficult. It has you encourage yourself rather than discourage or frighten yourself, and encouraging yourself naturally has you be more optimistic.

Write what crosses your mind:

> *Think of something you feel challenged by, or would like to be different.*

> *What is a gentle conversation I can have about how I can interact with this challenge?*

4. Be Positive With Yourself

What would life be like if... you were your own cheering section?

Olive came from a family of artists. Her mother was a sculptor, her father was a painter, and her older brother was a concert pianist. Needing to assert her independence, Olive vowed to have a career that had nothing to do with the arts. She became an advertising rep for a high-powered company and was very successful at her practical job. After a few years, though, she realized that she was missing part of her creative self-expression. She loved her job and had no desire to change it, but she needed a hobby.

Olive took the optimistic viewpoint that since everyone else in her family was artistic, she too must have artistic talent. She signed up for a painting course, but after just a few classes she found herself dreading it and knew that painting was not right for her. She remained optimistic, however, and simply decided to try another medium. Because her mother was a sculptor, she thought she would try sculpting next—but soon she found herself slogging through class without much interest. She quit the sculpting class and decided to try the violin. Soon she realized that learning an instrument was more than she was willing to take on and that she was too old to ever be as good as she wanted to be.

Olive tried several more media including needlepoint and interior decorating, but nothing felt totally right. Still, she kept her optimistic outlook, telling herself, "Each thing I discover is not right for me is leading me a step closer to what *is* right."

One day Olive was walking through the creative department of her advertising agency when she noticed a gorgeous, fluid work of art on someone's computer screen. Fascinated, she decided to learn about computer art herself. She signed up for a course, and unlike the other courses she'd tried, she found herself utterly absorbed. Soon she was spending all her spare time learning about computer art and experimenting with new information she found on the Internet.

Olive was delighted to find a creative expression that was authentic for her. She was especially glad that it was something no one else in her family had done, so it could be totally hers. She had no urge to turn her art to profit because she wanted to keep it joyous and fresh, for her entertainment and fulfillment in leisure time only. Eventually Olive realized that her quest for a hobby had taught her about more than her creative talent. She had learned that she could have what she needed in life, and enjoy the process of finding it. Her optimistic outlook had taken her where she wanted to go and kept her from giving up before she got there. She could powerfully use that same optimism in other areas of her life so she could continue to have more of what she wanted.

If, like Olive, you expect that the future will be to your liking, you can keep focused on the positive rather than the negative. Like Olive, we have the power to tell ourselves good stories about what life is sending us. By telling yourself good stories, you encourage your own optimism, and optimism gives you the power to go about having what you want. As you continue doing the Natural Power Work, an optimistic viewpoint can help you see that, even when things are hard, you are heading in the direction you want to go—and you are worth it.

Uncoverings

Write what crosses your mind:

Think of a time you brought yourself through an experience by being positive.

What do you notice?

A dilemma I am in now is…

How can I use optimism to help myself through it?

5. Return Your Energy to Yourself

Now that you have begun to choose a gentler, more positive way of viewing your life, you may start noticing you have more energy for yourself. These new ways of looking are allowing you to begin releasing the energy you may have been using up by feeling confused, comparing yourself to others, powerfully restricting yourself, expecting perfection, not being your essential self, holding up unsupportive scoreboards, telling yourself negative stories, and expecting the worst. Releasing the ways you have been using your energy against yourself has you beginning to take back your power. When you use your energy for yourself, you are free to do what is authentic for you, to treat yourself well, and to have more of what you want in life.

Uncoverings

Think about, meditate on, and practice each of the following ways of being with yourself. Pick one a day.

I am quieting my mind.

I am reminding myself that I am doing the best I can.

I am being gentle with myself.

I am being positive with myself.

I am returning energy to myself.

Part Two

~

The Past:

How You Formed Your
Concept of Power

a powerful woman
is actively engaged in creating a life
that is authentic for her.

a powerful woman

separates herself from the influences
of her past so she can be
her true self.

3

~

Our Dilemma as Women Today

Our Shifting Culture

Feminism burst the doors off of our cultural restrictions and expectations. The modern feminist movement has its roots in the abolitionist movement of the mid-nineteenth century. Women working to free the African-Americans couldn't help noticing the similarities between slavery and their own situation. In the nineteenth and early twentieth centuries, the suffragists led the American feminist movement with the goal of obtaining the vote for women. After women were granted the vote in 1920, the women's movement quieted. In the Depression era of the 1930s, the image of the independent career woman enjoyed brief popularity. Women's career opportunities were limited, but the idea of women working outside the home was no longer shocking—but of course poor women always worked. When the United States entered World War II, women were summoned to work in the factories by the smiling, muscled image of "Rosie the Riveter." Their labor was crucial to the war effort, and for many women it was the first time they felt needed and appreciated in the public sector.

When the men returned home in 1945 they needed their jobs back, and women were encouraged to return to the home. Women who needed to work were often relegated to their "pink-collar" clerical jobs. The 1950s was the era of home and family. It was patriotic to have children to replenish those lost in the war. Hollywood, the media, and the advertising industry produced the image of the perfect wife and mother to support the postwar economy. All a woman needed to achieve happiness was a house in the suburbs with the right appliances, the right car, and the right kind of dish soap and cake mix. Women who had to work outside the home were generally limited to low-paying, low-prestige jobs. Women wanting more than "pink-collar" jobs were generally limited to teaching and nursing—and even those jobs were seen as temporary, something to give up once she married.

Under the placid surface of 1950s living surged tides of discontent that would erupt in the 1960s with the civil rights movement and the modern women's movement. In 1961 President Kennedy appointed Eleanor Roosevelt to head the first President's Commission on the Status of Women. The commission found evidence of discrimination against women in several areas including employment, the law, and lack of adequate childcare facilities. In 1962 Helen Gurley Brown, editor of *Cosmopolitan* magazine, published *Sex and the Single Girl*, opening up the possibility for women to enjoy sex out of wedlock.

Betty Friedan published her groundbreaking book, *The Feminine Mystique*, in 1963, putting her finger on "the problem that had no name," the quiet dissatisfaction of the suburban housewife. Suddenly women realized they were not alone and that their discontent was shared by thousands, perhaps millions, of other American housewives. A revolution was born.

In 1964 Congress passed the Civil Rights Act that included a clause prohibiting discrimination in employment on the basis of race, color, religion, national origin—and sex. Immediately women began to petition the Equal Employment Opportunity Commission (EEOC) with complaints of unfair treatment, but they were largely ignored or ridiculed. In response to the EEOC's lack of action, the National Organization for Women was founded in 1966.

The next few years saw the women's movement swing into action. Women emerged again as a force in the political arena, forming consciousness-raising groups where they shared their personal experiences and discussed political implications. Armed with new support and knowledge, they demanded equal access to resources, equal pay for equal work, tax credit for childcare, and more. Women's studies courses were introduced at universities. In 1972 Gloria Steinem's influential *Ms.* magazine released its first issue amidst a whirlwind of controversy. Conservatives, both male and female, saw feminists as masculine and threatening. The Equal Rights Amendment failed as federal legislation in 1972.

The controversy increased when the Supreme Court established a woman's right to abortion with their *Roe v. Wade* decision in 1973. This decision served to intensify the developing split between conservative and radical women, yet gains continued in the battle for women's rights. The American women's movement had worldwide impact. In 1975 the United Nations declared the first Year of the Woman, sponsored by the U.N. Commission on the Status of Women. The First International Conference on Women was held in Mexico City, kicking off the United Nations Decade for Women (1975–1984). For the first time, women's needs were being examined on a global level. In the United States, women were entering the work force in record numbers and the concept of "Superwoman" was born. She was a mythic figure who could do it all, combining a high-powered career with home and family. In 1984 Geraldine Ferraro became the first woman to run for national office as running mate to presidential candidate Walter Mondale.

The 1990s saw women's concerns remain at the forefront of America's political and economic concerns. The issue of sexual harassment emerged with Anita Hill's explosive denunciation of Clarence Thomas during his U.S Supreme Court confirmation hearings in 1991. Universities established women's studies as part of their core curriculum, while the public schools incorporated women's history and issues into theirs. Issues such as rights for working women, welfare rights, health care, women and AIDS, the feminization of poverty, and child care are still vying for attention on the national political agenda. While women were struggling to find how to combine work, relationships, and motherhood, debates raged over the state of the feminist movement. Some declared feminism dead while others countered that it was only the beginning. The word "feminist" sparked controversy—it was demonized by the media and embraced by others who believed in feminism's basic tenet of equality between women and men.

Feminism got us here, and we are grateful. The work now is for each of us to step into our own power, knowing we need to create new models for how to be. The examples our parents set for us may no longer apply, and the cultural norms we looked to as we grew up also no longer fit. We often end up feeling as if there were something wrong with us because we don't have it all figured out. It is powerful to explore the nature of our dilemma and to look at the personal and cultural history that has us acting or reacting to our constantly shifting lives.

Uncoverings

How has feminism influenced me?

How has feminism changed the lives of the women around me?

Action or Reaction

What would life be like if...
you had to lead the life that your mother or grand-mother led?

The prospect of reliving your mother's or grandmother's life can help you see how restricted their lives were and how far we have come. Most women today don't want to lead the life our mothers and grandmothers led. We see how their choices were limited and we see that they deserved more possibility in life. Many of us observed our mothers' lives and from a very young age vowed to have a different experience. What we may not realize is that by living in reaction to our mothers' and grandmothers' lives we limit our own choices. We may be so afraid of going through what we saw them go through that we make decisions in our lives that may not be authentic for us. Now we realize that we want lives in which we can define ourselves, rather than letting our reactions and circumstances choose for us.

Our mothers and grandmothers had rules, spoken or unspoken, that laid out what they needed to do in order to be a woman: get married and have children in that order, keep an orderly house, feed and nurture their children, be a support to their husbands. Women who didn't conform to those rules had labels: "spinster," "old maid," "whore," "loose woman," "bad mother," "lazy wife," "divorcée." One woman in our group had an aunt who was invariably referred to as "Poor Aunt Ruth Who Doesn't Have Any Children." Didn't we all have some version of Aunt Ruth in our families—a woman who didn't fit into the cultural norms and was seen as an aberration, someone to be pitied or scorned?

We are no longer called "old maids" if we reach forty without marrying and having children, yet we have new concerns that our mothers and grandmothers never had to face. We worry that having a relationship means giving up autonomy, and that having children means giving up independence. How do we choose between

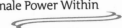

a career and children, or how do we incorporate both into our lives? Our dilemma is compounded by the fact that we are the first generations to have the freedom to ask these questions. Whether to put children or career first was not a typical question for our mothers or grandmothers. If they didn't want to be "Poor Aunt Ruth Who Doesn't Have Any Children," they knew exactly what they needed to do.

What is important for all of us to realize is that until we can free ourselves from living in reaction to our mothers' lives, we won't be able to make choices that are authentic for us in our own lives. You cannot avoid being influenced by your mother's role or by her perception of what a woman's role should be. Either you are reacting to her by saying, "No way, I'll never live the way she did and make the choices she made," or you are reacting to her by consciously or unconsciously repeating her patterns—or some of both. If staying home with the children looks too much like what your mother did, you may choose not to have children at all—even if it would be authentic for you to raise a family. On the other hand, you may choose to stay home with the children because that is what your mother did—even if you would prefer to have focused on your career. Making extreme choices in either direction is a reaction to the past. You now have the opportunity to map your own life, and you also have the opportunity to have your life include elements of what is seen as traditionally female and traditionally male without having either one be a burden or a restriction.

What would life be like if…
you made all your choices from what fit you well,
rather than from a reaction to the women who came
before you?

In the late 1980s, women began to whisper, "I want to stay home with my children." They whispered it because it seemed like a betrayal of what feminism had opened up for them, and implied that they were not Superwoman. Now women are not only saying it out loud, they are also doing it. Increasing numbers of women are quitting their jobs or changing their work situation in order to be home with their children. With today's technology, it's much easier to work from home, and increasing numbers of women are doing this at least part of the time. This trend points to the fact that as women we have many facets to our lives. We have the opportunity today to incorporate all aspects of what is important to us into the breadth of our experience. It may be that completely separating career and child rearing doesn't work for us, and that what we are working toward is a situation that combines both in a more organic way.

If you choose to have making a home and nurturing others be a central part of your life, does that mean that you are falling back into the roles of your mother and grandmother? Fear of regressing to the past keeps us tiptoeing around the subject, afraid we will be negating the gains of feminism by making a choice that may feel more fulfilling for us. But the difference is that today we do have choices. As women, we have the wonderful opportunity to have our lives be multifaceted. And one of the facets of our lives can be our desire to nest and nurture. If you look at your life as a creative, ongoing process, then the choice to stay home becomes simply one more expression of who you really are. It may be that later you will redesign your life again in a totally different way. And the woman sitting next to you will probably choose something entirely different.

Uncoverings

What would life be like to lead the life my mother or grand-
    mother led?

What would life be like if I made all my choices from what
    fit me well rather than from a reaction to the women who
    came before me?

Becoming What You See

How is your life just like your mother's?

How is your life the opposite of your mother's?

Like a duckling imitating the mama duck, you have made choices and taken action in your life based on what you saw your parents do. The mama duck goes "waddle, waddle," and the baby duck goes "waddle, waddle." Even if you think you haven't copied your parents, it is inevitable that you have to some extent. Your parents were your role models for how to be in life. You looked up out of the confusion and stimulation of childhood and saw your mother and decided how to be, relieved to know how a woman should behave. We take on our parents' struggles, almost as if they were contagious and caught like a cold. Saying "I'll never be like my mother" or "I'll be just like my mother" keeps you living in reaction to her. Saying "I'll make it up to my mother by living the life she could never have" or "I'll never be like my mother so everyone knows she didn't do a good job" also keeps you living in reaction.

Cassie, a fifty-year-old consultant, learned early in life that being a woman meant having to fall back on her own resources. Cassie was the third of the five girls her mother had before finally giving birth to a boy—and then proceeding to have two more boys in rapid succession. Cassie's father looked around at his eight children and realized he had a dilemma. He didn't have the financial resources to give all the children the best opportunities and education, so he would have to choose between them. Because it was the 1950s, the choice was clear.

"I can't send you to college because I have to focus on the boys," he told the girls. "The boys will have to grow up and have a way to support a family of their own, so they need a college education. You have the chance to meet men who will take care of you."

Cassie, however, was determined to get an education and have a career of her own. Observing her parents' financial struggles, she vowed to herself never to be a burden on a man, and to always have the resources to take care of herself. Her parents supported her in her desires even while making it clear they couldn't assist her financially. "If you want something, you need to use your own resources to go out and get it," they told her.

Cassie went to college and then become an extremely successful businesswoman, eventually starting her own company. She flew all over the world for business and, when at home, often worked from 8 a.m. until midnight. She had achieved her goal of being successful and financially independent, and she certainly wasn't a burden to a man. In fact, she didn't have time to have men in her life at all. Because all she did was work, she never had the chance to meet men socially. The men she met professionally were often married, and they tended to look at her as "one of the guys" because she was so successful and in charge of every situation.

When she was facing turning fifty alone, Cassie realized she was finally willing to make it a priority to rearrange her life in a way that would make space for a man. She came to Life Works and began the process of coming to understand why her life was the way it was. As she grew more aware, she began to see that the roles her mother and father modeled for her were still running her life today. Because Cassie saw her mother as a burden on her father financially, she equated being a burden with having a relationship with a man. She was so afraid of giving up control that she scared men away. Her "I can take care of myself" persona didn't allow anyone else in. As she did the Natural Power Work, Cassie saw she could begin making choices about how to live her life instead of believing her parents' model was the only way. Last year Cassie married, became a stepmother of three, took on a business manager and a housekeeper, and has dinner with her husband and stepchildren most evenings.

Adrian laughingly called herself a "gypsy." By age thirty-eight she had lived in seven different cities and had moved several times within each city—always looking for something a little better that might be waiting around the corner. As a freelance writer she could take her work with her wherever she went. She quickly grew dissatisfied with any place, though, and would soon feel that urge to move on that kept her permanently living out of boxes.

The last time she moved, however, Adrian was surprised to find she felt really sad. She usually didn't let herself get attached to people or places, but she had made some really good friends in her last place and she wasn't very interested in meeting anyone new. She found herself wondering for the first time if all her moving had to do with running away from things. As she explored this idea, she realized that getting close to people made her uncomfortable. Her parents had moved around a lot when she was growing up, constantly looking for a better house, a more lucrative job market, and better schools for the children. Because they would often move in the middle of the school year, Adrian often had trouble adjusting and making friends. After a while, she just stopped trying.

A light bulb went off for Adrian when she realized she had taken on her parents' pattern of restlessness in her adult life. She always believed there was something better around the next bend, down the next block, or in the next city—exactly as her parents had. She never allowed herself to get close to people because she would let them know from the start that she was only passing through. Recognizing that she was living out her parents' pattern was an immense relief for Adrian. She could finally see that she had simply carried on living the only way she knew how.

Now that she could see the pattern, she had the freedom to make different decisions. Taking a deep breath, she picked up the phone and dialed the number of a friend in the city she'd just left. "I'm coming back," she announced. "I'm coming home."

Your parents set up a way of being in the world that worked for them in the only way they knew how. It is inevitable that you absorbed at least some of the ways they patterned for you. If they worked from dawn to dusk and saved every penny, never spending anything on themselves, you had a reaction to that—perhaps either by following their role and becoming a frugal workaholic, or by rebelling against that role and becoming a shameless spender. If your parents lived in a strictly traditional arrangement of mother staying home and father working, you had a reaction to that—perhaps either by marrying and staying home with your children, or by vowing never to marry and having a successful career instead.

Either way, you end up tied into a way of life based on following or not following the roles your parents patterned for you. What you may not have realized is that you have more than those two options. There is a wide range of ways to be between the extremes of frugality and spending, tradition and rebellion. Identifying your parents' roles and seeing how you have been limiting yourself by living in reaction to them will free you to have more choices and more options for living an authentic life.

Uncoverings

How is my life just like my mother's?

How is my life the opposite of my mother's?

How my mother saw her role as a woman was…

How my mother felt as a woman was…

How my mother expressed her power was…

How my mother limited her power was…

Maternal Line

How has your mother influenced how you are as a woman?

Have you ever looked in the mirror and seen your mother? Whatever your mother's response to her life, you made a decision at many points either to pattern your life on the life she had, or to live the life she never had. In any case, you have probably been living your life in response to your mother's life on some level. Our mothers were our models for womanhood. We are often consciously or unconsciously living our lives in reaction to our mothers' lives. This can stop us from knowing as individuals what is authentic for us—what will make us happy, fulfilled, and satisfied.

Susan, a forty-two-year-old theatrical producer, got mixed messages about being a woman in the world. Her mother had an exciting, creative job as a fashion editor that Susan admired—but she always told her daughter that having children was the most important thing a woman could do. When she was in the fifth grade, Susan's teacher called her mother to inform her that her daughter was acting up in class, picking quarrels with other students and often refusing to obey instructions. Susan's mother immediately gave up her job to stay at home and care for her, convinced that her absence and not puberty was the reason for her daughter's wayward behavior.

Susan knew her mother had given up her career for her. She felt guilty, but also resentful that her mother had given up her glamorous job. "The lesson I learned was you can't have it all," she says. "I've solved it up until now by focusing on my career and not having children."

Andrea, a fifty-eight-year-old scientist, didn't recognize how completely she had followed her mother's model for how to be in life until a boyfriend told her, "You're too critical. You push people away by criticizing them all the time." The word "critical" hit Andrea like a ton of bricks, and she realized she was living life based on her mother's use of criticism as a way to control.

Andrea's father had died when she was quite young, leaving her mother with six children to bring up on her own. Her mother was angry that she had been left all alone to cope, and she expressed her anger through constant criticism of her children. She told them they should treat her better, she deserved better kids, they weren't doing as much as they should, and on and on. "Growing up, I learned that to be critical was one way to go about living life," says Andrea. "If life got difficult, I could cope through criticizing myself and others."

As an adult, Andrea took on her mother's critical approach in her personal and professional interactions. She saw self-criticism as a way to motivate herself and get herself to do better, and crit-

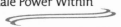

icism of others as a way to get them to perform better or do something for her. She couldn't understand why she couldn't sustain a relationship with a man or keep employees at her firm when all she was trying to do was help them improve themselves. Finally, she came to see that she had become like her mother, pushing away the very people she wanted to attract and nurture, and often getting negative results when she thought she should be getting positive results. When she let go of this pattern she got surprising results. Recently an employee told her, "Andrea, we were just saying how much easier it is to talk to you these days. We're not afraid to come to your office anymore."

How your mother saw her role as a woman has influenced the choices you have made about your life. Your mother didn't have the same choices that you have. Some mothers whispered to their daughters, "Don't rush into marriage. There's no need to do it too soon," or "Don't have children right away." Some mothers were silent, too involved in their own struggle to give advice on how to be a woman. Others encouraged their daughters to make decisions different from the ones they had made. More important than what your mother *said* was how she *behaved* and the role she took in your family—and how she matched up that role with the role your father thought she ought to have.

Sloane, a thirty-four-year-old therapist, had a "perfect mother." Everyone would say to her mother, "You are such a perfect housewife!" and after she gave a party, everyone would say, "Ellen is just the perfect hostess." When her mother took Sloane to her swim meets, the other mothers would comment on how she interacted with Sloane, saying, "Oh, you're such a perfect mother."

With such a "perfect mother," how could Sloane ever be better at motherhood and wifehood than her mother was? Facing this need to be a perfect mother and housewife, she chose to be the exact opposite of her mother. She vowed to never get married, to have her own career, to never give parties, and to never have children—and therefore to never fall short in comparison to her mother. In this way she severely limited her choices for living her own life. It wasn't until later that she realized she actually enjoyed cooking, and it took her ten years to agree to marry the man she knew was right for her. By living in reaction to her mother, Sloane restricted herself in her own life.

What did I learn about being a woman from my mother?

What did I learn about power from my mother?

Am I living the life my mother would have wanted?

Did I vow not to be like my mother?

What does she have that I would like to have and don't?

What choices have I made that are like hers?

What choices have I made that are opposite to hers?

How my mother influenced the way I am as a woman is...

Daddy's Little Girl

How has your father influenced the way you are as a woman?

Many women find that, in addition to living in reaction to their mother's life, they are living in reaction to their father's view of their mother and of women in general. If your father expected your mother to cater to his every need, you learned that to be a woman meant rushing around to take care of the man in your life. If your father respected your mother and valued her contribution to the household, you learned that a woman's work had inherent value. Your father influenced you in spoken and unspoken ways—by what he told you, what you saw him do at home, how he thought about your mother as a woman, what he said to you about women in the world, how he treated women in the world, and how he treated you. These ways might have been contradictory, because there is often a difference between what men say and how they feel. Men sometimes feel more vulnerable to women than they are comfortable admitting.

Some men raise their daughters so they can do anything, and some men raise their daughters to be wives and mothers, perhaps ignoring their uniqueness and individuality. They may focus their attention more on the sons in the family, believing, like Cassie's father, that the sons needed to be trained for independence, while the daughters would grow up to be taken care of by a man. Some men raise their daughters to be "Daddy's little girl," setting her up to believe that no man will ever be good enough because he can never treat her as well as her father did.

If your father raised you to be "Daddy's little girl," the unrealistic expectations that that set up could create a block to finding a satisfying relationship with a man later in life. You might end up being angry with men because they don't measure up. If your father was a "womanizer," you may have absorbed the belief that to get love from a man you had to be sexy. This may have created in you a pattern of reaction that involved being sexy and playing up to men, or deciding not to be sexy and stifling the part of yourself that enjoyed your sexuality. If your father didn't respect your mother, you might have learned that as a woman you didn't count for much. You might have carried out that belief by not living up to your potential, or you might have reacted against it by becoming an overachiever who has to be the best at everything.

Liz grew up believing that a man would always take care of her because that was her father's role in her mother's life. It didn't occur to her that she would actually have to make a living until she graduated from college and realized there was no one taking care of her anymore. She resented the fact that her father had patterned one thing by taking care of her mother and had not prepared her for other options. Developing a career of her own seemed overwhelming, so she opted to marry the man she'd been dating even though she wasn't sure that marriage was what she wanted.

Fathers don't need to speak their expectations for them to be sensed and understood. What you heard your father say around you, and how he acted toward you, your mother, and other women indicated his attitudes. If his mother or other women in his family worked, that would influence his attitude toward women's careers and whether he expected your mother to contribute financially to the household. Clues to your father's attitude during your childhood can lie in his response to his neighbor's wife working, or his reaction when a colleague's wife went back to school.

When it became apparent that women could have careers, the easiest place for girls to look for models was their fathers' professions. Many women went into business in imitation of their fathers either at a conscious or an unconscious level. Jackie, an independent business owner, absorbed her father's small business values watching him run his own accounting firm. Jackie and her sister Vivian both carried on the small business tradition they'd seen their father model—Jackie by creating her own marketing firm, and Vivian by working as an accountant for a small business owner.

Vivian and Jackie grew up steeped in her father's love of cars. He had little money, but as a young man he had won a Cadillac in a contest—a moment which was one of his life's highlights. He knew every make and model of car on the road and made a game out of teaching them to his two daughters. Though neither Vivian nor her sister consciously pursued a career in automobiles, Vivian ended up working in the accounting department at General Motors and her sister worked for a tire manufacturer.

Jackie and Vivian unconsciously chose careers that reflected their father's interests, perhaps from the desire to please "Daddy." Other women took the opposite route. Anne's father was a bank president who encouraged her to go into the financial field, insisting it was the only way to make a successful living. In rebellion, Anne chose to focus on her creative talents and pursued a career in graphic design. Only when she reached her mid-thirties did Anne realize she had deliberately turned away from finance, something she was actually interested in, to prove to her father she could make a successful living as a creative person. Recognizing this allowed her to rethink her choices and look at ways of combining her creativity with her interest in finance.

Until you can see that the choices you have made in life have to do with a reaction to the roles your mother and father patterned for you, you'll have some struggle creating an authentic expression of yourself. By identifying your parents' beliefs and actions, and seeing the way they influenced you, you can move out of reaction and into creation.

Uncoverings

How my father saw a woman's role was...

How my father treated women was...

How my father thought and spoke about women was...

What I learned about women and power from my father was...

Am I living the life my father wanted for me, or the opposite?

Am I living my life like my father's?

How my father influenced the way I am as a woman is...

Donna Reed, Superwoman, and Madonna

What influences did the media have on how you are as a woman?

You followed your parents' examples like a baby duck waddling after its mother, but your parents were not your only influences. Your concept of what it is to be a woman was also formed by the cultural influences of the film and television industries and the books and magazines you read. Every generation has its own cultural icons that either reflect the current ideals and help shape them, or rebel against the current ideals and help deconstruct them. As Hollywood gained influence and television found its way into American homes, suddenly there were images of what we "should" all be striving for in a way that had not been there before.

Films and television often reinforce the cultural times. The movies, sitcoms, and advertisements you watched growing up had a hand in molding your adult experience of womanhood. Those of us in the baby boomer generation absorbed the cultural milieu of the 1950s, when women's goals in life usually revolved around getting or keeping a man and being happy in the home. Though cultural times were changing in the 1960s, television and film often portrayed the status quo. In the 1950s and 1960s, women on television were usually housewives, sex objects, or both—*I Love Lucy, Bewitched, I Dream of Jeannie, Ozzie and Harriet,* and *Father Knows Best.* Leading ladies in the movies were exotic or ditsy sex objects whose main goal was to attract a man—Marilyn Monroe in *How to Marry a Millionaire* and Doris Day in *Please Don't Eat the Daisies.*

Exceptions included independent Katharine Hepburn characters and rebellious Bette Davis characters that kept planting the seeds of what was possible for women—yet the happy ending still usually meant she wound up with the man. A single career woman was often a laughable figure, like Rhoda on *The Mary Tyler Moore Show* or Miss Hathaway in *The Beverly Hillbillies.* Rosemarie on the *Dick Van Dyke* show was unattractive, outspoken, and sassy. In the film *Funny Face,* Kay Thompson's character is a single magazine editor who is strong and independent. She doesn't have a man, and no one falls in love with her by the end of the movie.

Television and magazine advertisements were aimed to keep women thinking they needed the latest model of vacuum cleaner or the best laundry detergent. Romance novels emphasized women's dependence and weakness. Only a few countercultural role models slipped in, such as the independent and adventure-loving Nancy Drew. She gave many girls the opportunity to think about leading nontraditional lives.

Lara, a single business owner of fifty, remembers being fascinated with the strong, rebellious, independent images of movie stars such as Ava Gardner and Ida Lupino. Though she was mesmerized by their strength, she knew she couldn't use them for role models because they always played the "bad women." The characters they played always ended up either in jail or dead at the end of the movie. "Ava Gardner never ended up with the guy," Lara recalls. "He always ended up with the blond ingenue." The stronger and more independent the woman in the film, the greater the price she paid—and the price was often death. At the very least she would end up alone, which was seen as a terrible fate for women. Still, Lara retained the image of the strong women played by Gardner and Lupino as something she would aspire to in her own life—without the unhappy ending.

During the 1960s things began to change. Though the predominant culture still encouraged women to keep traditional roles, "the times they were a-changin'." Images of women in the popular culture slowly began to shift, giving radical ideas to girls growing up in this time. Suddenly it seemed possible that we didn't have to live like our mothers, that there could be other choices. And as feminism swept into the 1970s, bringing with it changes deep at the heart of the culture, women flooded into the work force and the political arena.

Women born in the late 1960s and 1970s grew up with a much broader range of cultural icons. Those of us born in the 1960s and beyond were faced with a confusing mix of traditional female roles and a radically transformed culture. In the 1970s women on television could do more things—be a superhero, a detective, or a taxi driver. But no matter what women were doing, they were still either sexy and ditsy or intelligent and unattractive—and they were usually controlled by a male authority figure. On television, *Charlie's Angels* had three women as its tough detectives, but all three were sex objects who gladly bent to the will of an invisible, controlling male. Linda Carter as Wonder Woman was strong and brave, but she wore what amounted to a bathing suit and looked charming at all times. *M*A*S*H* showed women in the military, but they were all nurses who served mainly as diverting sex objects for the male doctors.

Movies started to shift as women had more powerful roles, but women's roles still involved being attractive to men. The Walt Disney ideal of princesses in distress or drudges transformed to go to the ball continued to surface in the popular imagination. Carrie Fisher as Princess Leia in *Star Wars* was strong and feminine, but she still needed Han Solo to rescue her. Olivia Newton-John in *Grease* changed herself from an innocent, sensitive, intelligent girl into a leather-clad vixen to get the man she wanted. In a twist on the traditional portrayal of women as housewives, the 1975 movie *Stepford Wives* presented a horrifying picture of evil underneath the well-groomed exterior of a town's perfect wives.

By the 1980s women were portrayed on television and in movies as having a wide variety of careers. It was still their sex appeal, though, that helped them get what they wanted—such as Melanie Griffith's portrayal of a sexy young woman taking over her boss's position in *Working Girl*. As the 80s progressed, movies continued to reflect women's increasing presence in the workplace and the dilemmas they faced there. The 1989 movie *Baby Boom* was the first major film to examine women's whispered desire to leave the corporate workplace and stay home.

On television, the explosion of MTV onto the scene in 1980 radically affected adolescent and even preadolescent youth. "I was twelve when MTV came onto the scene," says Erin, a thirty-two-year-old small business owner. "My friends and I stopped watching sitcoms or soap operas and started watching MTV all the time. It was fabulous because the female singers on MTV could express their sexuality and power in new ways. I mean, to see Madonna just throwing everyone for a loop in her 'Like a Virgin' video was so exciting for us. Women could express themselves and be popular! We all either wanted to be Madonna or reviled her as a pop sellout, but in any case she had an effect we couldn't ignore."

Strong female icons, such as Madonna and the androgynous Annie Lennox of the Eurythmics, provided girls with role models radically different from any they had seen before. But MTV also carried out the cultural norm of women being svelte, sexy, and almost always craving a man. MTV, along with the proliferation of women's magazines, focused on appearance, glamour, and fashion; continuing the cultural belief that, above all, a woman needed to be attractive and find herself a man—an underlying current that hadn't changed since the 1950s.

Some famous women have worked hard to make the media a more female place. In 1972 Gloria Steinem co-founded *Ms.* magazine. As the first women's magazine not dedicated to beauty, fashion, or homemaking, it gave women a forum for discussing serious issues. More recently, Oprah Winfrey changed the face of talk shows from in-your-face confrontations to forums for healing. Lifetime television for women and the newer Oxygen channel often provide the human side of the stories they cover, focusing on nourishing women's real lives, rather than on putting forward ideals they can never reach.

Today's pop culture portrays women as independent, successful, and powerful in ways they never would have been portrayed forty years ago—and also just as involved with being attractive, sexy, and concerned with pleasing a man as they would have forty years ago.

It would be powerful for you to identify the cultural influences that shaped you and notice how things have changed or not changed. There is still a lot of inequality in how women are treated and perceived in popular culture. The more each of us focuses inward and comes into our own power, the less power we will give to social and cultural ideals. As we become our fully authentic selves, the worry of not measuring up to those ideals will disappear.

Uncoverings

My favorite movies from my childhood and early adolescence were...

What did they teach me about being a woman?

My favorite heroines were...

What did they teach me about being a woman?

My favorite television shows were...

What did they teach me about being a woman?

My favorite television characters were...

What did they teach me about being a woman?

Cultural standards I was pressured by were...

I responded to them by...

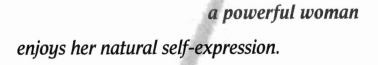

*a powerful woman
enjoys her natural self-expression.*

*a powerful woman
knows she is worth going through
the hard part.*

4

What You Lost Along the Way

Invisible Ties That Bind

What would your life have been like if...
your parents had encouraged you to be yourself?

In the last chapter you looked at the influence your parents had on the life you've chosen and at the cultural history that shaped you. As we get more specific, we'll be exploring your family's unique combination of dynamics that still holds you in its grip today. By exploring your family's history, you can begin to free yourself to investigate what is authentic for you rather than remaining fixed in a familiar pattern of reaction to your childhood.

Most of us spent at least part of our childhood being told it wasn't okay to be ourselves, and those voices are still working to keep us from living authentic lives. No matter how much support we got in life, we remember the times we fell short and the people who were displeased with us. To create a life for yourself that is authentic and fulfilling means being willing to look at the history that holds you back.

Exploring your family's history and how it affects you today does not mean blaming your parents for everything that is difficult in your life. You may be angry with them, and you may have every right to be angry. On the other hand, you may *not* be angry and it may be good for you to allow yourself to be angry. If it is difficult for you to say anything negative about your parents, it would be healthy for you to be able to do so. Being angry doesn't mean placing blame—it means just feeling the feeling you are having. It is important to keep in mind that your parents really were doing the best they could at the time. This may be difficult to accept, and you may find yourself asking in amazement, "*That* was the best they could do?" But if they could have done better, they would have—wouldn't they?

Your parents had their own histories that restricted them in their lives, but they might not have had the tools or the support to deal with it differently. They were human and they made mistakes, as you are human and you make mistakes. Somehow we all think our parents should have been perfect, and of course since they are human, they could not have been perfect. Accepting your parents' humanity will make it easier to put the past in the past.

Janet's parents divorced when she was ten and her father moved far away. When her mother remarried, Janet accepted her stepfather as her father figure and rarely thought about her birth father. One day when she was in her early thirties, he called her. She wasn't sure what to say to him and realized she was still angry with him for leaving. He seemed determined to develop a relationship with her, however, and started calling her every Sunday night. She grew to dread those awkward conversations and tried not to think of him in between their talks.

Soon afterward, Janet came to Life Works and attended weekly Gatherings and the Father Retreat. Gradually she realized she'd been angry with her father for leaving because she could no longer think of him as perfect. She didn't want him to be a flawed human being. Once Janet began learning to accept that her father was human and therefore made mistakes, she noticed a subtle shift in their relationship. She was able to listen to him better, and found that in turn he was able to listen to her. Today they have a more meaningful relationship. "It's not the fairy tale," Janet explains. "He's not perfect, and neither am I. But if I hadn't done the work, we never would have had a relationship at all."

Accepting that your parents are human doesn't mean glossing over the profound effect they had on how you have lived your life. You have reacted to them by being a good girl or by rebelling—and both reactions limit you.

What would your life have been like if...
you had belonged to a different family?

Your family's expectations of how you could and could not be in life have had a powerful influence on how you have lived. Like all families, your family has a style or way of being that creates invisible limitations for you. No glass ceiling at a corporation is stronger than the glass box that being a member of your family has set up for you. That glass box has you functioning within a certain set of rules, expectations, and beliefs that is comfortable for your family.

Antonia never seemed to be able to get herself into the black financially. She changed careers several times in her twenties and thirties, but her jobs always involved many work hours and low pay. She found herself saying things such as, "Oh, I'd love to go on that vacation with you, but I can't afford it," or "I really love that dress, but it's not in my budget this month." Eventually she began to wonder why she never seemed able to have the things she wanted when she worked hard every day. She noticed that her friends, who didn't necessarily make more money than she did, treated themselves to vacations and new clothes. Why was it that she was constantly broke?

One day as Antonia was walking past a large, beautiful Victorian house, she thought about the big house she had lived in until her parents got divorced and moved to smaller houses, then downsized to meager apartments. She remembered stories her grandmother had told her of the huge house in Vienna her grandmother's family had lived in until Hitler's invasion of Austria forced them to leave, forfeiting all of their immense wealth. Her grandmother had made her way to New York with her husband and Antonia's infant father, living in poverty in a tiny apartment in the unbearable summer heat.

As she did more work on herself, Antonia realized that her beliefs about wealth were based on the two events of her parents' divorce and her grandmother's exile. Because it was her family's pattern to have wealth and then lose it, Antonia was unconsciously keeping herself poor. If she were poor, she wouldn't have to live with the disappointment of having everything taken away from her. Antonia's identification of a family pattern allowed her to see her own choices differently. She was able to see that she had been living in reaction to the belief that it is impossible to have financial security.

Part of what makes change difficult is having to change the role you play in your family and the beliefs about life that your family instilled in you. You have already identified some of the roles you have played that may have held you back from being authentically yourself. Like everyone on the planet, you were raised in a family that has spoken or unspoken rules, regulations, ways of doing things, expectations, beliefs, traditions, superstitions, warnings, and controls. Your family's way of framing how you could and could not be in life has had a powerful influence on how you have lived. In order to function within your family, you adopted its rules, expectations, and beliefs as your own—perhaps without realizing it. You have probably also chosen friends and colleagues who reinforce your family way of being.

If you want to become more yourself and have more of what you want, you will probably find you need to free yourself from your family's limitations. This may mean that there is an emotional "leaving home" you have to do. When someone succeeds further than a family member has done or steps out of the family's restrictions, it means emotionally leaving the family in some way. We have all had ways of being rebellious, but being the opposite of your family way means you are still living in reference to it. In some aspects we are still good girls striving to have everyone feel safe and comfortable. As you continue the work of uncovering your natural power, it will help to keep in mind that these family limitations might have you resisting change in ways that until now would have been invisible to you.

Kimberly worked hard to become a successful stockbroker, denying herself a personal life and focusing on her career. On her fortieth birthday she went out to eat with some friends. Getting into bed by herself after dinner, she realized she was lonely. She had always thought her career would be enough, but now she knew she wanted someone to share her life with. Immediately she felt her heart start to race and her palms get sweaty. Terrified, she switched on the light. All she could hear was her mother's voice warning her, "There are no good men out there. They'll all screw you one way or another, so you're better off on your own."

As a teenager, Kimberly had watched her mother's marriage end in a messy and wrenching divorce. When her mother started dating, she complained about her dates constantly and admonished Kimberly never to get involved with a man. Watching her mother date was almost as humiliating and discouraging for Kimberly as watching her suffering during the divorce. Once the adult Kimberly realized her mother's divorce had set her up to expect marriage to end badly, she was able to find help so she could open herself to having a relationship.

Identifying the beliefs and patterns of your family can be a step in freeing yourself from the family influence. It may be that functioning within the belief systems your family set up for you

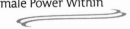

is limiting you in life. You may not even realize that it is limiting you. It is powerful to ask questions that reveal the invisible limitations you feel from your family. Each one of us has different questions we can ask ourselves that let us see the rules and regulations our family has provided.

Uncoverings

Ask yourself these questions. Some may not apply to your family, and there may be other questions not on the list that you would like to add.

How successful can I be and still be a member of my family?

How happy can I be and still be a member of my family?

How much money can I earn and still be a member of my family?

How much authority can I have and still be a member of my family?

How in control of my life can I be and still be a member of my family?

How gentle can I be and still be a member of my family?

How powerful can I be and still be a member of my family?

How authentically self-expressed can I be and still be a member of my family?

How well-respected can I be and still be a member of my family?

How famous can I be and still be a member of my family?

How happily married can I be and still be a member of my family?

Can I be childless and still be a member of my family?

How cooperatively can I live and still be a member of my family?

How confident can I be and still be a member of my family?

How enviable can I be and still be a member of my family?

How tender a woman can I be and still be a member of my family?

How independent a woman can I be and still be a member of my family?

How generous can I be and still be a member of my family?

How self-loving can I be and still be a member of my family?

How wealthy can I be and still be a member of my family?

How strong a woman can I be and still be a member of my family?

Who Pulled the Rug?

Think of a time...
in your childhood when you lost your sense of worth.

Every child loses her dignity, value, worthiness, and entitlement somewhere along the way. You had it once, because like everyone, in the earliest years of childhood, you had a strong sense of your own value. Then life started happening to you—and as you were reprimanded, criticized, unacknowledged, corrected, and ignored, the innate sense of worth you were born with was diminished over and over again. The people who brought you up and influenced you probably had no intention of reducing your sense of worth and value. They were just doing what they knew how to do to raise you the best way they could. And today you are still living with the effects of your upbringing.

If people who felt undeserving raised you, you will probably feel unworthy. If you were an unplanned child, you may have sensed that your parents had somehow rearranged their lives for you. You may have felt you needed to prove your value to your parents. If you had a sibling born after you, you may have noticed that all your parents' attention went to your sibling and that suddenly your value seemed to go down.

Emma's two brothers were nine and eleven years old when she was born, and she knew from the beginning that she was a mistake. Whenever her brothers did well at school or at a track meet, her parents praised them and celebrated with them. When Emma brought home her report card with straight A's, however, her parents barely noticed. Emma felt that her two brothers could do no wrong in her parents' eyes, and she could do nothing right. She did everything she could think of to try to make them approve of her. She tried helping her mother with the housework, baking cookies, and doing her homework without prompting. Yet her efforts often brought only blame—for singeing a shirt she'd ironed, using up all the eggs in the house in her baking attempts, and bringing her noisy friends home. Her parents rarely showed affection for her, either physically or verbally.

Emma found herself constantly wondering, "What could I do differently so my parents will love me?" It was clear she would never please them and that the harder she tried, the less appreciative they seemed. Eventually, she realized the only thing to do was escape. She graduated from high school early and went far away to college, where she started building her life up from the shattered remains of her self-esteem. She couldn't use her power well if she didn't feel worthy.

You may remember an event in your childhood that took the wind out of your sails—perhaps to such an extent that you still feel it today. The ongoing pattern of Emma's invisibility in her family resulted in her losing her sense of value, but sometimes what causes a woman to lose her sense of value is a single catastrophic event. If you forgot your lines while performing in the school play or if you were really proud of a Popsicle-stick sculpture you made and your parents laughed at it, all your enjoyment of being the center of attention would likely have been overwhelmed by the shame or hurt of that incident. It may be that it was not one specific instance that let the air out of your balloon, but that you were in a situation that happened over and over again to eventually deflate you. You might have reminded your parents of themselves, so they tried to correct their own mistakes by correcting you. Having a parent who picked on you constantly, or having an unpredictable mother who kept you walking on eggshells in anticipation of an outburst, would have the capacity to cut into your sense of who you were.

Think of a time…
when you lost your sense of dignity.

Children keenly feel the sense of their own dignity, and parents might not recognize that their interactions with a child can damage that dignity. Parents don't always appreciate the essence of a child, and even if your parents did appreciate you, there was a time when they didn't—which is the time you remember. If you were humiliated in front of others, if your parents spanked you, if you were not listened to, or if your desires were ridiculed, you probably lost your sense of dignity in each of those situations.

If you don't feel deserving today, there was probably an event in your childhood that set you up to feel that way. Loretta, a clothing designer, deeply desired a pair of platform shoes she found at a garage sale when she was six. She was fascinated by the high cork heels and the shiny white straps, and begged her mother for them. Her mother looked at them in horror, but seeing the longing in Loretta's eyes, she seemed to relent and bought them.

Loretta sat in the back of the car with the shoes in her lap while her mother continued to look around the sale. Suddenly her mother came up to her and gestured to a young girl standing next to her looking dejected. "Susie really wants those shoes, Loretta," her mother said. "She had just run home to get the money when we saw the shoes and bought them. Wouldn't it be nice of you to give them to her?"

Loretta's heart gave a lurch, but what could she do with her mother and the girl looking pleadingly at her? She handed them over and cried silently later. She was sure she must have done something wrong not to deserve those beautiful shoes. From then on, whenever she really wanted something she didn't allow herself to tell anyone about it. She felt strange whenever someone gave her a gift because she was sure she didn't deserve it and she knew it could be taken away. For years she wore nothing but old cast-off clothing.

Exploring the times you lost your sense of worth can lead to a deeper understanding of why you may not feel worthy of having a happy and fulfilled life today. Finding these times doesn't mean blaming your parents. Loretta's mother had reasons of her own for taking the shoes back, just as your parents had reasons for doing what they did. You may never know those reasons, but understanding that your parents were doing their best allows you to explore the past without blame. After all, wonderful people do some awful things—ourselves included.

Your parents were not the only ones who had you lose your sense of dignity, worth, and value. Sarcastic remarks from a teacher, being taunted or bullied by other children, or being punished at school are all ways you might have experienced scarring humiliation.

Beatrice remembers her fourth-grade gym class as one of the worst experiences of her life—one that still affects her today. "The male gym teacher made fun of anyone who wasn't good at sports," she recalls. "He would let the most popular girls pick teams, and I was always the last to be picked. Finally when I was the only one left, the team who got me would groan. Mr. Henderson never did anything to stop it. In fact, he encouraged kids to pick on me and would torture me and other klutzy kids on purpose, making us go through what he called the 'gauntlet' where we had to run through a double line of kids all swatting at us with tennis rackets."

Mr. Henderson's behavior had a lasting effect on Beatrice. To this day she is afraid to try any competitive sports, even though she would like to take up golf. "I finally got over thinking I was a complete nerdy klutz in my twenties, when I started running and dancing and realized I was actually quite coordinated," Beatrice says. "But I still can't bring myself to participate in my company's annual tennis tournament or even to play a pickup game of badminton with friends. I'm working on it, though, and the more I heal the old wounds the more willing I am to try new things."

Like Emma, Loretta, and Beatrice, you experienced events in your childhood that may still be holding you back today. Those times that you weren't listened to, when you were punished without anyone hearing your side of the story, when your younger brother was valued over you—those are the times when you lost your sense of worth.

Uncoverings

Think of times...

> *Times I lost my power*
> *Times I lost my sense of dignity*
> *Times I lost my feelings of deserving*
> *Times I lost my sense of value*
>
> *Based on these experiences, the decisions I made about myself and my power were...*

Living Between the Lines

Who was uncomfortable when you were expressing yourself fully and successfully?

An old adage says that you spend the first half of your life being embarrassed by your parents, and the second half being embarrassed by your children. Your parents may have been embarrassed when you expressed yourself freely. If they were uncomfortable with their own self-expression, they were certainly uncomfortable with yours.

Your authentic self-expression was limited every time you wanted to speak your piece and you weren't allowed to, every time you wanted to voice an opinion and no one would listen, and every time you wanted to explain yourself and you were silenced. Your authentic self-expression was limited if you were creating art out of clay and you were told to "take that dirty mess outside," or if you were singing out loud with great gusto and you were told to hush. Your authentic self-expression was limited when you didn't win the trophy, when you were laughed at, and also when you felt envied. You may find it difficult to believe that people envied you, but they did—and their envy may have been a powerful deterrent to your authentic self-expression.

Blake, an editor in her early thirties, recalled an experience of another's envy that powerfully affected her. As a child, Blake's involvement in her local Brownie troop was a source of pride and fulfillment for her. She earned badges for her creative and athletic prowess and often won praise from the troop leaders. When she was ten, she found herself confronted by Nellie, another Brownie whose mother was a troop leader. "My mother says you're not a good Brownie and that you're too noisy and rambunctious," Nellie informed her. Blake was devastated. She had always enjoyed the high spirits she experienced when she was participating, and she had never thought of her actions as "noisy" or "rambunctious."

In retrospect, Blake can see that Nellie probably insulted her out of spite due to Nellie's envy of Blake's success and popularity in the troop. Yet the remark affected Blake's sense of self well into her adult life. She found herself often wondering if she was being too loud or if her natural exuberance was offensive to others, and she often censored herself because she didn't want to be seen as obnoxious. Nellie's envious spite had such power that it kept Blake from fully expressing herself for much of her life.

What childhood limitations placed on you have stayed with you, influencing you to make decisions in your life that limit who you are?

Early training may have informed you that it was not okay to be yourself, and because you were impressionable you learned the

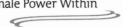

lesson well. You may have developed habits that stop you from being yourself in some way, and you probably surround yourself with some people who will ensure that you don't go beyond a certain boundary.

Pamela's mother was an amateur painter who had a small following of admirers. One day, Pamela's junior high art teacher called her mother to tell her how well Pamela had been doing in art class. "She's a natural painter," the teacher enthused. "You should really consider sending her to private art classes." When Pamela arrived home, her mother confronted her.

"You didn't tell me you were taking painting at school," she said.

Pamela shrugged. "It's one of my electives. I like it. Hey, my teacher told me one of my paintings looked like a Matisse. Wait—I've got it in my bag. See?"

Her mother looked at the painting and snorted. "It looks like a third-grader's painting to me," she said. "Why don't you stop wasting your energy on this foolishness and concentrate on your academic subjects."

Though Pamela was hurt and confused, she accepted her mother's judgment and steered away from art. Only in her adulthood did she understand that her mother had made fun of her painting not because it was not good, but because it was too good. It would not have been acceptable for Pamela to be a better painter than her mother was. As an obliging daughter, Pamela found other things to be good at in order to keep her relationship with her mother on stable ground.

Pamela powerfully kept herself away from something she was good at in order not to upset her mother. You may also have powerfully kept yourself away from something you may have been good at in order to keep someone around you happy. If you wanted to major in drama in college but everyone in your family had always majored in the sciences, your desire may have seemed impossible to fulfill. You may be powerfully limiting yourself by keeping yourself within your family's glass box because you learned as a child that to express yourself authentically could upset people. Upsetting others means they may decide they don't like you, and of course you want people to like you. Children must have their parents' approval to feel safe, and we often carry that desire for approval into adulthood. One element of becoming authentically self-expressed is making peace with the idea that not everyone can like you. Your self-expression will not be pleasing to everyone—but it will be pleasing to you.

If you had a parent who was strongly critical of you, you may have learned to stop expressing yourself in their presence. If you were ridiculed for your interests, you may have learned to stop expressing your desires. If your opinions were disdained or ignored, you may have learned not to trust your own impressions.

It is powerful to look at the times in your childhood when your authentic self-expression was limited, stifled, or ignored. Look for experiences as far back as you can remember, because the earlier ones were what formed the patterns you live out today. Understanding what happened back then to have you living the way you live now can help liberate you from your past.

Uncoverings

Who was uncomfortable when I was expressing myself fully and successfully?

When I was young...

>*Who felt harmed when I was being (expressing) my true self, and when?*

>*Who felt threatened by my being (expressing) myself, and when?*

>*What my mother did to control my natural expression was...*

>*What my father did to control my natural expression was...*

>*What others did to control my natural expression was...*

Based on these questions and answers, what I learned about expressing myself and being powerful was...

Who would be uncomfortable now if I were being my powerful self?

Remember, these questions are designed to allow memories and feelings to come forward. No one is judging your answers or checking to see if you finished each uncovering. If you feel a little overwhelmed, or if your answers are just skimming the surface, that's okay. We encourage you to look over all the questions, but know that you can return to them anytime and fill in missing pieces.

Part Three

~

The Practice:

Everyday Tools for Releasing Your Power

a powerful woman

accepts her humanity and the
humanity of others.

a powerful woman

sees situations as opportunities for
growth, healing, and stretching.

5

⌒

Locating Your Power Centers

A New Way of Seeing Who You Are

What would life be like if...
you could fully accept that you are human?

As you begin to identify ways you have defined yourself until now, to see how our cultural shifts have shaped you, and to discover ways you have lived within the framework of your family's limitations, you are beginning to uncover the layers that have kept you from knowing your essence. If your sense of worthiness was taken away, and your self-expression was stifled in childhood, then parts of you have been lost along the way. We have found that working with the chakras is one of the very best ways to find these lost aspects and uncover ones that you may not even know exist.

Chakras are the body's seven energy centers, located from the base of the trunk (the anal chakra) to the space just above the physical body at the crown of head (crown chakra). They serve as your windows to the world, places in your body that have you connect to the world in different ways.

In this chapter we will explain the qualities of each chakra and how you can use them to help yourself. A light entered your body the moment you were born and will leave your body when you pass. By becoming aware of the energy flowing through the chakras, you can see yourself as this light. The chakra meditation at the end of this chapter is designed to help you do that—to stretch the boundaries and frontiers of who you are, and ground yourself in the present moment.

If you are familiar with the chakras, you may have noticed that our view is more psychological than others. While the ancient concept of the chakras originates in some forms of Hinduism and Buddhism, our modern approach focuses on understanding the qualities of each chakra as a way of seeing who we authentically are. We see chakras as a powerful way of explaining our humanity and understanding ourselves in a more accepting and forgiving way. Our interpretation of the chakra system is not intended as an absolute truth but as a model for understanding human nature.

You can use the chakra system as a way of understanding the essence of who you are—beyond the identities you have formed or the history that has kept you acting and reacting in certain ways. This new understanding allows different thoughts about yourself to come forward. And these different thoughts generate new feelings, which, in turn, may have you taking different action. By taking different action, you may create different results. The simple act of expanding your *perception* of yourself, then, can begin the process of bringing you what you want.

It will be useful to be open to seeing yourself differently as you read on.

Anal or Root Chakra

Think of a time...
  you felt safe and grounded.

The anal chakra, located at the base of the trunk, is where you experience life-or-death situations. In a crisis, two things happen: the mind becomes one-pointed, focusing only on what is dangerous about the situation; and the body prepares itself for Herculean feats by becoming filled with extraordinary energy. We have all heard stories of mothers lifting cars to get their children out from underneath, or of women running into raging fires to rescue their families. You may even have experienced something similar yourself. When the survival instinct kicks in and adrenaline rushes through the body, you are poised to act. This is a response you want in an emergency. It is powerful to acknowledge the anal chakra's response and be grateful that it can help you when you need it.

When we feel we are in danger, the body and mind react from the anal chakra, preparing for emergency action. This response is good and necessary when we really are in peril, but often situations that are not life-or-death trigger the anal chakra. The same

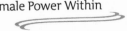

alarm goes off when you receive an unexpected letter from the IRS, if you can't find a document your boss asked for, or if the person you're dating doesn't call when they said they would. Your anal chakra gets triggered or "grabbed" by the situation, and adrenaline moves through your body. Your mind becomes obsessed with one idea, and your body is filled with energy that demands action. It is here that you may make decisions and take actions that are not healthy for you, because you are thoroughly involved in the upset of that situation. You may do something that will harm you, or take an action that you will be sorry for later.

Very few upsets in the anal chakra have to do with any real threat to your life. Most of us have only experienced one or two truly life-threatening moments. Yet in all probability you experience the feelings that accompany a life-or-death situation several times a week, or even several times a day.

The beginning of having power with an upset is being able to name what is going on. If you can name something, you can have power with it. If it goes unnoticed and not spoken about, it has power over you. If you can recognize that when you have a strong fear reaction the anal chakra is being "grabbed," you can know that what you are really experiencing is a call to deal with life and death danger, whether or not it is actually an emergency.

Think of a time...
in the past month when you experienced the life-or-death "grab" in the anal chakra—when your mind became one-pointed and obsessed, and the adrenaline rushed through your body, filling you with an extraordinary energy.

Did it feel like you were in great danger? Were you really in danger? When you are involved in an upset in the anal chakra, you lose power with yourself. If you can't find your driver's license when stopped by the police, you may experience the same body reaction as if someone you love just got run over by a car. You may not be able to stop the body's condition, and it may last an entire day. In the episodes when you feel triggered in the anal chakra, your mind obsesses, trying to control something that feels out of control. Your body wants to rush into action. You think you need to make a decision immediately. You may never think to stop and ask yourself if you really are in danger.

In the moment of acknowledging an "anal chakra grab," there is a separation between you and the experience—you are slightly outside of it instead of completely caught up in it. There is, then, awareness that your response is an exaggeration, that you are actually much safer than you feel, and that you are reacting in a way that is out of proportion to what has occurred.

Think of a decision…
you have made recently when you were feeling "grabbed."

When such a thing is happening, it is powerful to be able to step back and recognize what is happening. Might you have made a different decision if you knew that the situation was not life threatening? Instead of accepting the obsessive thoughts and doing something rash with your body's excess energy, you can say, "Ah, there's that obsessive thinking and the body wanting to take immediate action. I think I'm in danger—let me check. Am I in danger? No, I'm having an 'anal chakra grab'." Recognizing what is going on is the beginning of taking back your power.

Once you can recognize the anal chakra's signals, you have the ability to be grounded at any given moment. Grounding is the act of connecting yourself to yourself through the earth, as a tree is connected to the earth through its roots. Sometimes when you are frightened or nervous, you might feel light-headed. Grounding yourself by breathing, meditating, or drinking water can bring you back so you can see how to cope with a situation. Groundedness allows you the ability to know what to do and how to proceed.

Groundedness is a powerfully female place to come from for making decisions. When you are grounded, you can handle life instead of running away, hiding, or taking a male, forceful action that won't get you what you want. When the anal chakra calls you to action, instead of looking for who to blame or who to harm, you can breathe and let yourself be with the situation until an answer becomes clear. It may be that no action is necessary at the moment. You will only know that if you are grounded. When you are grounded, your life is easier because you are able to calm yourself in a stressful moment and choose well for yourself.

Doing the chakra meditation following this chapter will help you connect through the anal chakra, which will ground you.

Sexual Chakra

Think of a time...
you experienced being womanly.

Think of a time...
you experienced being nurturing.

The sexual chakra is the seat of your womanliness. It is located in your pelvic region, where your sexual organs produce and blend your hormones and where the ability to create life originates. The soft and tender light of your female power emanates from this chakra. Your female nature is like the uterus, which has the ability to expand to grow new life, and the pelvis, which has the ability to open when a woman gives birth. Giving birth to new life can take many forms. Stimulating growth in others, planting a garden, beginning a new project at work, or starting a new way of being are all ways of metaphorically giving birth. Your sexual chakra is the source of your creativity, which you express in your own unique ways—by having a child, hiring new staff, or writing a story. It enables you to see widely as you lean back and receive life with open arms, embracing what is coming toward you.

The power of your sexual chakra is in that female strength that we find hard to describe in words because it is unaccustomed to being acknowledged. That power is evident when you soothe a distressed friend, when you listen to what a child is saying, or when you praise an employee. It is a power that expresses itself by approaching a situation with tenderness rather than defensiveness or by allowing someone to support you when you need it. It is the power of acceptance, of being open to life, of being vulnerable.

Just as your sexual organs are hidden, so, often, is your power. It can be subtle and quiet, and it may only be noticed when it's missing because it doesn't demand attention. Whenever you help a conversation flow smoothly or really listen to someone, when you gently encourage people to work together or you provide care and tending to someone, you are expressing your subtle female power. What you did may go unnoticed, but if it hadn't been there, the quality of the experience would have been diminished and the outcome different.

Our female nature involves us in the *process* of life. We are attuned to process because we experience menstruation, gestation, childbirth, and menopause. This orientation to life gives us the ability to enjoy the ride, be in the moment, attend to the details, expect the path to turn, adjust to its fluctuations gracefully, and go with the flow. It is female to put a desire out into the universe, then lean back and open our arms to what the universe is sending us, embracing it and using it in the best way to have what we want—even if it doesn't look exactly the way we thought it would look.

When we are connected with our selves and not "grabbed," we are able to sit with a certain amount of ambiguity. We can follow the steps that will lead us to an answer, instead of immediately leaping to a solution. It is powerful for us to be able to lean back and say, "I don't know, let me take some time to think about that" or "Let's see how the situation evolves before coming to a solution." It is male to want answers right away. It is female to sit with a problem or situation, to let it get clear, to permit trial and error, and to accept that part of the process might be to get it wrong the first, third, or tenth time we try. Like foreplay, we can follow an experience and stay in the moment of it, expecting that it will bring us to the place we want to be. Enjoying the process allows us to relax into our lives, trusting that each step is taking us on the path we want to travel.

Being grounded in the anal chakra and centered in the sexual chakra has us be in the *now* of life, able to keep many plates spinning effortlessly. We can be relaxed, know who we are, lean back, expect that things will happen for us in a good way, and have all the time we need to be in the process rather than needing an instant result. We can trust that it will all happen—it's just a matter of time.

It is our birthright as women to have rich, full, varied, broad lives. We may have put ourselves into narrow boxes, but we are wide and expansive by nature. We have all had moments in our lives when we have been the female we know ourselves to be, and these moments are powerful. We can have more and more of these moments as we lean back and relax into our lives, knowing that we don't need to be worried, angry, or frightened and allowing ourselves to sit in awe of life's unfoldment.

Solar Plexus Chakra

Think of a time...
  when you expressed your will.

Think of a time...
when you expressed your willingness.

We get "gripped" in the anal chakra because we are responding not to the immediate situation in front of us, but to another, similar situation that happened in our childhood. The emotions connected with the early experience are stored in the solar plexus chakra, which is located in your midriff above your belly button. We call this emotional center your *psychological self*. It is the part of you that gets upset.

Whenever we are upset, we are experiencing a series of reactions to old emotional situations. When you got "gripped" in the anal chakra, responding to a life-or-death signal sent you into immediate action. When you were a child, the anal chakra's response helped you make quick decisions for how to act in frightening situations. If, for example, your mother sighed and glared at you, you knew you had done something wrong, and you would have to decide very quickly what to do about it so she wouldn't scold or punish you like she did the last time. You might have decided that what you needed to do was cry, apologize, and beg her to let you fix the problem. If this reaction worked and you escaped harsh punishment, you made it a rule to act that way in any similar situation. If it worked better to skulk away and hide in your room, you made slipping into the shadows a way of being in order to save yourself. The decisions you made became patterns of behavior that reside to this day in the solar plexus.

You made your childhood decisions based on what would protect you in the life-or-death grip of the moment, and on what you thought would ensure you would never have to feel that way again. The rules you made worked in the short term to keep you safe, but now they may be working against you. Assuming that every circumstance you come into will feel like the childhood circumstance felt, and reacting the way you did in childhood, keeps you stuck in certain patterns of behavior. Though some of these patterns might be working well for you, some might be holding you back from being more yourself.

You may have decided as a child that you had to be organized because it looked like life was falling apart around you. This need for organization might have helped you back then, and it may still be helpful in many ways today. Your boss may appreciate you for your organizational skills at work. On the other hand, needing to be organized all the time might cause strife at home when you yell at your husband for leaving his socks on the floor. If you have decided you are shy, it might feel comfortable and allow you to fade into the background. But if you are trying to meet people or apply for a high profile job, your shyness could keep you from getting what you want.

By making decisions based on what happened in the past and the reactions you had in the past, you are continually repeating your history. It is as if a part of you were frozen in an experience back then—and that part of you is still frozen today, unable to make a change or take an action different from a knee-jerk reaction to a past situation. The energy of the frozen part of you can only become available to you again when you can revisit the traumatic situation, heal it, and return your energy to yourself. We will help you do this over the course of the next few chapters.

Think of something...
that upset you recently.

Did you feel upset for more than a few minutes? If you did, you probably time traveled back into your history when a similar situation occurred. For example, someone may have yelled at you this morning and you felt wildly hurt and humiliated. Without knowing it, you time traveled back ten, twenty, thirty, forty, fifty, or sixty years into an original experience in which you were yelled at and humiliated. You then became engrossed in your experience of that past situation, and your upset was no longer about the present. You were probably completely mesmerized by your upset, and were unable to step back and look at it objectively.

How much energy do you use by getting upset every day, every week, every year?

Being mesmerized by your upsets disconnects you from your creative energy. It is easy to get engrossed by your emotional life and the circumstances you find yourself in. You are not alone! The next time you walk down the street, walk through a mall, or sit in traffic, take a look at the people around you. Do they look like they are totally in the moment and enjoying it? In all probability, they are somewhere lost in their past or their psychology, carrying on conversations with themselves about their emotional lives. Most people are lost in their thoughts, feelings, and internal conversation most of the time. The man standing next to you on the elevator might be absorbed in a humiliating memory of a seventh-grade dance, brought on by the canned elevator music. Only when he finds himself standing outside in the street will he again be in the present.

It is easy to get totally taken up by your upsets—by what you are thinking and feeling, how someone else is responding, what she said and what she did. But in doing this, you lose yourself. You powerfully engage in your psychological being, your solar plexus chakra, and believe that it is who you are. You may never take a moment to think that perhaps you are something greater than your psychological self, and that your psychological self is not you. The good news is that while you have a psychological self, it is only a part of you. It is not *who you are.* The psychological self that resides in the solar plexus is only one of your seven chakras—it is an *aspect* of who you are.

Your psychological self is the part of you that never got healed, so it keeps drawing toward you people and experiences that have you relive your childhood. The names and faces have changed, but your experience is the same. For example, you may attract a certain kind of romantic partner, perhaps one who leaves you for someone else when you get really attached to him—just as your father left you when you were six years old. Or maybe you attract a boss who verbally abuses you—just as your older sister did throughout your childhood. You may find yourself in a friendship where you get taken advantage of—just as the other children in your class took advantage of you by making you do their homework for them.

The solar plexus is where you express your will and willingness to have things happen. Will is the male aspect, which involves making something happen, and willingness is the female aspect, which involves being open and available for something to happen. You need both will and willingness to manifest what you want in life. Upsets stop you from expressing your will and willingness. Often the fear of having an upset may keep you from doing something that you want to do.

Think of something…
in the recent past that you didn't do because you
were afraid of the feelings it might provoke.

When you are upset, you lose your sense of safety and your relationship with yourself. You lose the connection to your creative energy, you are no longer in the present, and your ability to make decisions is stuck in your psychological self. There is nothing wrong with you when you get upset and lose the power of your will and willingness. Human beings limit themselves, because every human has a psychological process that can stop them from expressing their will and willingness. It is part of being human to have ways we limit ourselves. Being aware that we do this is a necessary step toward living an authentic life.

When you know that your psychological self is only an aspect of you, you can open yourself to experiencing the power of all the chakras. Until now, you have probably lived most of your life making decisions from the life-or-death reaction in the anal chakra and the historical experiences in the solar plexus. Knowing that you are not your psychological self can free you from being mesmerized by your upsets, to see that you have other options for making decisions and taking action that will help you have what you want.

By meditating and breathing, you can clean the window of the solar plexus and see that you have other options for how to respond to challenging situations.

Heart Chakra

Think of a time...
when you responded in an openhearted way.

When your heart is open, you can feel love for yourself and others. Love for yourself means being on your own side, helping yourself have what is good for you that you want. It doesn't mean having what is good for you that you *don't* want, or having what you want that is *not* good for you. Loving yourself means having a heartfelt, handholding relationship with yourself. Loving someone else means being on their side, helping them have what is good for them that they want. It is not helping them have what is good for them that they *don't* want, what they want that is *not* good for them, or what's good for them that you want them to have but they don't.

Think of a time...
when you were loving toward yourself.

Think of a time...
when you were loving toward someone else.

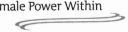

When we feel moved or when we make a heartfelt statement, it is natural to place our hand on our heart. This tunes us into the heart chakra, the place where we experience all the aspects of love for ourselves and love for others, and where we receive love from someone else. The heart chakra is where we experience compassion, forgiveness, gratefulness, generosity, the ability to be moved and inspired, and love itself. It is also where we experience the more vulnerable side of love, which involves regret, disappointment, and heartbreak. Each of these aspects of love are subtly different and important to have a heartfelt relationship with yourself and others.

Compassion

Think of a time...
you felt compassion.

Think of a time...
someone was compassionate to you.

Working with the heart chakra opens us to feelings of love and compassion. It's difficult to define compassion in words because it is only accessible when our hearts are open, and often they're not because we've experienced disappointment and heartbreak. Whenever we are mesmerized by our time-traveled reaction to our history, our hearts are not open. When we are completely involved in our thoughts, our feelings, and the body sensations that accompany them, our hearts are not open. When we are angry with someone, or feel frightened that they will leave us, when we are feeling defensive or self-conscious, our hearts are not open. And when our hearts are not open we cannot feel compassion.

It is powerful to have compassion for the human condition, and for yourself as a human being. Being human is incredibly difficult and complicated, in part because we have the ability to reflect on our actions. We have a critical voice that judges what we do and how we do it, what we say and how we say it, what we wear and how it looks on us, and on and on, all day long. This is not necessarily only a negative ability, because we also have a discerning voice that can help us do something better. It is a great thing to be able to change ourselves by observing and reflecting on what we do. Unfortunately, though, we usually use that discerning voice against ourselves, berating ourselves for not doing it better, for not saying something different, for not wearing the right clothes, or for not being good enough. We undermine ourselves by fearing the future, expecting a negative outcome, and discouraging ourselves from trying.

The good news about the ability to reflect is that we can make choices and decisions, we can change our minds, and we can improve our lives by making changes. A dog doesn't have the option to change his bark to a more pleasing timbre, stop his habit of begging for scraps at the table, or wag his tail so that it doesn't knock knickknacks off the coffee table. We have incredible resources for change in our ability to reflect on the way we do things, the consequences of our actions, and how our actions could produce different results in the future. The bad news about our ability to reflect is that we most often use that ability against ourselves, that we become self-critical and judgmental, and this can make our lives very difficult.

Instead of looking at a situation as an experience for learning, the self-critical voice tells us all the ways in which we could have done it better, the reasons why we didn't do it better, and that perhaps it will never be better because we are just not good enough. It is tragic that we beat ourselves up, and it is amazing that we can accomplish so much in life considering the overwhelming negativity of the conversations we sometimes have with ourselves and how we handle our expectations about the future.

You deserve compassion. As a woman, you are very complicated, and you live with this complexity every day, all day. The complexity is added to by the fact that you are living in a time when each woman is being called to bring forth her authenticity. You probably won't get where you are going in a straight line. Your path will zigzag as you acquire new wisdom, learn new methods, and transform your life. What is right for you at thirty won't necessarily be right for you at forty-five, and what is right for you at forty-five won't necessarily be right for you at sixty. There is no firm plan for you to follow anymore, which gives you a freedom that comes with this extraordinary opportunity. Our hearts need to be open to ourselves and other women for being alive at this interesting time. Our hearts need to be open to men for their part in the changing dynamics of our lives, for their desire to be involved in our lives, and for their position at the brink of changing roles.

What would life be like if...
you were compassionate with yourself?

Forgiveness

What would life be like if...
you could forgive your own mistakes readily and
easily?

What would life be like if...
you could forgive the mistakes of others readily and
easily?

Without a road map for this journey to authenticity we need extraordinary compassion *and* we need forgiveness as we make mistakes along the way. This is a trial-and-error universe, and making mistakes is part of the process of being human on this planet. If making mistakes is part of life, then forgiveness also needs to be part of life, or we will build up walls of old hurts and grudges that will close off our hearts.

Without forgiveness, it is impossible to move beyond old hurts. Because it may be easier to feel compassion for someone else than for yourself, it also may be easier to forgive someone else than to forgive yourself. Self-forgiveness means acknowledging that you are not perfect, acknowledging that you are human and therefore you make mistakes. This is difficult for many of us, who expect that there is such a thing as perfection. We are all perfectionists, to some degree, about ourselves, and this perfectionism is terribly destructive. Forgiveness involves acknowledging that you are on this planet to learn, that life presents you with many lessons, and that you can't learn without making mistakes. Mistakes are often a sign that you are on a road you've never walked before, so trial and error are good and necessary elements of growth. Would you attempt more change in your life if you knew in advance that you would forgive yourself?

What would life be like if...
you didn't hold your mistakes against yourself?

Gratefulness

What would life be like if...
you could actually be grateful for a mistake you
made because that mistake led you to discover new
things about yourself?

Another quality that helps our hearts be open to all the experiences life has to offer is gratefulness. Gratefulness makes things smoother in life, and gratefulness helps our hearts be open to all the experiences that life has to offer. Life offers us experiences that are difficult as well as experiences that are enjoyable, and both kinds of experiences can have great value. Being grateful can open us to look at difficult experiences in a new way, allowing us to see that it is often the most difficult and uncomfortable experiences in life that lead us to new horizons we hadn't dreamed of before.

Gratefulness means not rushing through life blindly, but leaning back a little to enjoy the moment. By stopping to notice small things you are grateful for, you can enjoy everyday life much more fully. Maybe you really enjoy the feeling of smooth, cool sheets against your skin. Taking a moment to be grateful for the feeling of the sheets on your body before you get up in the morning could change the tone of your whole day. If you love a hot shower with delicious-smelling body cleanser, gratitude for that experience can help you enjoy it, rather than running through the day ahead in your mind and barely noticing that you're in the shower. Being grateful means being in the moment. Have you ever eaten a meal without noticing what you are eating, or had a pleasant exchange with someone and not remembered a word you said afterwards? Our minds are racing all day, and it is easy to miss the small moments that make our lives more enjoyable.

Slowing down or bringing your mind into the present allows you to notice, and noticing allows gratitude. Many things remain nameless because they are there every day, and for those things we can be grateful. Does someone in your neighborhood plant beautiful flower gardens? If you walk or drive past the flowers and don't notice them, you are missing out, but noticing the flowers allows appreciation for the fact that someone took the time and effort to make your surroundings beautiful.

You work hard in life, and like many of us, you may not allow yourself the pleasure of gratefulness for the results of your work.

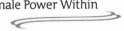

It's so easy to rush on to the next project, or the next dinner party, or the next promotion, without noticing the results that have manifested from the effort you have already invested. Noticing what is in your life that you have worked hard for is a powerful way to be grateful.

What would life be like if...
you were grateful for a yearning, knowing it was a
signal that what you desire is already on its way?

There may be things that you yearn for that are not yet in your life. Your mind can conceive of something in an instant, but it takes time and sometimes effort to manifest it on a physical level. We tend to think of yearning as a lack of fulfillment, but it is really a signal that what you want is already on its way. Yearning is a way of stimulating ourselves to open to what is coming toward us and to be grateful for its approach. Yearning for something gives you time to pave the way for it physically, psychologically, and psychically. It can give you the time you need to clear the path for its arrival.

Think of something...
that you used to yearn for that has come into your life.

Allowing gratefulness for what has already manifested that you yearned for, and what is on its way toward you that has not showed up yet, lets you enjoy the process rather than only striving for results. Gratefulness allows you to enjoy the moment that you are in, even if everything you want isn't here yet. Being in the moment is a place of power because you are totally present and available to experience what you are here to experience.

Generosity

Think of a time...
when you gave generously and openly to someone
who received your gift with pleasure. Recall the feeling of pleasure you had in giving to that person.

Gratefulness allows you to be open to generosity, because when someone is giving generously, they need a receiver whose heart is open and grateful for their generosity. True generosity is pleasure in giving *and* pleasure in receiving. Swami Satchidananda, a great Indian teacher, says that giving with the expectation of receiving something in return is a business transaction, but giving something for the pleasure of it is generosity. For many, it is easier to give than to receive, but receiving with pleasure is also generous.

Think of a time...
when you received something so that the giver had the experience of generosity.

If someone gives you a compliment, it is generous of you to receive it. If you give someone a compliment, it is generous of them to receive it. Giving someone a compliment and having them brush it off with "Oh, this old thing?" doesn't feel pleasurable. Giving someone a compliment and having them accept it gracefully feels satisfying, because you have given them something with an open heart and they have received it with an open heart.

Sometimes it might be easier to be generous with others than with yourself. Being generous with yourself means giving yourself the benefit of the doubt, not hurting yourself if it looks like you've made a mistake. Being generous with yourself means allowing for mistakes. Being generous with yourself means recognizing that it takes time to change, and allowing for the time it takes.

Being Able to Be Moved and Inspired

Think about a time...
when you were moved or inspired by something someone did.

What in you has inspired someone else?

You might be moved and inspired when people take life into their own hands, or when people do things beyond their own expectations. Watching the dignified struggle of others is often deeply moving, and it inspires us to keep on in our own struggles. There is great dignity in the ability to be vulnerable and go through the hard parts of life. Because we all share the human experience, it is inspiring to see another person be human and accomplish something despite the odds. It can also be uncomfortable to be so moved. We keenly feel the vulnerability of our human condition, and witnessing human moments reminds us that we, too, may need to risk being humiliated to get where we want to go.

It is impossible to avoid vulnerability and humiliation if we want to be fully expressed human beings. The ability to tolerate some discomfort will allow us to move through the hard parts where perhaps our struggle will move and inspire others. If we are unwilling to go through the hard parts, we avoid not only the discomfort but also the reward. We often don't do what we desire to do because it requires a period of vulnerability and humiliation. Seeing that others can go through it can inspire us to move forward with equal courage.

As each of us does our work, we will change others' lives because we all add to the collective vibration of being female. Observing each other and supporting each other through our periods of trial and error allows us to be secure in the knowledge that if she can make it through this, so can we. In the Gatherings we are often awed by the wonder of a woman going through her process and emerging more fully herself. The ability to be moved and inspired has us share and learn from our collective experiences.

Love Itself

When your heart is open, you can experience love for yourself and others. When your heart is open, you can experience all the warm, supportive facets of love that include compassion, forgiveness, gratefulness, generosity, and being moved and inspired. When your heart is open, you can make decisions and take action in your life based on what is truly good for you. Your heart is where you know what is good for you because it is where you experience being on your own side.

What would life be like if,...
when you were in an upset, you could draw your energy up from the survival instinct in the anal chakra, and come through the historical associations in the solar plexus to the heart?

What would life be like if,...
next time, you placed your hand on your heart and asked, "Is this good for me?"

Throat Chakra

Think of a time...
  when you lost yourself in an experience, when you were so involved in it that you lost all sense of time.

Think of a time...
  when you lost yourself in an experience so fully that you were not in the least self-conscious, and the self-critical and reflective voice was totally absent because you were so absorbed in the activity.

Think of a time...
  you responded authentically.

You don't have to search outside yourself to find your authentic self-expression. The beautiful expression you are here to share will begin to emerge when you start making decisions and taking actions in your life based on answers from the throat chakra. The throat chakra is the center of authentic self-expression, the place where you can be in touch with your true nature and your potential. When your throat chakra is open to the world, you can express something magnificent.

Your throat is an intense place in your body because your nerves and your breath pass through it, connecting your trunk to your brain. You may notice that you get "choked up" when something really touches you, or that you have to clear your throat before saying something important. Speech, one of your most important means of self-expression, comes from the throat.

When the window of your throat chakra is open, you can be fully aware of who you have always been and who you are designed to be. You can know what you knew when you were an unselfconscious infant or toddler who expressed herself without reservation. When you were very young, you let forth joyous sounds of laughter, shrieking, crowing, or gurgling when you were delighted with something. When you were unhappy, you cried or screamed without inhibition. Soon, though, you were told to hush—not to laugh so loudly, not to cry, not to yell. Your naturally expressive self was dulled by your efforts to comply with the adult rules and expectations that ran your life.

You learned to stifle your voice in the hopes of being accepted, approved of, liked, and rewarded. Even if you have achieved these things, however, there is something in you that knows it is not enough. You want to express something fantastic that no one else is here to express in quite the same way—and your natural self-expression might have nothing to do with people accepting you, approving of you, liking you, or rewarding you.

To the extent that you have had to repress your natural self-expression, you have dulled the light of your essential self. Your throat is often tense with words left unsaid, words said that did not resonate well with you, songs unsung, projects left unfinished, dreams not realized. When you do the chakra meditation, the light that is you will move into your throat, relaxing it and opening up space for your authentic expression to emerge.

The throat chakra holds the potential for happiness, contentment, fulfillment, and satisfaction. If you don't feel happy, content, fulfilled, and satisfied, you may feel it in the throat. In some way you are unable to express your true nature. Maybe you have a job that feels confining to you, or you are in a relationship that doesn't support you, or you have no outlet for your creativity. What uses you up most in any of these situations is the frustrated desire to express your true nature. It is agony not to be able to express who you really are.

The world needs your contribution. If you don't offer it, no one else ever can. Imagine if Bach had never composed, Marie Curie had never experimented, Amelia Earhart had never flown, Picasso had never painted, Jane Austen had never written, or Audrey Hepburn had never acted. Your contribution may not be earth shattering, and yet it is as important as the contribution of anyone who has ever lived. Your relatives, friends, partners, and coworkers want and need your expression to enhance and stimulate their own experience of life.

Try placing your hand gently on your throat and asking, "What is right for me?" You might find that you are here to stimulate volunteer groups into action, to listen and guide others through problems, to rear children, to produce a work of art, to be active in politics, to play an instrument, or to be a loving daughter. You may be here to accomplish many different and seemingly unrelated things in your lifetime, and you may have one singular expression that is consistent throughout. Your expression may take many different forms as you grow, stretch, and uncover more of your power. One thing you will find to be true is that your offering will not look like anyone else's, so comparing yourself to others will not have you come to what is true for you. Your truth is within you, and you can find it when you open, clear, illuminate, and breathe into your throat chakra.

What would life be like if...
next time you needed to make a decision or take an
action, you put your hand on your throat and asked,
"What is right for me?"

Psychic Chakra or Third Eye

Think of a time...
when you used your intuition.

The psychic chakra, or third eye, is where you experience psychic awareness—what is called the sixth sense. The third eye is located directly above the bridge of your nose, just above and between your eyebrows. Psychic information can also enter through the third ear, located at the base of the skull. The psychic chakra forms a column between the third eye and the third ear, and this column passes through the pineal gland, which is located directly below the crown of the head. The pineal gland stimulates psychic awareness.

We all possess psychic ability to some degree. Intuition is an aspect of the sixth sense, when you know that you know what you know without being able to explain how you know it. In a psychic experience you might instinctively know that you can or cannot trust someone, you might enter a room you have never been in before and know exactly where everything is, or you may have a déjà vu—the stimulating feeling that everything that is happening has happened this way before in a thought or a dream.

Psychic information is constantly being channeled to you through your third eye and your third ear. If you think back over the past couple of weeks, they probably contain some experience of psychic awareness, such as knowing who is on the other end of the phone before you pick it up, or writing to someone you haven't been in contact with for years only to hear news of them the next day. You may dismiss these occurrences as accident or coincidence, but it would be powerful to accept them as aspects of your natural psychic ability. When that ability is trusted, tested, and worked with, it can help you feel safe because it provides you with another way to help yourself know what is good and right for you. You can access unseen information that can help point you in the right direction, receive something coming your way, or make a decision about the future.

It is difficult to speak about the psychic chakra in our culture because we don't have sufficient language to describe it. In societies where the spiritual is more valued and attended to, people rely heavily on their intuition and acknowledge it as a valid way to know something. They trust what they experience through the sixth sense as much as what they can see, hear, feel, touch, or taste. In our culture it can feel frightening to trust in our psychic ability because we are accustomed to looking outside ourselves for proof that something exists. It is against our training to trust from the inside out because science tells us to trust only from the outside in. We sometimes trust that something exists only if we can prove it empirically, even if we have a knowingness inside about what is true.

It would be powerful for you to trust in your knowingness. As a woman, intuition is your birthright. Women have long relied on intuition to help us know when someone is in trouble, what kind of healing a person needs, and how to best deal with a situation in the moment. This knowingness is subtle and might easily be missed or dismissed if you are not tuned in to it. When you are open and available to your innate knowingness through your psychic chakra, you have yet another powerful place you can go to help you manifest what you want in your life.

What would life be like if...
you used your intuition or psychic information to
help you make choices?

Crown Chakra

Think of a time...
you were in nature and through your body you felt it
was good to be alive.

If you have ever taken a solitary walk in the woods while listening to the birds twitter and the leaves rustle gently overhead, if you have ever taken a deep, deep breath and allowed a peace to fill your being, or if you have ever been with a group of people with whom you felt totally comfortable and connected, you have experienced the profound sense of well-being that comes through the crown chakra. The crown chakra, located just above your head at about the place where you would balance a ball, has you connected to everyone and everything. When you are having the experience that all is right with the world and it is good to be alive, or when you are feeling that everything coming your way is good, you are living from the crown chakra point of view.

It is in the crown that you experience "at-one-ment," a feeling of oneness with the universe. The crown chakra allows you to feel a deep sense of well-being and gives you knowledge that all is right with the world. Unfortunately, you may only have this kind of experience a few moments in a year, if that. It is possible, however, to have more and more of these moments. You can invite them into your life, not by changing anything you are doing, but by changing your connection to it. Changing your connection to it starts with being open to different ways of looking.

What would life be like if...
you could look at everything that happens in life as supportive of you in some way?

The crown chakra point of view has you in the flow of life, holding everything that happens in your life as ultimately for your well-being. With the point of view that everything coming into your life can be good, you can always reshape what happens to you. Unpleasant experiences have the ability to be fabulous if you use them well. You can use them to rearrange your thinking, to heal something from the past, to see what you are being asked to focus on in your life, to disconnect from or reestablish an attachment, or to build strength by developing a muscle different from one that you are accustomed to using.

Think of a pivotal moment...
that changed the course of your life.

It is the pivotal moments in life that often feel the worst because you have to get through the hard part before you can move ahead. As you look back on a turning point in your life you can see that it was a learning spot that might have been calling for you to release and heal something in your history, shift a belief you held, understand a motivation you'd been living by without realizing it, fall more in love with yourself and accept yourself unconditionally, learn to tolerate your feelings, understand your power more fully, or realize that a fact you had been living by was not really true.

By living from the point of view that life is offering you exactly what you need to learn and being willing to learn from it, you can experience oneness, connectedness, and a profound experience of well-being. Coming into the flow of life by seeing that every situation has value, no matter how you feel about it, allows you to feel more calm and connected to life. You can stand in the middle of your life rather than using yourself up by avoiding things. It is female to embrace life, knowing that you are able to handle what comes toward you and having the support of other people who already have it handled.

If you know everything coming your way can be used for your good, you don't need to be afraid of what might look difficult. You can relax into the fact that there will always be challenges and difficulties because life is a progressive process of growth and understanding. Accepting this will allow you to use your energy to have more of what you want in your life instead of using it up praying for the day when difficult things will stop happening. That day will not come, but that doesn't mean life has to be full of suffering. Being in the flow has you know that when something difficult happens, you're up for the challenge. You are strong, awake, alive, present in the moment, and ready for what is coming.

Being in the flow of life allows you to see uncomfortable experiences as potentially having positive outcome. Feeling bad doesn't necessarily mean a bad thing is happening, and feeling good doesn't necessarily mean a good thing is happening. If you get into significant credit card debt it will probably feel bad, but if you are in the flow of life you can see that it gives you the opportunity to learn how to better manage your finances. It might feel bad to pay your credit card company the money you owe, but a bad thing is not necessarily happening. It might feel good to spend the money you owe on a new outfit, but a good thing is not necessarily happening. Deciding what is good for you based on how you feel doesn't always support your growth, so being in the flow allows you to have a wider view of what is happening.

Leaning back and embracing what comes toward you opens you up to experiencing optimism—a knowledge that life is on your side, even when it is unpleasant. You can encourage experiences of connectedness by being willing and open to seeing that all life's offerings are for your benefit, that everything is for the best.

What would life be like...
   if you could more often access the wisdom that
   comes through the crown chakra?

What would life be like if...
   you could make decisions and take action in your
   life from a point of view that the experiences you are
   having are ultimately for your well-being?

Uncoverings

Seven chakras, seven days: Over the next week, take one chakra each day, in sequence, and reflect on it. What do you discover about being human?

> *Anal Chakra*
> *Sexual Chakra*
> *Solar Plexus Chakra*
> *Heart Chakra*
> *Throat Chakra*
> *Psychic Chakra*
> *Crown Chakra*

Remember: These uncoverings are designed to stimulate thinking and encourage deep reflection. They are not a contest or a race. If you don't respond immediately to a question, just try to open yourself to it and see what comes.

Seeing Yourself as the Light

Think of a time...
   you knew that you were greater than your thoughts
   and emotional responses to life.

Discovering your authentic self is a process of stripping away the ways you have always seen yourself. Until now you have probably been living as if your psychological self is who you are, and this belief has kept you limited. You know now that you are not your emotional reactions to real situations, you are not the identities you have constructed to explain yourself to the world, you are not the history you have lived through, you are not the rules and beliefs you made up as a child, you are not your family, and you are not what others expect of you. You *have* ways of being in the world, but they are not *who you are.* So who are you exactly?

You are the light that moves through the chakras. That light is the essential self you have been from the moment you were born, the light that has been dimmed and stifled by your experience. You can brighten, extend, stretch, and free this light so your essence can shine. Concentrating on seeing yourself as the light will help you be in a place of healing whatever keeps it from shining steadily. Knowing yourself as the light will allow you to know what needs healing and to access your authentic self. Doing the following chakra meditation will have you experience yourself as the light. The light will enter through the crown chakra and will move through your body, connecting all the chakras and making the energy in them available to you.

The chakra meditation grounds you in the present and in the body, has you experientially know yourself as the chakras, helps you release toxic stress, and reminds you of the aspects of your power and where they are located. Doing this meditation on a regular basis will have your life change because you will know more about each area beyond what we have explained here. You will have your own unique experience of the power in each chakra and you will be able to develop and stretch that experience. Your ability to separate yourself from your psychology, your solar plexus chakra, will develop so that eventually, when you are in a situation triggered by your psychology, you will be able to help yourself make a different choice. Your life can take on a different texture when you remember to put your hand on your heart and on your throat to find out what you should be doing.

If you build a practice of doing the chakra meditation, you might notice that after a while it doesn't feel like a practice anymore but like something you look forward to as an important part of your day. Women at Life Works who have been doing the meditation for years report that it has changed their lives in profound ways. How the practice of doing the meditation will affect you personally has yet to be seen, but certainly you will experience stress reduction and an improved relationship with yourself. Having a deeper connection with yourself will change the texture of your everyday life, and as the texture changes your relationship with yourself will continue to change. Thus the practice of chakra meditation has a cumulative, exponentially powerful effect.

It would work well to read through the chakra meditation first, then close your eyes and try it. It will take about 10 minutes to do. The first time you do it, you may want to read through it more than once before closing your eyes to make sure you take it all in.

If you find it difficult to do this meditation on your own, you can order a tape that will guide you through it. The ordering information is located at the back of the book. You could also make an audiotape of yourself reading the meditation in a slow, gentle voice. That way, you listen to your own voice as you do the meditation.

Chakra Meditation

Allow yourself to be comfortable where you are sitting. Let yourself be in a relaxed position and one in which you will be able to remain awake. When you are ready, close your eyes and uncross your hands and ankles. You can have your legs crossed and make sure your ankles are not crossed. Open your hands, turning the palms upward so they can receive energy. Notice your breath exactly the way it is, then allow yourself to slow your breath down and deepen it by exhaling twice as long as you inhale. If you inhale for a count of three, exhale for a count of six. Concentrating on slowing your exhaling breath will calm your body.

Noticing a brilliant and gentle light over the top of your head, imagine the crown about the place where you would balance a ball. Very gracefully and very gently, the crown opens to the light as a rose opens to the sun, one petal at a time. The light comes into the crown to clear and clean and open, to call attention to the part of the body that has you feel connected to everyone and everything, an experience that all is right with the world, that it is good to be alive, a deep, deep feeling of well-being. This kind of feeling usually comes with a nice, deep breath, and you may have this feeling when you are out in nature, sometimes with certain groups of people, sometimes during certain activities. It is from the crown chakra that you can view all experiences as for your well-being, that everything that is coming toward you is good for you ultimately. When focused on that way, all experiences will help you have your life be more and more the way you want it to be.

And now... allow yourself to breathe, and as you breathe, light and energy moves into the third eye, and goes from the third eye through the pineal gland and back to the third ear at the base of your skull, clearing, cleaning, and opening. Calling attention to the part of your body that has you be connected to your ability to use your intuition, to know that you know what you know without being able to explain how you know, a deep inner knowing. This is the part of you that is open to psychic information, the information of the sixth sense, the information we can't quite find the words to describe, yet you experience knowing something. You are always receiving psychic information and you are getting to trust this sixth sense. Every day something crosses your experience that you have some information about, and you could never tell how you know what you know.

And now... allow yourself to breathe again, and as you breathe, light and energy moves down to the throat. The throat relaxes and the throat opens, calling attention to the part of your body that allows you to connect to your true nature, who you are and who you have always been. The you, the light that entered your body the moment you were born, the light that no one could take their eyes off of, the light that everyone was drawn to, the you that you have always been and will always be. It is the essence of yourself that is unique and special. There is nobody like you; there is nobody who is here to contribute what you are here to contribute. Every time you are in some way connected to your true and authentic self, you are being fulfilled. Every time you are expressing your unique, authentic self, you are feeling satisfaction, happiness, and contentment. You are designed to do what is natural for you and what is easy for you. The light that was there the moment you were born and will pass from your body when you pass, this light that you are has been frozen by the trauma that you experienced in your childhood, that light is trapped by the defenses you designed in order to navigate through your life, that light is trapped by the personality that you designed so you could cope in your world. That light exists and wants to stream through your body as it did when you were very young. It wants you to remember who you are and who you have always been, your authentic self.

And now... allow yourself to breathe again, and as you breathe, light and energy moves down into the heart. The heart feels very taken care of by the light, the heart feels very supported by the light. The heart rests into a pillow of light. The light comes into the heart to clear past wounds, to clear past disappointments, to clear past heartbreak, to clear the past regrets, thinking that remembering them will help you in the future, yet remembering them keeps you from living fully in the present. The only way to be sure you are taking care of yourself in the future is to be present now, and now, and now, so when the future is here you will be in the present, now. As the light does the work of healing the past and returning the past to the past, think of compassion... think of forgiveness... think of being grateful... think of being generous... think of being moved and inspired... Think of love itself, of being on your own side, helping you have what is good for you that you want.

For a moment, sense the light in the upper chakras and notice the clarity and peacefulness of the light. Know that this is the light that streams through the whole body, and for a moment identify yourself as the light. When you know you are the light, you can separate yourself from your psychological self, separate yourself from being your psychological reactions to the situations you are in, and push yourself away slightly so you can observe your psychological self. The moment you observe your thoughts, your feelings, and your body sensations, you have the power to know that you are much more than your psychological reactions. Knowing yourself as the light permits you to have choices you've never had before, permits you to return you to your natural power, permits you to be yourself. The moment you identify yourself as the light that moves through the chakras, you are able to access and use the power of *all* your chakras.

Identifying yourself as the light, bring the light from the crown down through the heart, down into the solar plexus, the part of your body through which you express your will, the chakra through which you express your willingness. What is in your way of expressing your will and your willingness is your psychological reaction to your experiences, the upsets you have. It is here that we attract toward us those people, those circumstances that we expect, that repeat our childhood experiences. The people, the circumstances are different but the experience is the same so they can be healed from the past to the present.

And now... allow yourself to breathe again, and as you breathe, light and energy moves down into the sexual chakra, the part of the body that has you connected to your womanliness, to your female nature. Slowly, gradually, you are becoming accustomed to knowing your female power. Our power is very subtle... it makes no sound, it has no force; we are unaccustomed to knowing our power as power and may only know its power when it is missing. If you are in a situation that needs nurturing and there is no nurturing, you can sense how powerful nurturing is. There is power in your tenderness, there is power in your softness, there is power in your nurturing, there is power in your envisioning, there is power in your ability to empower, there is power in your natural ability to heal, there is power in your ability to stimulate communication, there is power in your ability to encourage cooperation. If you knew how powerful you were, you would not be frightened. You would lean back and receive life as it comes, you would embrace each experience knowing it is for your benefit, you would deal with each situation gracefully, then let it go. Image this part of your body as healthy, toxins released and the hormones balanced so your moods can be more steady.

And now... allow yourself to breathe down one more time, and as you breathe, bringing light and energy down into the anal chakra, releasing the anus, which is often tight. It is here that you experience life-or-death situations. This is where you experience being grounded in this three-dimensional reality we live in. It is here that you respond to some experiences as if they are a matter of life or death. When this happens, adrenaline rushes through your body and you become very off-centered, you are confused, your mind is one-pointed and obsessed, your body feels very energized as it prepares for action, able and ready for Herculean efforts. It is then that you need to ground yourself. You now imagine yourself like a tree, and as the tree grows, it deepens its roots down into the ground. Imagine that you too have roots down into the ground so that you are grounded in this world. The nature of the grounding, what makes up the roots, is your relationship with yourself, the knowledge that you can help yourself, that you can take care of yourself, that you will love yourself through difficult situations, that you can count on yourself. This knowledge grounds you in the world.

The next few times you exhale, release toxins from your whole body, allowing yourself to make a sound. Then, allowing light and energy to go from the anal chakra to the sexual chakra, from the sexual chakra to the solar plexus, from the solar plexus to the heart, from the heart to the throat, from the throat to the third eye, and from the third eye to the crown, and down again, feeling the light streaming down, and up, and down again. This is the light that you are; this is the light you have always been. This is the light that appeared inside you the moment you were born, this is the light that will leave your body when you pass. Knowing yourself as this light enables you to put your psychological self in perspective, allows you to know that you are greater than your psychological reactions, that you have extraordinary resources in each of the chakras that you can access at any time. By knowing yourself as the light, you can return to yourself and ask yourself what to do in any circumstance, what is good for you and right for you that reflects your authentic self.

Allow any good feelings to remain in your body. Allow any good thoughts to remain in your mind. Allow any pleasurable body sensations to remain in your body. Slowly begin to bring yourself back to being in this room by noticing where your body touches the furniture, the floor. Notice any sounds around you, and the light on your eyelids. When you are ready, open your eyes.

Uncoverings

It works well to do this meditation regularly or when you want to be in touch with yourself, when you need to feel grounded, when you are upset or feel stress, and when you want to relax.

After the meditation ask yourself:

> *What did I notice?*
> *What images seemed meaningful?*
> *What did I learn about myself?*

Write in your notebook.

After doing this meditation for a week ask yourself:

> *What did I notice?*

After doing this meditation for a month ask yourself:

> *What do I notice about my relationship to myself?*

a powerful woman
is aware of when she is repeating
an historical experience and
uses it to heal her past.

a powerful woman

is gentle with herself.

6

⁓

Getting to Know the Little Girl Within

Seeing yourself as the light that moves through the chakras will enable you to know yourself, your psychological self, as one aspect of yourself, not who you are. The psychological self we call the *little girl*.

Your Little Girl

What do you think of...
when you think of yourself as a little girl?

Whenever we get upset out of proportion to the seriousness of a situation, or when we are upset for more than three minutes, it is as if we are a little girl again—the little girl who was powerless to change what was happening around her. Every woman has a little girl in her, just as every man has a little boy in him. That little girl lives in your solar plexus and her reactions are part of your psychological self—the part of you that has emotional reactions to real situations and draws your history to repeat itself. Your little girl is the aspect of you that is rooted in the past. When you get upset in the present, she is the one who is upset because she never had the chance to heal the original experience.

Now is a good time to take out pictures of yourself as a little girl.

When you are totally taken up by an upset, you lose your power because you are reacting from your solar plexus where your history resides. You have become a little girl again and you cannot access the power of your other chakras. Our model allows you to see that when you are upset it is your little girl, not the adult you, who is upset. That little girl is living in the past and she feels as powerless as she felt in childhood. She shows up when she is in an experience that is similar in some way to an upsetting childhood experience that has not yet healed.

We're not talking about the delightful, creative, curious child who was the authentic expression of you. We're talking about the aspect of you that has been hurt, humiliated, lied to, criticized, threatened, neglected, disappointed, scolded, and blamed. She is the part of you that has made mistakes, experienced failure, and feels insecure. She sometimes feels unworthy, hopeless, discouraged, wrong, betrayed, and rejected. The little girl is made up of your psychological responses to your childhood, and she makes decisions about your life based on her past experiences.

When you are in an upset, you are having a conversation with yourself. You might say, "I'm just not strong enough to deal with this," "I'm too stupid, I'll never get it," or "There must be something wrong with me." But who was really saying these things? Your wise, compassionate adult self would not say these things. It is your little girl who thinks she is not strong enough, not smart enough, and just plain wrong. She is repeating the things she was told or that she told herself in a similar experience in her childhood.

When you are upset you are being distracted by something in the past that may not have relevance to the present and therefore stops you from proceeding powerfully and lovingly forward. If it's time to ask for a raise and you can't bring yourself to do it because the idea makes you feel humiliated, you are powerfully holding yourself back from something that would benefit you. Any time you are upset for more than three minutes, you have time-traveled into the past. Looking at what might have happened in the past to your little girl that has her feeling so humiliated can help you move beyond it to take positive action.

You can begin by noticing the conversation you are having with yourself. Your little girl might be saying, "What makes you think you're so special?" If you think back to who might have said that to you in the past, you might discover yourself back in first grade, walking single file to the lunchroom. It's hot dog day and you are so excited that you skip joyfully ahead. Your teacher, frustrated from trying to keep thirty-two children in order, runs after you and grabs your arm, saying, "Get back in line with everyone else. What makes you think you're so special?" The other children snicker as the teacher escorts you to the back of the line. You vow to yourself that you will never again push yourself to the front of the line where people will notice you. To this day, your little girl is living out that vow. Her fear of humiliation is keeping you so mesmerized by your upsets that you may have trouble doing what you need to do to have what you want.

When your little girl is upset, she is having an emotional reaction to a real situation. Her reaction is valid—but the intensity of the upset is based on a situation that happened ten, twenty, or fifty years ago. She experiences a series of thoughts, feelings, and body sensations that have her travel back to the early incident that is recalled and stimulated by the present. If your boss chastises you, if your partner disagrees with you, or if a friend accuses you of something that pulls you into an upset—it is not the adult you who is standing in front of that person. You are a child again, looking up at an angry or accusatory adult who seems bigger and more powerful than you.

Your little girl feels the same feelings, thinks the same thoughts, and responds to circumstances in the same way as she did when she was a child. She experiences over and over again the same upsets that she has in the past because she attracts people and circumstances that will remind her of the past. She knows she is not old enough to take care of herself, so in order to deal with an upset she returns to the way of coping that she developed in her past. She makes all the same assumptions that she made in the past because she never developed another way of taking care of herself. She responds to the person in front of her as she did to her mother, her father, her siblings, her best friend, or her first-grade teacher—because she sees the person in front of her as if they were someone from the past.

Uncoverings

What did you like about yourself as a little girl?
What was hard for you as a little girl?

She Is Not You

What would life be like if...
you knew that your little girl is not who you are but an aspect of you?

Your little girl is the aspect of you who gets upset. She is *not you.* Knowing this will make all the difference in the world. Your little girl recognizes that she is not strong enough, old enough, or wise enough to take care of herself. She is already relieved that you are beginning to understand that she is only one aspect of you. She is the part of you that is frozen in time, the part of you that has you continually relive your past. Setting your little girl apart from you leaves space for you to have compassion for her, because if you see her as other than you, you then have a chance to help her. You can open your heart to the precious little girl who was harmed in life, who feels helpless about her circumstances, and who did the best she could with the resources she had.

You can begin to see that having a relationship with your little girl allows you to have power with your upsets instead of feeling powerless in them. Looking at pictures of her will help you connect with her. It would be powerful to spend some time to find these pictures. If a sibling, aunt, cousin, or parent has them, see if you can borrow them for a while, and make a color copy of them so you have your own copies. If you can't find them or don't have access to them right now, it would work to conjure up a mental picture of the little girl, draw a picture of her, or describe her in writing.

It is best if you can find pictures of your little girl at different ages and at different stages of her childhood and girlhood. Maybe there is a picture of her as an infant or a toddler where you can see her light shining out at the camera. As she gets older, you may be able to see the light receding farther and farther within her. The pictures that are most difficult to look at might be the most powerful to connect with. Remember to find those pictures where she looks awkward and unattractive, the ones you would never show to someone you want to impress. Pictures in which she looks sad or angry, or in which she is trying too hard to look happy, may be the ones you need to connect with, because she is the one who needs to be healed. It is the sullen, resentful, awkward, shy, or rebellious little girl who needs healing—the little girl who felt traumatized, unknown, misunderstood, and neglected.

You may find it difficult to feel compassion for her right now. If it is difficult, it is because there is another aspect of the little girl that finds it hard to look at herself. You may feel angry, impatient, or disgusted with the little girl. You may even feel hatred for her, because she is the one who gets upset and does the wrong thing. If you feel hatred for your little girl, the one who hates her is another helpless little girl who does not know what to do to save herself. Your compassionate adult self would never feel angry, impatient, or disgusted with the little girl.

As you sit with the pictures of your little girl, see what it is like to refer to her in the third person, as "she." When we share our pictures in the Natural Power Workshop, we sit in small circles of four women, where we tell each other about the little girl using the third person. Talking about the little girl as "she" is sometimes difficult and is always valuable. Setting your little girl slightly outside of you by referring to her in the third person allows you not to be her—and if you are not her you begin to know yourself as other than her. Observe her expression in each of the pictures and see if you can remember, or imagine, how she is feeling. She is most deserving of your love and compassion. Let yourself sit with the pictures of your hurt little girl, and allow yourself to really see her as you open to soothe her and help her understand she is not alone.

Your little girl may feel that there is something wrong with her because she didn't get what she wanted. She may blame herself for her suffering, thinking that if only she were smarter, more male, more obedient, more athletic, less outspoken, or more charming, everything would have been different. As your adult self, you can feel great compassion for the little girl who suffered and who has never had a chance to heal.

Your little girl developed ways of dealing with the feelings she had that were overwhelming for her, and she deals with those feelings in the same way today. It will be powerful for you to identify the ways your little girl has learned to cope with her feelings by finishing the sentences below.

Uncoverings

When my little girl is hurt, she…

When my little girl is scared, she…

When my little girl is angry, she…

When my little girl is humiliated, she…

When my little girl is sad, she…

When my little girl is joyful, she…

Is my heart open to be compassionate to this little girl?

Her Protection

Think of a time...
**in your childhood when experiences were happening
too fast for you to figure them out.**

Think of a time...
**you had to protect yourself the best way you could
against the constant bombardment of experiences.**

When you were a little girl, life happened to you so fast that
you didn't have time to make sense of it, so you created ways to
cope. In childhood you inevitably found yourself in uncomfortable situations involving parents, peers, or teachers, and had to
make quick decisions about how to act. Not only did you have to
decide how to act in the present, but also you had to decide how
to prevent the situation from happening again in the future because you knew you couldn't live through that experience again.
The systems you developed to cope with challenging experiences
became what we call your *defenses*.

In childhood, life was like a tennis match, and the tennis balls
were the events that were constantly happening to you. When you
first started out in life, you were standing behind the net with
balls flying at you very fast. No one told you exactly how to hit
the balls or how to avoid getting hit by them, so you learned to
dodge the balls and swing at them as best you could. Later, as you
accumulated experience and learned how to play the game, the
ball seemed to be sailing over the net more slowly. You had time
to consider your move, get into position, and hit the ball so that
it would go where you wanted it to go.

On the first day of school, perhaps a group of "cool" kids was
formed, and they didn't choose you. This rejection hurt your feelings, so you had to figure out how to get through it this time. In
addition, you wanted to find a way not to be hurt the next time—
because there would certainly be a next time. Maybe you got angry with the other kids and told them they were all stupid, and
you didn't want to hang around with them anyway. Maybe you got
very quiet and withdrew into yourself so that no one would notice you. This situation helped to form your personality. If you got
angry and felt better, you developed anger and an "I don't care
anyway" attitude as a defense against being hurt. If being quiet re-

moved you from the situation, you may have developed shyness and a feeling that there was something wrong with you as a defense. Perhaps you organized a group of friends and established a club with your own secret password. Because the "cool" kids rejected you, you may have developed "I'm a special person" as a defense, finding ways to prove you were superior to others.

Later in life, you would begin to define yourself by the defenses you'd developed, identifying yourself as "I'm an angry person" or "I'm a shy person." You might voice the beliefs you developed about yourself in this early experience by saying "I'm not a group person," "The group I belong to is more special," or "I'm a loner and I prefer doing things on my own." Or you might have gone to the other extreme to compensate for the childhood hurt. You might have developed an overly outgoing personality or a desire to please others in order to ensure that you would be included. Yet you might not be naturally shy, angry, special, a loner, or independent. As a "group person," you might really like to be alone more, but you can't know that about yourself because you have grown so accustomed to identifying yourself by your defenses. If you imagine yourself as one of Michelangelo's partially finished statues, you can see your defenses as part of what makes up the excess stone that has you trapped. Your defenses keep you from being fully yourself, and releasing yourself from their limitations will free you to come into your power.

As an adult you have the opportunity to make new, considered decisions about your life, but you may be so entrenched in acting out your history that you don't even realize you have options. Your defenses may have become so much a part of you that you believe they *are* you. Much of who you know yourself to be are your defenses—but your defenses are not who you are. They are systems created in the past by the little girl who was doing her best to negotiate in the world. She created certain ways of looking and thinking that helped her cope with childhood situations and gave her a way to respond. She created behaviors that allowed her to feel in control of situations over which she had no control. Her defenses are a result of vows, promises, and decisions made in the moment to avoid uncomfortable feelings.

Everyone copes with situations differently and develops different defenses, but everyone develops them. No one gets through childhood without being hurt or traumatized in some way. Even if you had a terrific childhood, there were people and events that confused, hurt, or frightened you. Everyone needs to heal their childhood. Your little girl had to develop defenses, and she did so to save herself—and she did it brilliantly. Whatever design she made, she made it for survival.

Uncoverings

Think of times in my childhood when I felt harmed or frightened.

What defenses did I design to take care of myself?

Creative Solutions

What would life be like if...
you could see that every single person on the planet has developed defenses in order to help them be in the world?

What would life be like if...
you knew that every single person has had to hide the light that is their essence in order to survive in their families, in their schools, and with their friends?

Looking at others to identify defense systems is often easier than identifying them in yourself. Think of someone you have a hard time with. What really bothers you about that person is not their essence but their defenses. If someone yells at you all the time, it is because they developed yelling as a defense. If someone whines, it is because they developed whining as a defense. They might be "a nice person" as a defense, they might have procrastination as a defense, or they might be critical or stubborn. Seeing that their troublesome behavior stems from their defenses can allow you to have compassion for them and can give you the option not to get hooked by their behavior.

Take a moment to think of something you don't like about yourself.

If you look at this aspect of yourself as a defense you created to survive rather than who you are, it may change the feelings you have toward your little girl trying to cope. It begins to be easier to have compassion for that little girl. She needed a compassionate, wise adult back then—and she needs you now. She needs the you who has compassion, forgiveness, patience, and unconditional love, the you who can see a defense as something that she developed in childhood and not something that defines who she is. She needs the you who can stop blaming her because you see that she created her defenses out of necessity.

Defenses are as varied as the people who develop them. If Valerie is consistently denied her desires, she may learn to sulk until she gets her way. If Lisa lives in an atmosphere of distrust where she is accused of things she did not do, she might learn to be sneaky. If Suzanne's brother constantly torments her, she could learn to fight back and to approach situations with force. In any of these examples, there is more than one way to respond. Valerie responds to denial of desires by sulking, but another girl in the same situation might learn to scream and cry until she gets her way. In Lisa's place, another girl might try to be as good as possible and never upset anyone, thereby suppressing her own feelings. Someone else in Suzanne's situation may shrink into herself and become a victim of life. There are myriad ways in which we construct the elaborate defense systems that allow us to negotiate life—yet they are not *who you are*.

Defenses limit your potential by keeping you stuck in a stagnant relationship with your life. Those limitations probably feel comfortable for you because they are known and familiar. Like Linus's blanket in the *Peanuts* cartoon, your defenses keep you feeling safe because you and others know what to expect. Linus uses his blanket as protection against having real interactions with others. If he's uncomfortable, he can just stick his thumb in his mouth and retreat behind his blanket. If he let go of his blanket, he might have to start interacting with others more directly, and this might feel uncomfortable for everyone.

"I'm a late person," "I'm a perfectionist," "I'm clumsy," "I'm oversensitive," "I'm impatient," and "I'm an overachiever" are all descriptions of defenses that keep you feeling safe and comfortable. Defining yourself allows you to know how to act and allows others to know how to react to you. They describe an aspect of the personality you constructed in your childhood that has you interact with the world in a certain way. But even if your descriptions seem to be positive, they keep you in a strict mold that may limit you. Saying "I'm confident and outgoing" doesn't leave you much space to be timid, shy, fearful, or introspective when circumstances call for those true responses.

Shannon, an artist, defines herself as a "sensitive person." She takes in birds that have fallen from their nests and stray dogs that have been hit by cars. She sends money to every charity that asks her, even if she's never heard of it. She values the fact that she is finely tuned to others' feelings, and prides herself on never offending anyone. She always says yes when someone asks her for a favor because she can identify with their need—even if is inconvenient for her. When her sister needs to talk, or her friends need to vent, she is always there to listen and sympathize—often at the expense of getting her painting done.

Sometimes Shannon finds herself tired and worn out from taking care of everyone else's needs. She overcommits herself to goodwill projects and resents not having enough time to work on her own paintings. Sometimes she wishes she could just say no to those asking for help or tell her sister she has to get off the phone. But because Shannon believes that sensitive is *who she is*, she finds it impossible to express the part of her that could care less about things. She doesn't recognize that her extraordinary sensitivity is a defense that keeps her from having to draw boundaries with people and concentrate on her own life. If instead of saying "I'm a sensitive person" she said, "I tend to be sensitive to others' needs and desires," she would allow herself room to choose differently.

Josephine grew up with parents whose lives were messy and out of control. Her father was usually absent on business, and her mother drank heavily whenever he was gone. She didn't do housework and rarely cooked meals. When Josephine's father was home, her parents fought often and furiously. From a very young age Josephine felt responsible for keeping things under control in the house. She cleaned and attempted to cook so that when her father came home he wouldn't be angry. She hid her mother's bottles so she wouldn't be able to drink. She tried to intervene in her parents' arguments so she could make peace between them.

As an adult, Josephine sees herself as a "peacemaker." Strong feelings make her uncomfortable and she hates confrontations of any kind. She is the one who smoothes over everyone's difficulties, who tries to make sure everyone is feeling okay so there won't be any fights, and who sweeps all the dirt under the carpet.

What Josephine doesn't know is that her peacemaking is actually a form of control. The need to control others' feelings is a defense she developed amid the chaos of her childhood. Now this control is detrimental to her, because her need to have everyone feel okay has her ignoring her own feelings and her own needs while she attempts to control everyone and everything around her. Men leave her because she worries so much about what they need, what they are feeling, and what they are doing that they feel smothered. What would happen if Josephine could know that her need to be a peacemaker was a defense from her childhood, and that she has other options for how to be in the world?

Mae changed jobs frequently—not because she didn't perform well, but because she grew dissatisfied quickly. No job seemed to use her unique combination of talents well, and she didn't want to settle for something mediocre. When her friends would ask her why she quit, she would reply, "I'm just not clear about what I want to do for work."

After Mae quit her latest job at an art gallery, her friend Helen confronted her.

"Mae, that was a really great job. I don't see why you had to quit, and I'm concerned that you're sabotaging yourself by quitting all the time," Helen said. "Eventually it will catch up to you and no one will hire you anymore."

Mae, offended by Helen's forthright statement, stomped off in a huff. Later that day as she was going through the want ads, however, she found Helen's words revolving through her mind. Reluctantly, she started to see the truth in them. She called Helen to apologize and asked her for advice.

"Well, I think you're afraid of something," Helen said. "It seems to me you might want to get some help from a professional to figure out what the problem is."

Mae took Helen's advice and came to Life Works, where in the course of her work she was finally able to admit she was afraid. As she explored deeper, she discovered that her "not being clear about work" kept her from facing the real problem, which was fear of rejection. If she committed to one job, she realized, she would have to face the possibility of not doing well and of being passed over for raises and promotions. Uncovering the real source of her problem allowed Mae to work with it so she could find a job that would be fulfilling and not let her fear make her leave.

What are some of the defenses you've designed?

How have they served you?

How have they limited you?

Healing Your Little Girl

How do your defenses use up your energy and get in the way of being your true self?

Can you see that your defenses limit the choices you make in your life? The irony of your defenses is that you created them to make yourself feel better, but they often end up making you feel worse. Defenses are not logical—they are psychological. The logic of psychological defenses has you frequently ending up having exactly what you are trying not to have. If you don't want to be disappointed, you may have as a defense an attitude of "I don't expect anything, because it won't work out anyway." You have this attitude in order to protect yourself from disappointment. The only problem is, it doesn't work! When did expecting you would be disappointed ever stop you from being disappointed? You only end up being unhappy during the process and disappointed in the result.

Your little girl created her defense systems for self-preservation, but now they can backfire and end up harming you. They may limit what you can experience from life by limiting what you attract into your life or what you repel from it. They can limit how you experience something as well as how you respond to it, which can limit other people's responses to you. They keep what is possible small and create a glass ceiling on your success.

Marianne's parents were first-generation Americans fighting their way up the social ladder. Material success proved their worthiness in their newly suburban lifestyles. Just as her mother had to have the most beautiful flower garden on the block or her father had to drive the fanciest car of any of his friends, Marianne had to be the smartest, most talented, and most coordinated child in school. If she got a "B" on her report card, didn't get the lead in a school play, or didn't make a goal at soccer practice, she was punished. Marianne hated it when her parents weren't pleased with her, so she vowed she would never allow herself to fail. Because she had to avoid failure at all costs, she constructed an elaborate system of procrastination. If she never started anything, she could never be directly accused of failing.

As an adult, Marianne's procrastination kept her in a frustrating cycle of unfinished projects. By putting off doing a project for work, she ensured that she would not fail. She would stall progress by not beginning in time to finish the job well and then get upset and angry with herself for putting it off. Feeling upset and angry used her energy and drained her of her resources so she couldn't even begin. Then, if her boss didn't like it, she could say to herself, "Oh well, it didn't work because I only gave it a few minutes of my time." This way, she could blame lack of time instead of taking responsibility for her possible failure to produce the desired result.

Marianne lost several jobs before realizing she needed to change her behavior. After doing the Life Works Workshop, she could see that she kept herself in a pattern of procrastination because it was familiar. She was still reacting to her parents' expectations and living in fear of punishment for failure. By trying to avoid failure and the punishment she was sure would follow, she was managing to get herself fired over and over again. Ironically, the defense she'd developed was having the opposite effect than the one she intended. Seeing that pattern helped Marianne develop new ways of coping with the pressure to succeed.

Florence's greatest desire was to get married. At thirty-eight, many of her friends had already "tied the knot," and every time Florence went to one of their weddings she found herself gritting her teeth underneath her smile to keep herself from crying. Why did her friends seem able to find men who could commit when her relationships always ended in disaster, one after the other?

When her last single friend got married, Florence was despondent. She dragged around for weeks, crying whenever she was alone and paying little attention to her work. Finally she couldn't stand the way she was behaving anymore, so she sat down with herself and took a look at why she wasn't married. She wrote a list of all the men she had been in relationship with since graduating from college, and then wrote about the situation she had found them in and how the relationship had ended.

What Florence found surprised her. She realized that although she had been saying she wanted a man who could commit, she picked men who were unavailable—either because they were emotionally distant or because they were in a relationship already. She had even dated married men, perhaps thinking that if they were married they weren't afraid of commitment.

Florence decided to seek help in ending her cycle of picking unavailable men. She came to Life Works and began doing deep work on herself. As she started identifying her defenses, she was surprised to discover she had a dilemma about whether or not to have children. As the oldest of seven children, she vowed that she would never have her mother's life. It was this dilemma that had her little girl choose unavailable men so she would never have to decide about having children. It had been a hidden conversation, a motivation she did not consciously know she had.

Once she brought her hidden conversation to light, Florence was able to work with herself differently. She saw that her real dilemma was not finding a man who would commit, but questioning in herself about whether or not to have children. She saw that fixating on finding a man had become a defense against her real dilemma. Once she identified the defense, she was able to have open conversations with herself about having children.

Cissy had dreams of becoming a high-level executive with her own corner office and a staff at her command. She worked diligently at her advertising job and received a few modest promotions, but fifteen years into her career she wasn't where she wanted to be. She couldn't figure out why she hadn't been promoted to vice president. She'd worked hard, been pleasant to everyone, and given the firm her all—only to see younger, less hardworking people promoted in her stead. Cissy started asking friends and colleagues why they thought she wasn't getting the recognition she deserved. Almost all of them told her, "You're too nice. If you want to get ahead in this business you have to be willing to push yourself forward and take all opportunities, even if people are envious and talk behind your back."

Cissy was floored by their feedback. She had always defined herself as "a nice person," and she believed that respecting others and working hard would get her where she needed to go. How could she risk offending someone or take a job they wanted if she was "a nice person?" Nice people didn't scheme to get ahead, and nice people didn't put themselves forward at the expense of someone else. Later, after working on herself, Cissy realized that by defining herself as "nice" she had cut out any possibility of being bold or forward. She had limited herself by living by the defense of "nice" that she had developed so that everyone would like her. By changing her description to "I am often pleasant and polite," she left herself more leeway to act boldly and expand her options for taking action in life.

The intention of Natural Power Work is to release the light trapped inside you so your true self can shine. Understanding this will help you feel compassion for your humanity and the humanity of others. Part of being human is to move away from who we really are, and eventually coming back to it. Meanwhile, we are identified as our psychological selves. Our undertaking now is to reconnect with our higher selves and heal the parts of us that have been harmed.

Uncoverings

I use the defense of criticism in order to...

Defenses that use up energy and are in the way of being my true self are...

Defenses I'd feel uncomfortable without are...

Pictures

It is empowering to have pictures of your little girl around your living space. It will help you keep her in your consciousness, and serve as a reminder to be in contact with her. It will help to keep a photo in this book and in your notebook.

Place her pictures in various places around your living space, and put a picture of her in your billfold or in your checkbook. It is especially powerful to put a picture of her in your bedroom, where you can see her when you wake up in the morning and go to sleep at night. You will be able to connect with your little girl more fully if you notice her at least every day. You can take a few moments upon awakening to contemplate the picture, allowing yourself to be with your little girl as you begin the day.

Daily ask yourself to notice something about her that you haven't noticed before. What is special about her? Your little girl is sweet, delightful, and innocent. She deserves your compassion for all she had to go through. As you connect with her more and more, you will be able to open your heart wider and wider.

a powerful woman
knows she is the light and sees
others as the light.

a powerful woman

knows herself as the higher self always
available to the little girl.

7

Accessing Your Higher Self

Your Guide

Think of a time...
when you saw a child express herself unselfconsciously.

Now that you have begun to experience yourself as the light, you have a pretty good idea of who you are *not*. You have a cultural and a family history that keep you acting and reacting to life in certain ways—yet it is not you. You have a psychological self we call the little girl who has emotional reactions to real situations—yet she is not you. You have defenses that have helped your little girl cope with life—yet they are not you.

You are someone essential and wondrous, someone greater than the ways you have tended to define yourself. You are someone so special that there is no way to really describe the essence of who you are except by saying that you are like an absolutely unique and beautiful ray of light. You are the light that moves through the chakras. We call this light your *higher self*.

Your higher self was with you the moment you were born. When you were an infant no one could take their eyes off of that light—everyone was drawn by the light to pay attention to you. It is this light that has people be attracted to you today, and when you are expressing your authentic self you radiate its glow. This is the light that moves through the chakras. It has always been there and will pass from your body when you pass away.

Think of the last time you were with an infant or a toddler. Wasn't it a delight to watch and interact with her? When children are very young, before life has happened to them, they radiate a light that is a pure expression of themselves. A child might run in circles pretending to be an airplane, chuckle to herself delightedly while pulling her dress up over her head, or practice saying "no" in all different moods and tones. Before age two and a half or three, most children have not yet learned to censor what they say or do. They have not yet developed a critical voice dictating their actions, and generally they have not yet learned to be self-conscious and self-critical. They are the unselfconscious expression of themselves—the amusing, delighted, curious, creative expression of their essence.

You, too, once radiated a light that was the pure expression of yourself. That light still flickers within you, although your experience in life may have obscured it. Doing the chakra meditation can expand your experience so the light flows through your body once again. When you are aware of the light moving freely through your body and when you know that this light is who you are, you have the ability to access power from all of the chakras. Your higher self can experience groundedness and centeredness in the anal chakra, creativity and nurturing in the sexual chakra, will and willingness in the solar plexus, extraordinary compassion and love in the heart chakra, what is true and authentic for you in the throat chakra, psychic awareness and knowingness in the third eye chakra, and wisdom and a connection to everyone and everything, along with an acknowledgment that all experiences when used well are for the best, through the crown chakra. When you are your higher self, you are wise, compassionate, loving, and nonjudgmental.

Uncoverings

Watch infants, toddlers, and young children playing.

Look for their "light."

Watch them express themselves unselfconsciously.

Look for their delight, creativity, and curiosity.

Notice the uniqueness of each child.

Creating a Relationship With Yourself

Think of a time...
   when you were wise for someone else.

Who is this higher self? She is that part of you who knows you as no one else can ever know you, because she has been there

through every experience you have ever had. She has great compassion for you, and her heart is totally open to you. Because you have been mesmerized by your psychology, your higher self has not always been available to you, yet she has always been there. She knows what is good and true for you, yet she does not judge you for the choices you have made that weren't good and true for you. She knows you were doing the best you could at any given time, because if you could have done better, wouldn't you have done better? Times when you were wise for someone else were probably times when she was able to come forward most lovingly.

Think of a time...
when you were able to be completely present with another person, a time when you had great wisdom and compassion for them.

Your higher self is the wise woman in you who is able to be there totally for someone, to soothe and advise them from a place of unconditional love. It is often easier to be present for someone else when they are upset than to be present for yourself. When your little girl is upset, you, the higher self, can be there for her, too. When she is upset she needs compassion, wise advice, and soothing—and you, the higher self, can always provide that, just as you do for others. When you don't feel like you can take care of yourself anymore, remember, it is the little girl who feels this way. She isn't strong enough, doesn't have enough experience, and was never supported to get through tough circumstances on her own. But you, the higher self, are always able to take care of her because you are not caught up in repeating your history. You are wise, loving, and compassionate. You never get tired or angry, and you are totally compassionate and nonjudgmental. You are always available to guide your little girl and hold her hand through the hard parts. You have available to you the power of all the chakras.

Women who have done the Natural Power Work often say that putting the little girl outside of themselves and creating a relationship with her is the most valuable part of the Work. Knowing themselves as the light allows them to parent themselves in ways they weren't parented in childhood. Because they can separate themselves from the upsetting situation and see that it is the little girl who is upset, they can be present for themselves in the same way they would be present for a friend in distress. "It was a revelation to me that I could have the ability to take care of myself no matter what because I had this higher self—this adult self—who could take care of the little girl," says Portia, a forty-two-year-old hospital administrator. "The little girl has someone to take care of her when life gets scary. It's made a big difference in the way I see my life and in the way my life happens."

Gretchen, a thirty-three-year-old teacher, says that knowing she is her higher self has allowed her to stop criticizing herself and start helping herself. "It's incredibly liberating to have the little girl be a part of me but not be who I am," she explains. "When I'm procrastinating, or when I think there's no way I can do it, I can identify that it's the little girl who doesn't think she can do it. Realizing it's her allows me to be the wise higher self who can help her. I can calm her down and ask her why she doesn't want to do it. The question becomes, 'What does she need right now?' instead of 'What's wrong with me?' And that makes all the difference in the world."

If you feel tired of taking care of yourself, know that it is not *you* who is tired, it's your little girl, and she is tired because she has been trying to parent herself all along. She is tired because she doesn't have the resources to take good care of herself, and she knows she shouldn't have to.

You, the higher self, are the one who has the capability and energy to take care of your life. You, the higher self, are never tired because you are a never-ending stream of light. You, the higher self, hold the ability to access power from all the chakras, and you possess all the wisdom that you have accumulated throughout your life. Your little girl wants to be nurtured and guided by you. Your little girl wants to confide in you and know that you will listen to her. You, the higher self, can help her heal.

When your little girl is upset, she wants to be soothed and comforted. You have the ability to soothe and comfort her as no one else can because you have been through all of her experiences with her. You know exactly how she feels, and you know how she felt every moment in her past. Your little girl knows what will make her happy, and as you build a relationship with her, she will grow to trust you. Once she trusts you, she will tell you exactly what you can do to make her happy, relieved, and satisfied. She is relieved right now as you read, just because you are finally recognizing her for who she is and recognizing that who you are is the higher self.

Think about a situation...

that was difficult for you as a little girl. Imagine what it would have been like if you had available a grown-up, wise self to explain what was really going on.

Perhaps there was a neighborhood bully who called you terrible names that hurt and humiliated you. You believed that what she called you was true, because otherwise, why would she be calling you those awful things? If your wise higher self—the one that you would become one day—were there, she could have told you that the bully was only acting the way she did because she felt afraid and inadequate, and that her behavior actually had nothing to do with you. Her father bullied her at home and told her she was no good, so in order to make herself feel better, she did the same to you. Wouldn't knowing this have made you feel better?

Instead of believing the things the bully called you, instead of letting her have power over you, you might have been able to shrug off the names. You might even have felt compassion for the bully because you understood that she was hurt and humiliated, so she felt compelled to hurt and humiliate someone else. Without a wise guide, this incident would have caused you to create defenses that would further hide your light. If you'd had the higher self's guidance, you would have been able to understand it for what it was, and you wouldn't have had to carry its consequences with you into the present.

Unfortunately, your little girl did not have a wise guide to explain to her what was really going on in the millions of things that happened to her. If she had, your life would be different now. You would not have had to rearrange yourself for the people around you or think badly of yourself. You could have understood what was going on around you differently. When your mother yelled at you for being "too sensitive," you would have had someone to explain to you that it was April 14 and taxes were due the next day. Your parents hadn't prepared ahead for it, so they were frantic, and they had no patience for you. That's why you were called "too sensitive"—not because it was true.

Although your little girl did not have a guide in her childhood, it is not too late for her to have that experience. Your little girl makes herself present whenever you are upset and you time travel into your history. Every time she is present, you have an opportunity to heal what happened to her in the past. And you can now be that wise and compassionate presence for your little girl. As an adult, you have an opportunity to soothe and guide your little girl exactly the way that she wants to be soothed and guided. By providing your little girl with the love and understanding that she didn't receive in her childhood, you can heal your past. And by healing the past you have more possibility in the present, and therefore you can change what happens in the future.

Uncoverings

> Imagine yourself as the higher self. She looks like you look when you look in the mirror—but probably just a little bit different.

> Think of a time I was wise but probably for somebody else: when I was able to be completely present with another person, a time when I had great wisdom and compassion for them.

> Think about a situation that was difficult for me as a little girl. Imagine what it would have been like if I had available a grown-up, wise self to explain what was really going on.

Meditation

The visualization that follows is designed to help you connect with your little girl. It is meant to be done daily, along with the chakra meditation. Ideally, you will do them one after the other. Both should take about 15 minutes. The chakra meditation (see chapter 5, p. 126) allows the light to move freely through the chakras, which prepares you for meeting your little girl in the visualization. In the visualization, you, the higher self, will have an opportunity to meet your little girl and begin to develop your relationship with her. Allow yourself time to sit with any memories, pictures, emotions, or thoughts that came up.

By doing the meditation and visualization every day, they become part of the practice you can cultivate to come into your powerful self. As with the chakra meditation, you can purchase an audiotape from us (see ordering information at the back of the

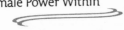

book) or, if you prefer, you can tape the meditation yourself and use the tape in your daily practice.

Healing Your Past Visualization

Keeping your eyes closed after the chakra meditation... As you stay in the light, relax again and notice your breath, feeling the light streaming through your body. Become comfortable in your seat. With your eyes closed, wiggle around so you can find a position you can remain awake in.

Imagine yourself as your higher self, seeing yourself as you pass a mirror. Who you see looks like you, she is very similar to the way you look now, but there might be something slightly different about you, the higher self... perhaps a certain glow, perhaps a different style of hair, perhaps different clothing, yet you know it is you by gazing at yourself as you pass the mirror. You experience the light that moves through the chakras. You know yourself as the light, and you experience the grounding that you are as the light.

And you look in front of you, and not very far away, but somewhat in the distance, you see your little girl playing at something that she loves to play at. And you see her in the distance, and you start walking toward her very, very slowly. You don't get near her for a very long time, but as you approach her, you see her, and you see something about her that you may have never noticed before. You watch her and you notice that your heart opens to her.

You have great compassion for her, for how difficult it was to be a little girl in your family. You have compassion for how confused she was so often as she had to negotiate through whatever it was she was living through.... Compassion toward her because she must have made mistakes, because she is human... Compassion for her because she was uncomfortable with her feelings... Compassion for her because she was criticized and blamed... Compassion for her because she didn't know what she thought she needed to know... Compassion for her because she experienced humiliation... Compassion for her because she thought there was something wrong with her. Back then, when she was young, she needed you to hold her hand and see her through some very difficult situations. Now for a moment you feel the love you have for her in your heart, you feel that you accept her fully and completely, and you are feeling the desire to be in her presence whenever she needs you, because she is still walking through life reexperiencing things that happened in the past, now in the present, in her adult life.

You walk a little more slowly still as you approach her, and at a certain point when you are close enough that she can see you, allow her to notice you, and she has whatever response to seeing you that she has, because most likely you are a stranger. Just notice her response to you, the higher self. Some little girls get close very quickly; some little girls take time to connect. One is not better than the other, just notice how she is. See what it is you see about her that you have never noticed before. Something rises to the surface that gives you some insight into her or how she dealt with her childhood. Perhaps you see the powerful desire she has to be in a relationship with you.

Sit down, and allow her to get as close as she is comfortable getting. However that is, it is up to her. Explain to her that you are who she will be when she grows up, that you are the adult that she will be. Explain to her that you have been with her every moment of her childhood, that you have always been there even though you did not make yourself known, that you were not available for her to connect with then but you can be available now. Tell her that you have a desire to help her through the difficulties that she has, and allow her to respond to your telling her that. However she responds is the right response. She experiences the love that you feel in your heart for her, and she begins to feel her heart opening, allowing her to feel the love going from your heart to her heart to your heart to her heart. Let her know that you are now available to her any time she needs you, that you would like to walk hand in hand with her through each of her experiences.

Let her for a moment ask you a question or say something that she would like you to know, as she experiences your connection with her from your heart to her heart to your heart. Perhaps she feels some sense of relief because she no longer is alone, that there is someone available who knows her better than anyone else could ever know her, that there is someone available who has lived in every one of the experiences that she has had and will have, that she knows that you know her in a way that no one else can know her because you know exactly how she feels about everything. You know exactly what worries her, and where in her body she feels that worry. You know exactly what makes her happy, and where in her body she feels that happiness. You are her and she is you, you are aspects of the same person. She is the psychological self; you are the higher self. She needs you. Now you can heal those things in the past by committing to her to be present, letting her know to reach for you, presencing yourself in her life at any moment that she is in an upset or in need of a hand to hold.

Again, allow her to say something, or ask something, and you can respond. Feeling the love in your heart for her, sensing the connection you have to her. If possible, being physical with her, but not pushing that if it makes her uncomfortable. Letting her know that you are available, that she needs to be open to your showing up. Asking her to wake you up to her needs, and again allowing her to say anything she wants to say to you and ask anything she wants to ask you. Feeling your heart connection, and sensing how the little girl feels about meeting you and knowing you. As the higher self, letting the little girl know that you will be meeting with her again soon, and that she will have the chance to be connected with you again. That there might even be a time between now and then, that she might want your attention, and that you are available to her. You know it is she who is upset and not you, and therefore you can help her as the higher self, as the light that moves through the chakras. Keeping yourself connected to the experience of being your higher self and having your heart be open to this little girl, allowing any of the pleasant, comfortable feelings in your body to remain, allowing any body sensations that are comforting and soothing to remain, allowing any thoughts that are pleasant, soothing, or empowering to remain. Slowly bring yourself back to being in the room by feeling yourself sitting or leaning, noticing the parts of your body touching the floor, or the chair, noticing the sounds around the room and the light on your eyelids. When you feel ready, open your eyes.

Uncoverings

It would support your practice to take some time each day to write in your notebook about the meeting between your higher self and your little girl. Any reaction you have is valuable. It may take some time to be able to visualize your higher self and your little girl together. Allow yourself to notice non-judgmentally, and write about your experience. If you write each day after doing the visualization, you will be able to see the growth of your relationship with your little girl. Your notebook entries will be helpful reminders when you check in with yourself about what has changed.

After doing this meditation for a week ask yourself:

What did I notice?

After doing this meditation for a month, ask yourself:

What do I notice about my relationship to myself?

a powerful woman
enjoys her feelings and observes
her thoughts.

a powerful woman

*knows just because she feels bad, it doesn't
mean a bad thing is happening, and just
because she feels good, it doesn't mean
a good thing is happening.*

8

~

Taking Back Your Power

Now that you are seeing yourself as the light and developing a relationship with your little girl, you can benefit from the Natural Power model for understanding and dealing with upsets. Our model will help you understand why your little girl gets upset and how to use her upsets as a way to heal the past. Once you can heal the original experience, the energy you were using on the upset returns to you, the higher self, to use for yourself.

Think of the last time you were really upset.

When you were in the upset, didn't it seem like it might go on forever? When you are mesmerized by your upsets, they can distract you and have you make choices that are not good for you. You might even feel like it's so bad you will die. When you are that upset, you lose perspective. Our model allows you to gain objectivity, which returns your power to you. When you have a more objective viewpoint you will have the chance to make different choices and take action that is better for you.

Traveling Through Time

What is it that is so compelling about your upsets?

Have you ever seen a friend get really upset about something and wondered, "Why is she so upset? That situation is really no big deal." The reason something can upset your friend, seemingly out of proportion, while the same thing would only upset you slightly or not at all is that the upset comes from her history, and you don't have anything in your history that causes you to get upset about that particular thing.

Upsets are a series of thoughts, feelings, and body sensations. As we've explained, any time you are upset for more than three minutes, you have time-traveled into your history. The thoughts, feelings, and body sensations of the past similar experience are intruding into the present and coloring the experience you are having right now. The thoughts you are thinking are the thoughts you had then, the feelings are the feelings you had then, and the body sensations are the same ones you had then. You are now mesmerized by the past and have lost contact with the present. You are no longer responding only to the situation at hand, but rather to a similar situation that happened long ago.

Veronica was having dinner at a fancy restaurant with her friend Tammy. When the waiter served Tammy her glass of red wine, she was in the middle of an animated gesture that caught the wine glass and tipped it over. A red stain spread over the white tablecloth. The waiter rushed to clean it up and Veronica helped with her napkin. After the waiter left, she noticed Tammy was crying.

"Tammy, what's the matter?" Veronica asked in surprise. "You're not upset that you spilled the wine, are you? It could happen to anyone."

Tammy blew her nose in her napkin. "You don't understand," she said. "It's so humiliating. The waiter thought I was a real klutz and everyone is staring at me." She rose abruptly and grabbed her coat. "I'm sorry, but I've got to go. I just can't stay after doing something so embarrassing."

After Tammy left, Veronica looked around at the other diners, who were all quietly chatting and eating their own meals. She couldn't understand the depth of Tammy's upset. Only later did Tammy explain that what upset her was her associations of the past. As a child, she went through an awkward stage when she would spill her milk every night at dinner. Her father would yell at her and sometimes banish her from the table. Her brother called her a "klutz" and made fun of her. To this day, whenever she spills something she can hear their angry or mocking voices telling her she's done it again.

Spilling things doesn't have historical associations for Veronica, so if it had been she who spilled the wine she might have had an upset of the moment, but she wouldn't have time-traveled into her history. She might have said, "Oh, darn!", laughed out of embarrassment, and moved on with her dinner. These upsets of the moment bother you briefly and then you forget about them.

But when you are in an upset that goes deeper than that of the moment, you are once again the little girl who experienced something similar in her past, like Tammy experiencing her father yelling at her for spilling her milk. When your little girl is upset she experiences a series of thoughts, feelings, and body sensations that stem from the solar plexus and render her powerless to access other chakras. Because she never resolved the original situation, her reaction is the same. Reacting from the solar plexus keeps you repeating your history and unable to move forward powerfully in life. But that doesn't need to happen anymore. Now you can learn to have power with your upsets.

Knowing Thoughts for What They Are

How much of your energy is taken up by the thoughts you are having?

Our thoughts provide a commentary about what is going on. When you are upset you have thoughts that may add to the intensity of your reaction. If your secretary calls you to say your boss is headed into your office with a face like a thundercloud, your first thought might be, "I'm going to get in trouble." If your partner gets angry with you, you might think, "There's something wrong with me." If your offer on the new house wasn't accepted, your thought might be, "Nothing ever turns out the way I want it to."

Thoughts are the mind's way of analyzing, judging, criticizing, and projecting into the future. Their descriptions are sometimes highly subjective and inaccurate. Our thoughts are shaped by decisions or vows we have made in the past and by the ideas or rationale that got us through it the first time.

What we may not realize is that our thoughts are not the truth. We believe everything we think and tend to honor our thoughts as though they were words from God—not realizing that much of what we think has no relevance, does not empower us, and is not kind. A thought such as "I look like a fool" only makes what you are doing harder and may not reflect the truth, but you probably believe it anyway—because if you're thinking it, it must be true.

It is our thoughts that cause us to suffer, not our feelings. Feelings such as pain or fear may only be experienced briefly, but when the feeling is followed by a thought such as "It will always be this way," it turns into a story that causes suffering. People commit suicide *not* because of their feelings but because of thoughts like "I can't bear these feelings a moment longer" and "Nothing will ever change." If your partner leaves you for someone else or your boss fires you, you will probably experience rejection. Rejection is a combination of feelings and thoughts. You might be feeling pain, humiliation, sadness, or anger—but what causes your suffering is the thoughts you have about it. "He fired me because I'm not good enough," "This always happens to me," and "No one will ever want to stay with me" are all thoughts that cause pain to turn into rejection, which has you suffer.

Your thoughts often serve to deaden your experience of feelings. If you feel hurt when you hear something a coworker said about you behind your back, you are having an appropriate response to a real situation, but you might find yourself immediately going to a thought such as "Here we go again" that distracts you from feeling the pain. That thought could quickly turn into a story such as, "Why is this happening to me again? This is just like that time in junior high when Sally told my boyfriend she saw me kissing another boy underneath the bleachers. I guess it just goes to show that I can't trust anyone. I'm going to stop making personal phone calls from work. Maybe I should try to find another job." You have now removed yourself from your feelings by rehashing your history and worrying about the future. You are suffering because your thoughts have you believing everyone is untrustworthy just because your coworker said something hurtful. It would have been more supportive to allow yourself to feel the pain briefly and disregard the thoughts, then move on.

Thoughts are merely a series of syllables strung together to become chatter. Thoughts strung together become stories you tell yourself that you believe. If you think you won't get the lead in the community theater production of *Grease* because you don't have Olivia Newton-John's singing voice, you are telling yourself a story about the director's expectations and about your own vocal ability. That story may limit you because if you prepare for the audition believing that your voice isn't good enough for the part, chances are you will never even try out.

As human beings we *empower* our thoughts by paying attention to them, believing them to be true, and taking action from that "truth." Yet we always have a choice. We don't have to let our thoughts have power over us. Our female nature allows us to lean back and see what is really going on.

You can *disempower* a thought by first hearing it as a thought, and then announcing it as a thought. Once you have identified the thought, you can check it against the real situation to see if it is something you know for sure, whether it could be true, or if it is just historically correct and not accurate in the present moment. You can then take appropriate action based on this analysis.

If the thought continues to hound you, work on ignoring it completely. Concentrating on noticing every detail of what is happening in the moment helps you get back into the present and ignore the persistent thought.

Knowing that thoughts are just thoughts and not the truth allows you to hear them without empowering them. To end suffering it is necessary to choose which thoughts to empower. Thoughts such as "It's always like this" or "There's something wrong with me" move you away from the feeling you are experiencing. If you can't feel your feelings, you can't heal the original experience and end your suffering.

Uncoverings

Think about today.

Recall the time you spent:

>   *criticizing*
>   *comparing*
>   *going over what happened*
>   *rehearsing for what is to come*
>   *avoiding feeling bad*

Experiencing Feelings

What would life be like if...
you could feel enlivened by having your feelings?

In our model for upsets there are only six true feelings: fear, anger, sadness, pain, humiliation, and joy. Any other "feelings" are either variations of these six feelings or a combination of feelings and thoughts. Embarrassment is a variation of humiliation, and fury is a variation of anger. Guilt, rejection, and loneliness are combinations of feelings and thoughts. If you are experiencing a true feeling, it will move through your body and spend itself in three minutes or less. Any time it lasts longer, you will know you have time-traveled and are having thoughts and telling yourself stories about it that are involving you in an upset.

Recall, if you can, the last time you watched an infant for a few minutes. A baby will often go through several feelings in a few moments, letting the feelings express themselves naturally without judgment. She may laugh one moment and cry the next, screw up her face in discomfort, then smile in contentment for no apparent reason. Because a baby has no thoughts, her feelings move freely without getting jammed in the body.

Feelings are good, healthy responses to real situations. They stimulate you and let you know you're alive. A true feeling is enlivening because it connects you to life and helps you understand what is happening to you. Feelings are the closest you come to having instincts. Fear alerts you to check if you are in danger. Anger and pain are two different responses that alert you to see if you are being harmed. Sadness indicates a loss. Humiliation tells you that you've done something wrong. Joy wakes you up to see if something good is happening. You may not have experienced your feelings as enlivening, and this is partly because feelings have a bad rap. The next time you have a feeling, try allowing yourself simply to experience it. You will find that it will move through your body in three minutes or less and that you are then able to move on to the next experience.

Think of a time...

in your childhood when you were told not to feel the way you were feeling, or that you shouldn't be feeling that way.

Many of us were brought up to believe that our feelings are bad, so we try to deaden them. Our parents may have said things like "Don't be sad" or "Don't feel bad." Children know what they feel, but are often told they shouldn't feel that way, or even that they can't possibly feel the way they are feeling. "You can't be mad about such a silly thing," "I'll give you something to feel bad about," or "You shouldn't let that upset you" are statements that negate or judge feelings.

Children are often punished for displaying feelings and learn early on to suppress them. Other children suppress feelings because they are raised in a family where feelings are out of control. If you

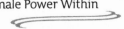

were in a family where feelings caused emotional or physical abuse, you might have learned that having feelings was dangerous, so you deadened your own for reasons of self-preservation.

Parents often try to control their children's feelings because they are uncomfortable with their own feelings. If they are uncomfortable with their own feelings, they will certainly be uncomfortable when a child displays feelings by screaming in anger or wailing in pain—especially in public.

Imagine if you had been raised to feel your feelings without judging the experience as bad. If anger didn't "feel bad," you might have experienced its energy as stimulating and invigorating. If you had come home from school angry about an injustice and your mother had said, "Wow, let's get out some pillows and punch out that anger. Whoopee! Now really wham those pillows," you might have experienced your anger as a valid response to the real situation that energized you. If you'd awakened at night afraid of a monster under your bed and your father had held you and said, "Wow, fear really gets your blood pumping, doesn't it? Don't you feel fully alive right now?" you would have had a different relationship to it. Maybe the two of you could have sat on your bed huddled together, experiencing the shivery feeling of fear.

The anger or fear might have left you feeling invigorated and refreshed because you really *felt* your feelings and they were honored. They would have flowed through your body and been released. It is important to feel your feelings. If your mother had shushed you and punished you for being angry, you would have had to deaden and stuff that anger. If your father had made fun of you for being afraid, you would have learned to hide your fear—even from yourself. When we deaden our feelings, we deaden a part of ourselves and keep the toxic energy of the emotion in our bodies rather than releasing it. Over a period of time, this stored energy can become detrimental to our health.

We all tend to honor and believe in our feelings as if they were the truth, but it is often the case that feelings don't really describe what is happening. If you are avoiding buying a new car because the salesmen intimidate you and you're afraid of appearing ignorant, you believe in the truth of your fear. If you could feel the fear and do it anyway, you might find out you enjoy the process of car shopping and that it's not a fearful experience at all. It is important to know that feelings don't necessarily describe the truth.

Because you were taught to label certain feelings as "bad," you have probably made many choices in your life based on not wanting to feel bad. Who wants to feel bad, after all? Yet if your feelings don't always accurately describe the truth, it could be that just because you feel good doesn't mean a good thing is happening—and just because you feel bad doesn't mean a bad thing is happening. It might, for example, feel really good to leave a smoldering message for a friend you are angry with, but it could be that a good thing is not happening. You might regret leaving that message later, and your relationship with that friend could be compromised. It might feel really bad to get fired, but it could be that a good thing is happening. Having to reevaluate what you are doing for work, relying on your own resources, and looking for a new job might lead you to new avenues you never would have explored otherwise.

It would be powerful to start noticing how many things you don't do that would be good for you to do because you are unwilling to feel bad. If going to a singles dance fills you with terror, you might decide to stay home even though you want to meet new people. If the sadness you feel when you see homeless people overwhelms you, you might not volunteer at your local shelter even though you want to help others. Even joy can stop you, because joy can be as difficult to tolerate as the other feelings. If you feel great joy while dancing wildly at a party, you might feel embarrassed or uncomfortable afterward and vow not to do it again.

Feeling your feelings doesn't mean you should take them out on someone else. Feeling your anger doesn't mean screaming at the person who happens to be standing opposite you. It does mean letting yourself experience what it is you are feeling without being influenced by the thoughts you are having, then being able to take considered action once the feeling has spent itself. Part of feeling your feelings is learning how to manage them.

Kelly, an editor, couldn't ignore her assistant Daniella's increasingly careless behavior. She was often late, forgot to do assigned work, and sometimes failed to deliver messages from clients. But Kelly found herself unwilling to take her to task. Every day she would vow to talk to her and every day she let it slide. After a few months, she finally sat herself down to examine the situation. Why was it so difficult for her to confront Daniella?

Kelly realized that she was afraid of this confrontation because in her childhood she had bossed her sister around, and in consequence her sister had withdrawn her love and stopped playing with her. She was afraid to talk to her assistant because she didn't want to experience the same feeling of loss. She was afraid Daniella would be angry with her and she assumed she would have to experience the sadness of watching Daniella withdraw. Because she didn't want to feel sadness, she had remained in an increasingly frustrating situation instead of taking action to change it. What if Kelly had allowed herself to feel bad and done it anyway?

It is important to feel your feelings. When you stop yourself from feeling, you are deadening a piece of yourself and keeping the toxic energy in your body instead of letting it pass through. Don't you feel better after having a good cry? If you can become friends with your feelings by letting them pass through your body and at the same time become increasingly in charge of your thoughts, you will have the possibility of less suffering and you will be able to manage your upsets differently.

Uncoverings

My mother's response to feelings was…

My father's response to feelings was…

My family's orientation to feelings was…

Think of a time when I…

> *enjoyed being angry*
>
> *had a good cry*
>
> *felt frightened and excited at the same time*
>
> *felt better after expressing a feeling*

Think of times I felt enlivened by and connected through my feelings.

Energy Moving Through Your Body

What body sensations do you have when you are scared?

Imagine that you are standing at the edge of a cliff overlooking the Grand Canyon. As you look down and down, your body has reactions that may include dizziness, butterflies in the stomach, sweating, or muscles gripping. You may experience a reaction just from reading about it. This physical reaction is what we call a *body sensation*. Whenever you are having a feeling, it is accompanied by a body sensation, and that sensation may make you uncomfortable.

Everyone experiences body sensations differently, but if you are feeling your feelings it is inevitable that they will stimulate a physical reaction. It would be powerful to start noticing the body sensations that accompany your feelings. Fear may make the hair stand up on the back of your neck or goose bumps rise up on your arms. Anger tends to raise blood pressure, making your veins pop and your head start to throb. Pain can feel like a stab in the heart. Sadness can have you feel like there is a great weight dragging you down. Joy might send butterflies fluttering in your stomach.

Part of the reason we think feelings feel bad is that we can't stand the body sensations that accompany them. Think about the last time you felt humiliation, the feeling many people are most reluctant to experience. What might have made humiliation so excruciating was not the feeling itself but the body sensations that accompanied it. Pia, a forty-four-year-old airline pilot, describes humiliation as a process of shrinking into herself and away from her skin. The space between her skin and herself fills up with heat and everything on the surface dries up like a prune. Your experience of humiliation might be different, but undoubtedly it is equally uncomfortable. Most of us would rather stay in our comfort zones than feel humiliated.

Moving forward in life means being willing to risk humiliation because trying out something new involves the possibility of making mistakes. If you join a yoga class, you may have to risk looking ungraceful for a while. If you take up pottery, your pots may not look as good as the others in your class who have been doing it for a while. Learning to play an instrument might involve making ugly noises at first. You may have stopped yourself from stretching in life because you were unwilling to feel humiliation.

If you knew it was just a body sensation, you might be able to tolerate it. It is impossible to be human without feeling humiliation. If you can be willing to let some humiliation into your life, you give yourself a chance to move toward becoming more yourself. After all, the words "humiliation" and "human" come from the same root. Withstanding humiliation and doing it anyway gives you a much larger range of choices, which will have you be more powerful in your life.

It is natural to want to avoid feeling uncomfortable body sensations, especially when you are upset and your little girl gets in

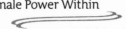

on the act. Your little girl had a small body that couldn't tolerate the enormity of the sensations produced by an upset. Now that you are in a larger body, you can deal more easily with the energy going through you—but your little girl doesn't know this. She responds as if she is still in a small body and can't tolerate the feelings, so she escapes them by having thoughts and telling stories that take her farther and farther away.

When, for example, a person you care about deeply separates herself from you, your little girl is brokenhearted. She feels so sad and believes she can't tolerate it, because that kind of sadness is very deep. Instead, she starts talking to herself and telling herself stories, saying things like, "There must be something wrong with me because this always happens to me. It happened with her, and her, and her. Everyone else seems to be able to handle situations like this, but I can't." She has now drifted miles away into thoughts that take her away from the real experience of the heartbreak. She is removed from the experience and doesn't have to feel the enormity of her feelings.

Having thoughts is not the only way we take ourselves away from the experience. If he doesn't call for a second date, you might get a bag of chips and settle in front of the television. If you don't get promoted, you might go out to a bar and have a few drinks. If your mother is harping on you about money again, you might go shopping for a new outfit. Alcohol, food, shopping, smoking, watching television, and reading fiction are some of the ways we distract ourselves from experiencing our body sensations. Yet running away only prolongs our suffering, because the original experience never gets healed. If we want to heal our upsets, we must be willing to quiet our thoughts and feel our feelings. The only way out is through.

Uncoverings

What are my body sensations when I am:

> *angry*
> *frightened*
> *sad*
> *humiliated*
> *hurt*
> *joyful*

Think of a time there was something I wanted to do but didn't
because I couldn't stand the body sensations I was having.

What I can do to help myself tolerate body sensations so that
I can take time to make the best choice for myself is...

Managing Your Upsets

What would life have been like if,...
when you were a child, the higher self had been
present every time you were upset to hold your hand
and take you through what was happening?

When you are in an upset, you have two choices for dealing with it. First, you can be fully in it, going into your thoughts and telling yourself stories that lead to potentially unhealthy or damaging actions. This is the model that you have probably been using until now, and it is the model that can keep you feeling stuck in life. When you are fully in the experience, you don't have objectivity in regard to the situation, so you believe your thoughts and the stories you tell yourself. You have a conversation with yourself like this one: "See? I'm right. This always happens to me. Everyone treats me like this. What's wrong with me?" Your thoughts take over, pushing away the original feelings and often stimulating new feelings. The feelings turn immediately into thoughts and take a well-worn path that almost assuredly will last longer than three minutes.

At this point, you have time-traveled into your history. You are reaffirming your experiences up until that point, staying in a comfort zone. No matter how miserable you feel in the known, it is less frightening than the unknown. So saying "everyone treats me like this" affirms what you think you know about yourself. Judging yourself adds a second dilemma to the one you are already experiencing. The first dilemma is the immediate situation, and the second one is "there's something wrong with me." Getting involved in the second dilemma ensures that the first one will never be solved and healed.

The second option for experiencing an upset is to recognize that the aspect of you that is upset is the little girl, your psychological self. The little girl is upset because she is playing historical thoughts like an endless tape in her head. Around and around go the thoughts, while she experiences the same feelings and body sensations she did in childhood. For the little girl, things are happening as fast as they did when she was a child. The tennis balls are flying over the net too fast for her to hit them or dodge them. She was helpless as a child, and she feels helpless now. The difference is that now you can presence yourself as the higher self to guide and reassure the little girl.

You, the higher self, can help your little girl by slowing down an upset to a point where it can be resolved. You can help her slow down the tennis balls so that she can relax. You can gently remind the little girl that not every tall man will act like her father, that not every boss is her sarcastic kindergarten teacher, or that not every girlfriend is stabbing her in the back as they did in junior high. You, the higher self, can provide alternatives. You can see that the person who is upsetting you is acting out of their defenses because that is all they know how to do. You, the higher self, know not to take things personally. Perhaps the person opposite you is in trouble, and that's why she is hurting or bullying you. Perhaps the person who didn't show up for an appointment has a valid reason, and she didn't miss the appointment on purpose to insult you.

If you, the higher self, are present during an upset, it becomes something more—it becomes an experience in which you wake up and heal your past. When something from your history shows up in a current upset, you could see that it is present because it wants to be healed. It is showing up to give you an opportunity to heal what happened when you were a child. You can be in the crown chakra point of view, which is that this situation is presenting itself today because you can heal it today.

The higher self has the ability to observe a situation objectively. The observer is the kind, openhearted you who is enlightened as to what is *really* going on versus what *you think* is going on or what seemed to be going on in the past. A little girl can't be objective about her own situation. She needs you, the higher self, to help her see an upset objectively.

When the water heater breaks down a week after the roof started leaking, the refrigerator gave up the ghost, and you received a cancellation notice for your insurance, your little girl might think it's the end of the world. She's eight years old again and her parents are fighting because they don't have the money to pay the mortgage. You, the higher self, can hold her in your lap and let her cry, or scream, and express herself however she needs to. You can soothe her as only you know how to soothe her. Then you can take a deep breath and access the wisdom and optimism of the crown chakra, sharing the knowledge that it will all work out for the best. Coming from this viewpoint you can help her see that she won't die from this upset, that you will work out a payment plan with the plumber, and that your paycheck is coming tomorrow so you can reinstate your insurance.

It may be difficult at first to find objectivity in the midst of an upset. Like anything new, it takes practice. You can start by taking a few minutes at the end of the day to sit with your little girl and go over an upset in hindsight. Maybe she screamed at the plumber in frustration when he informed you that you'd have to buy a new water heater. You, the higher self, may not have been able to presence yourself at that time. You can resolve the upset later by going over it with her in the evening when you are able to presence your higher self. Resolving it means slowing it down enough to look at each aspect: thoughts, feelings, body sensations, stories, and history. You can have a conversation about each aspect with your little girl and allow her to express herself about it.

Asking your little girl questions will give her the space to let you know what is going on for her. What thoughts did she have about the situation? Which of the six feelings did she experience, and what body sensations did they provoke? What stories did she tell herself based on the past? What in her history makes this upset big? Once the little girl has established the historical basis for the upset, you can help her see what might have been going on for the other people involved. You can offer reassurance by reminding her of other times she was able to fix what was broken.

Often, all your little girl needs is acknowledgment that she is feeling what she is feeling. If you have children or have ever interacted with them, you probably noticed that when they run to you with a problem, often they are comforted simply by your acknowledgment of their situation or their feelings. If Maude runs up to you saying, "Toni said something mean to me," you can soothe her by saying, "Oh, that's too bad. That must have felt awful." You may run to find Toni so you can talk with her about it and get her to apologize, but by that time, Maude may be playing happily with her friends again. She has forgotten all about the situation already, because her feelings were acknowledged. You can acknowledge your little girl's feelings by saying simply, "Poor thing," "That must have felt bad," or "Ah, that must have been hard."

Going over an upset in hindsight probably won't take longer than ten minutes, yet if you do it every day, you will begin to notice a profound difference in how you handle your upsets. Your little girl will begin to trust you, knowing that you will be there for her at the end of the day to deal with the upset. You may not even want to wait until the end of the day. If you can remove yourself from the upsetting situation, you can go over it with your little girl immediately. Bathrooms are great places to work with your little girl. One of our Gathering participants has what she calls a "prayer stall" at work—a stall in the women's room where she retreats to have conversations with her little girl when she gets upset. She emerges a few minutes later refreshed and ready to deal with the situation differently.

After a while, you will notice that you, the higher self, are able to show up *while* an upset is occurring. You may not be able to impact the experience, but you will be there as an objective observer. This stage can be frustrating, because you can see what is going on but you can't necessarily change what you are doing in that moment. Eventually, you will have the power to change what is happening in the moment. That is the point when the upset will no longer be an upset, because you are not lost in your history but can deal with the situation that is in front of you objectively and without judgment. You are not expending your precious energy on that upset, but are dealing with it as it comes and then letting it go.

When you do get upset, you can look at it different from how you have in the past. You can see that going through an upset is strengthening for you because it allows you to heal something from the past. Building a practice of handling your upsets with your little girl every day will allow your relationship with your little girl to grow and deepen, and it will allow you to process your upsets in a way that supports you in being more you. The less energy you need to expend on your upsets, the more energy you can use for things that are really worthwhile to you. The less you are taken up by your upsets, the more your essence can shine. You will be able to choose more authentically and experience being more powerful in your life. To know your power, it is essential to know your upsets for what they are.

Taking just one upset at the end of every day and slowing it down enough to shine a light on it can change your life.

The Anatomy of an Upset

Every day, after doing the Chakra meditation (p. 126) and the Healing Your Past visualization (p. 155), select one upset from the day and go over it with your little girl. The following instructions, The Anatomy of an Upset, will guide you. It works best to begin to go over an upset at night before you go to sleep so your unconscious can rearrange things while you are sleeping, but any other time works also.

After a while, you may want to start going over the upset right after it happens.

Eventually, you will be able to be present as the higher self in an upset, but you might not be able to change the course of your action. Then one day you will notice that you can change its course in the moment.

The Anatomy of an Upset uncoverings take only about 5 minutes to do, and the results, as you will see, are profound.

Uncoverings

Sit with your little girl and go over the following questions.

What thoughts were you having about this situation?

What thoughts were you having about yourself?

What feeling or feelings did you have (choose from anger, fear, sadness, pain, humiliation, and joy)? Let yourself feel the feeling.

What body sensations did you experience?

What stories are you telling yourself...

> *about you?*
> *about what this means?*
> *about someone else?*
> *about the outcome?*

What in your history have you time-traveled to? (If you cannot remember an experience in childhood that is similar, see if you can hypothesize what that experience might have been.)

Writing in your notebook may help.

Stories You Tell Yourself

Think of a time...
when you told yourself stories about a situation that
ended up being untrue.

The mind wants to keep busy, so it spends all day having thoughts and telling itself stories. Unfortunately, the stories we tell ourselves tend to be negative and have us use up a lot of our essential energy. Because we believe our stories are true, we often react to situations based on the story we made up instead of on what is really happening. The good news is that you can have some power over the stories that your mind makes up all day, every day. Once you start recognizing the stories your mind is creating, you can decide to create alternative stories that will support and empower you.

Because your mind needs to tell stories, it would be powerful to recognize that you have choice about the stories. You have the ability to start telling yourself positive stories instead of stories that keep you limited. By changing your story you can influence what you allow into your life and what you keep out of your life. If you tell yourself "Nothing ever works out the way I want it to," there is a good chance your reality will bear that out—not because it is true, but because thinking it may have you see only situations that don't work while blinding you to situations that might work for you. If instead you say, "It will all work out, it's just a matter of time," you are opening yourself to relax into your experience of the present and trust that the future will bring you what you want.

When you begin to hold your experiences differently, the stories you tell yourself can work for you instead of against you. You may have the same experiences, but seeing them from a different point of view can change how you interact with them. If you are up for a promotion at work, your mind might busy itself with stories such as, "I'm not sure if I'm ready to be the boss and wear a suit. It will change my relationship with my coworkers and I won't be able to go out for drinks with them after work anymore. It's so much responsibility, I don't know if I can handle it."

If you let your story stop here, you might turn down the promotion even if it would have been a good step in your career, or sabotage it in some way that you don't even realize what you are doing. If you can recognize that you are telling yourself a negative story and know that you could just as easily tell yourself a positive one, you could change the tone of your thoughts by adding, "The fact that this is uncomfortable must mean that change is happening, and that's probably a good thing. I might just have to let myself feel bad so a good thing will happen. In time, I will adjust to the change and I will be glad I let myself go through it." This positive story gives you the space to feel uncomfortable and to go ahead and do it anyway.

You are likely making up stories all the time without realizing it. If you are on your way to meet Mary, a friend you haven't seen in several years, the thought, "I'll see what happens when I get there," may only last a few seconds before your mind rushes to create a story about what will happen. You might start reviewing your history with Mary in your mind to find out how you can look good to her by knowing what she wants to talk about, how she will expect you to present yourself, and what she likes or doesn't like. You may have the whole conversation with Mary worked out in your head before you even meet with her. "Mary's going to make a snide comment about this dress, I know she is. She never approved of the way I dress. She'll probably think I look fat in it, and she'll look meaningfully at my hips when I order my lunch."

Once you've created the story and believe it, you will have the feelings it inspires. If you believe your own story about how you think Mary will act, you may feel frightened, angry, or humiliated before you even get to the restaurant. You will probably respond to her from the story in your head instead of what is actually happening. In fact, you may ignore anything she does or says that conflicts with the story. Afterward, you may wonder why you had such an uncomfortable time with your old college friend—but you remain right about how she feels about you.

Whenever you begin telling yourself stories, you have options. Instead of believing them you could intervene on your own behalf, realizing that the bad story was created out of your history. Perhaps your mother never felt good about herself in relationship to her friends. Recognizing that the thought wasn't really your own but one you caught from your mother allows you to separate from it. You can ground yourself by breathing and having light move through your chakras. Knowing you are the light will let you see that all Mary wants to do is be with her old college buddy. You can then have a delightful lunch with an old friend, renewing a relationship that wouldn't have been possible if you hadn't helped yourself.

We all listen to our stories as if they were true, expending a lot of energy on creating them and having emotional responses to them. Because most of our stories are negative, believing them keeps us emotionally wrought up much of the time, when the reality may not be upsetting at all.

What would life be like if...
you could listen to your story and say, "Well, that's an interesting story" instead of believing it?

How would it be to let the story be just a story and not allow it to hook you? Maybe you could meet Mary with a sense of calm and well-being that you've never had around her before, and because you weren't distracted by your emotional reaction to your story, she could respond differently to you.

It would be powerful to allow your stories to remain at arm's length so you could observe them. This would involve identifying the thoughts you have about something. A thought is your initial reaction before something becomes a story. If you change the thought, you can tell yourself a different story, and you will take a different action. While driving to meet Mary, if you had chosen the thought, "It's a gift to have the chance to renew this relationship," you would probably have told yourself a pleasant story and been in a cheerful frame of mind when you arrived at the restaurant.

How many thoughts do you have during the sixteen or eighteen hours you are awake that really matter?

If you imagine how many thoughts you have in a day, and how many of them are really valuable, you will see that most thoughts are not worth paying attention to. Very little of what you think is productive or to the point, and often has little basis in what is actually happening. Most thoughts are self-destructive or untrue— but you spend a bad day paying attention to them.

Our negative thoughts often come in the damaging form of self-criticism. Imagine taking a hammer and hitting yourself with it over and over, as hard as you can. You are angry with yourself, so you keep hitting your arm despite the pain you are causing. Eventually, though, you notice that the skin is broken and bruised, so you stop hitting yourself. Being self-critical is like beating yourself with a hammer, but because you don't see any blood you don't recognize the extent of the damage—and you may not stop.

If someone you knew was being abused this way, you would feel immense sympathy and concern for her. What you may not have realized is that your little girl is worthy of the same compassion. She believes her negative thoughts and often blames herself for everything that goes wrong. You, the higher self, can help her see that her negative thoughts and stories are not true.

On a Friday night your little girl might be telling herself, "I'm too quiet and dull. No one's interested in what an accountant does at work, so I have nothing to talk about. That's why no one likes me and I don't have a relationship. If only I were outgoing and witty like Zoe, I'd be popular. I might as well not even try to meet anyone because they'll all think I'm just a boring pencil pusher. I guess I'll just sit here and watch TV instead of going to the party."

Sitting with your little girl in a loving and compassionate way, you can soothingly explain that her thoughts are just thoughts and that her story isn't necessarily true. Understanding that she doesn't have to believe her story might allow her to have different feelings. You could help her create a different story like, "The fact that I tend to be quiet might fascinate someone and they might think I'm mysterious." Believing the positive story might have your little girl end up going to the party instead of staying home.

How you have your life happen has everything to do with which thoughts you pay attention to. Your mind wants answers to what will happen, so it looks to the only facts it has—which come from the past—to see what will happen in the future. And it is undoubtedly the negative thoughts that your mind will pay attention to, because the mind sifts through and brings the negative thoughts forward as a means of protection. "She'll reject me because the others always have" is a thought that keeps your life happening the way it has always happened rather than allowing it to happen differently. If you think she'll reject you, you will never make the call—and you will never have the opportunity to be charming, to exude confidence, and to believe some of the good things she said. If you ignored the negative thought or didn't give it credit, you might make the call—and you might have a chance to build a friendship with her.

Thoughts are like tapes that sometimes play so loudly you can't hear anything else. This was the case with Sylvia, a young

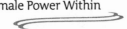

teacher who was having a difficult time with her husband and was considering leaving him. She couldn't think about anything else and was completely obsessed with her thoughts, while going automatically through the motions of her life. Sometimes she was listening so hard to her thoughts that she would drive all the way to work and not remember how she got there. One day she was crossing a busy intersection and as usual was thinking about her dilemma. She was thinking so loudly that she didn't hear the siren of the police car speeding toward her out of a cross street. The police car hit her sideways, catapulting her car into oncoming traffic. By a miracle, Sylvia was physically all right. But she realized that the "accident" had been a wake-up call. She needed to get her thoughts under control because her life depended on it.

It's the nature of the human mind to fill with thoughts, but you have the option of turning down the volume or changing the content. The more you pay attention to what your mind is saying and understand that you have choices about which thoughts to follow, the more control you can have in your life. If you are having negative thoughts playing in an endless tape in your head, you can take action to interrupt their flow. You could chant a positive phrase, hum loudly or sing to distract the thought, or you could simply observe the thought and count how many times you have it. Another tactic to interrupt the flow of thoughts is to start an objective commentary on what is going on around you. "The carpet is green, the walls are white, and my boss is talking. My legs are crossed and my pen is missing its top." It would also work well to write down your thoughts. If you are going to write them down, try writing at the top of the page, "Thoughts, not necessarily the truth." Then list all the intrusive thoughts you are having. Your mind may rebel, saying, "But these aren't thoughts—these are true!" or "This is *just* a thought?" In this process they will lose some of their power.

Being caught up in your thoughts and stories all day affects the quality of your life and your ability to have what you want. What you think when you enter a circumstance matters. People will respond to the thoughts you are having because your thoughts put out a vibration that influences your posture, how you walk, your facial expressions, and what you perceive. It would be powerful for you to explore good ways of interrupting your thoughts and to distance yourself from the stories you tell yourself. Choosing the thoughts that will empower you and rejecting the disempowering, negative thoughts will free up your precious energy and help you become more powerful.

Uncoverings

A situation I am uncomfortable about is…

What stories am I telling myself about this situation that makes me uncomfortable?

> Tell another story about the same situation that is uncomfortable to think about.
>
> Now tell a good story.
>
> Tell another good story.
>
> Tell a fantastic science fiction story.
>
> Tell a funny story.

What happens?

If my mind is going to make up a story anyway, what stops me from telling and staying with a good story?

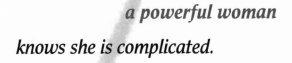

a powerful woman
knows she is complicated.

a powerful woman

lets herself take time to discover
an authentic solution.

9

⌒

Meeting Your Inner Committee

The Many Parts of Yourself

Think of a time...
**you were making an important decision and you had
many conflicting views about what to do.**

Sometimes it's not one internal voice speaking to us, telling us
stories, but many. When you are in an upset, for example, you
might have many different voices clamoring for you to take various actions. Identifying these conflicting voices and knowing how
to work with them will help you make good decisions.

It is natural and very female to have a variety of desires, expectations, feelings, and points of view about something. When
you are making a decision about your life you may find yourself
saying something like, "There's a part of me that wants to visit my
mother, but part of me doesn't," or "Part of me is on your side,
part of me doesn't care, and another part of me is really mad at
you." It is quite natural and normal to have two, or five, or ten different voices inside you all wanting different things. The voices
represent parts of yourself that come from the defenses you have
created, your reaction to childhood, the scorecards you've used,
your family way, the cultural influences that have shaped you,
what you are frightened of, and vows you made to yourself. We
call these parts of yourself your committee members.

Your committee members speak up when you are making
choices and decisions about your life, and many of them have good
and valid input into what you should or shouldn't do. Looking at
the various voices you have as if they are members of a committee will allow you to imagine them in dialogue together when you
are in the decision-making process. That way, you don't use up
your precious energy trying to figure out what to do amid a sea of

thoughts. Until now, you may have spent a lot of energy trying to figure out which committee member is the real voice—and by doing this, you may have been denying the parts of yourself that need to be included in making a decision. It would be a more empowering use of your energy to allow a conversation among all the committee members on your board, letting each one have her say.

Because your committee members are formed from your experiences, some of them are healthy for you and others are not. Coming to know and listen to all your committee members will allow you to give power to the ones who are most authentic and to heal the ones that are disempowering for you. When you are in debate about a decision, you can use the situation to discover all the opinions you have.

Holding a Meeting

In the Natural Power Work we suggest holding imaginary board meetings for your committee members on a somewhat regular basis so you can come to know your various voices. If you are trying to decide on the next action, it can be useful to imagine your committee members sitting on the floor in a circle discussing their views. You can have fun imagining the members, taking their personalities from the voices you hear. There may be one who is loud and demanding, accustomed to getting her way. Another is quiet and stubborn, holding onto a vow you made as a child. An impatient member might be bouncing up and down, not wanting to wait a moment longer to have what she wants and knowing she is willing to do anything to get it. And there may be one or more silent committee members who don't speak up at all. You can tell that the silent ones are there because you are stuck or because you keep on making the same decision over and over again and you are unhappy with the results.

When you need to make a decision about something, a good place to start is to lean back and listen to the different voices of committee members telling you their points of view. There may be a committee member who craves excitement and change, and another one who wants the safety of knowing what to expect. One committee member might want to be wildly successful, and another wants to be taken care of. You may have several committee members that represent your little girl at different ages, and you may have some that represent your higher self. Letting

all of them have their say is a step toward finding what is authentic for you so you can have what you want in your life.

If you are debating whether or not to quit your job and start a new career, your committee members will probably have a lot to say. Each committee member has her own agenda, and each has her own way of making herself heard. One committee member may jump for joy and yell, "Yes! You're finally doing it!" Another might cross her arms and say, "I don't know how you think you're actually going to do this," prompting another to respond, "You sound just like my mother." A cautious committee member may warn you, "Take it slowly and make a considered decision," while an impatient committee member drums her fingers on the table and says, "I can't stand it another minute, so you'd better decide right away." Another member, concerned, might try mediating between the conflicting interests, saying, "Come on, we can all compromise a little here." You may have a committee member who sits quietly through the meeting without expressing any opinions—then after the meeting, she does something to sabotage your decision.

The saboteur is a committee member who is unhappy with your decision, and since she didn't express her views at the meeting she gets back at you by taking action that is unhealthy or disempowering. She may do something that will harm the progress of your decision—such as to have you be late for an interview or forget to return an application on time. It could be that she is afraid and cannot express it out loud. Your saboteur may do any number of things to undermine your decision: compulsive shopping, eating something unhealthy, calling someone who isn't supportive, or any other action that is not good or authentic for you. She may be the committee member who does not have your best interests at heart because she is reacting out of your history. You may have a saboteur who goes for a cigarette at every stressful meeting, or you may have one who damages you by saying the wrong thing at the wrong time. These may be the committee members who are created out of your history and who you need to heal as you grow into your own power. As you continue to work with your little girl and heal the past, the committee members who do things that are harmful to you may gradually disappear.

When you are having a committee meeting, it is often the committee members who speak first and yell the loudest who get their way. It is probable, though, that these committee members are not the ones who will bring you to what is authentic. The first and loudest members are often coming from a knee-jerk life-or-death response in the anal chakra. It may be that you actually are in a life-or-death situation, and in that case you will want to listen to the voices shouting for immediate action. More often, however, the "anally grabbed" committee members are little girls who are driven by what has happened in your history. When these little girls shout, "Quick, run away right now!" they are responding historically and are not necessarily encouraging you to take action that will benefit you.

The loudest committee members are not the only ones who can have you taking disempowering action. As you get to know your committee members, you may find one or several members who remain silent—and their silence can keep you powerfully stuck in taking actions that repeat your history. Because they won't talk about it, the silent voices don't allow something new to happen. The way you can identify a silent committee member is by looking to see if you have what you want. If you don't have what you want, you can probably count on the fact that you have a committee member who is afraid of it or doesn't want it.

A committee member who never speaks may be remaining silent out of fear. She may keep you from trying something new because she is afraid to do it, but you might not have realized she is the one keeping you from trying something because she has never said so out loud. When you start having meetings and noticing who is there but not speaking, you can begin to encourage her to have her say. Expressing her fear will allow you, the higher self, to help her through it so you can choose action that will be good for you even if it feels frightening.

Your silent committee member might be the one who made a vow in response to a trauma you experienced. She may have vowed, "I'll never let this happen again"—and you might not even realize she made that vow. The committee member who made the vow may have been a little girl acting from the solar plexus. She made the best decision she knew how to make to take care of herself in that situation and in the future, a decision that may still be keeping you powerfully limited.

A committee member created from trauma may not speak up at all until years after an event has taken place, like the one Bertie discovered at age forty-five. Bertie had married in her early twenties and divorced after three years. The divorce was so painful for her that she vowed to herself never to get married again. Several years later she met Todd, a charming, considerate man who treated her with courtesy and kindness. She fell in love with him and eventually they began living together. He proposed to her on Valentine's Day, but Bertie said no. Todd understood her reluctance to marry, so they continued living together happily—yet every year on Valentine's Day Todd proposed again. Every year she said no, until finally on their fifth Valentine's Day she took the plunge and accepted.

The next morning Bertie was surprised to hear an internal voice saying, "You broke your vow! You promised me you would never marry again." Bertie realized she had a committee member who had been silently protecting her from another bad marriage ever since her divorce. She was surprised to remember vowing all those years ago, "I'll never get married again." She listened to the committee member's concerns and was able to reassure her that Todd was a good man with whom she could be happy. Released from her vow, she went ahead with planning her wedding, knowing she was doing the right thing.

The vow "I'll never get married again" had Bertie's protective committee member using a scorecard for happiness that involved staying unmarried—and that scorecard was in conflict with Bertie's scorecard for happiness, which involved marrying a good man. We all have committee members who hold up different scorecards to measure how we are doing. If you think about the immense array of choices women have in life today, it would be surprising if you didn't have committee members with different scorecards.

You get conflicting messages constantly in the media, from your friends, and in your family. *Cosmopolitan* magazine tells you to be sexy, *Ms.* magazine tells you to be independent, your friend June tells you to put yourself first, and your Aunt Ida tells you to stand by your man no matter what. You may have a committee member who thinks you should be married and have two children by now, and another committee member who thinks you should be CEO of your company already. One committee member may hold a scorecard that says your appearance is the most important, and another's scorecard says your financial success is the best way to measure how you are doing.

The committee members who are authentic for you can easily get buried under the powerful magnetism of the committee members who are based on your psychological self, in the anal and the solar plexus chakras. You might have a committee member who says, "We'd better decide right now" because she is afraid of being out of control. But sometimes it is good to sit with a question and let the decision evolve slowly. It would be good in that situation to listen to a committee member who says, "In time the answer will reveal itself."

It will be powerful for you to discover the committee members who have your best interest at heart. You can find these by putting your hand on your heart and asking, "What's good for me?" and putting your hand on your throat and asking "What's right for me?" The committee members who know what is good and right for you can then step forward to give you the answers.

Healing Committee Members

Growing into your authenticity means strengthening the committee members who have your best interest at heart and healing the committee members who have you take action that is disempowering or damaging for you. You will want to begin by identifying the committee members who need to be healed. They might appear as little girls, rebellious teens, or authoritarian adults. They are the ones who keep you from having what you want, by reacting strongly from the anal and the solar plexus chakras, by making a vow, or by sitting silently.

Once you have identified the committee members who need healing, you can go through the Anatomy of an Upset with each one. You will allow healing to begin as you go over their thoughts, feelings, body sensations, stories, and history. If a member is silent and you can't speak with her, you can form a hypothesis about what she might be saying by looking at your history, family way, and scoreboards. As you focus on your history, you may start getting flashes of your childhood that can illuminate a committee member for you. The stories your family tells about your childhood may help you to find what needs to be healed.

Bertie had to heal her committee member who took a vow never to marry again. In order to do this, she gave her committee member the name "Prudence" so she could visualize her better. Bertie formed hypotheses about why Prudence might have made the vow never to marry again. She knew that Prudence's vow may have come from experiencing her parents' marriage, which had been rocky and had ended in divorce when Bertie was eleven. Bertie realized that her own divorce might have traumatized Prudence into making the vow as well. She also postulated that Prudence might be holding onto church teachings she heard during childhood that said divorce was unacceptable. Another option was that Prudence had seen a close friend of hers go through a devastating divorce that caused major financial losses. Finally, Bertie realized that Prudence might be having a hidden conversation about having children that left her reluctant for Bertie to marry.

Once Bertie had formed her hypotheses, she sat down with Prudence and asked her directly whether her vow came from her parents' marriage, from Bertie's first marriage, from church teachings, from her friend's bad example, or from a fear of having children. As she began to identify that Prudence's reluctance came from her childhood experience of her parents' divorce, Bertie realized that there were several other committee members who had also been silently holding beliefs about marriage. She was able to work with each one to identify where the beliefs stemmed from and to go over the Anatomy of an Upset with them so they could heal.

Your committee members help you see the full complexity of what you are facing when you are trying to answer questions for yourself or attract something into your life that is uncomfortable or challenging for you. When you hold a committee meeting, you can fully flesh out the possibility of the voices, what might be holding you back, and what might have happened in your childhood to have you doing what you are doing. It is useful to write down the story of each committee member so you can see how she experiences what you are going through. Getting all the stories on paper can help you see who is on your side, who needs healing, and who needs to have her voice heard. Then you can make a decision either to honor a committee member's voice or work toward healing her.

If something you want is not showing up in your life, it is possible that you have a committee member who made a vow. It would be empowering for you to release yourself from the vows made by traumatized committee members, as Bertie released herself from her vow never to get married. You might have made a vow that sounds like, "I'll never be hurt like that again," "I'll never love anyone again," or "I'll never work for someone else again." Once you know you made a vow, you can reassure the little girl that you, the higher self, are there for her and you won't let the situation happen again in the same way. When a little girl makes a vow it is frozen in time, so it doesn't mature as you mature. Bertie had to reassure her little girl that it had been nineteen years since her divorce, and that she had grown and matured enough to have a successful marriage. Helping your little girl see that things have changed can soothe her so she knows she can be safe.

As you heal the committee members who need healing, they may gradually slip away. As you continue to consult the committee members who have your best interest at heart, they will grow stronger and more available. Eventually you might notice you don't have as many committee members, and that the ones you do have speak to what is authentic for you. You can be soothed in the process of making a decision because you will know that your voices all have valid opinions and that you will come to the decision that is good and right for you. You can make authentic choices that will allow you to have what you want.

Uncoverings

Over the next few days, try to notice when you are making a decision, and stop and spend time identifying the committee members involved. Create a chart like the sample one below:

Committee discussion: "Should I get married?"

Committee members' conversation	Where it came from	What is its motivation	How could it be dealt with
1. Silent, not marry	Vow after 1st marriage	Keep from feeling bad Keep from making mistake	Soothed by reality of the present
2. Hurry up and get married	Afraid it will never happen	Uncomfortable with feeling out of control	Check if there is a real reason to rush

Allow yourself to lean back and let all committee members have their say.

Proceed from the heart and throat chakras and ask yourself

What is good for me? (hand on heart)
What is right for me? (hand on throat)

Part Four

The Possibility:

Tools and Ways of Looking That Support Your Power

a powerful woman

*knows how powerfully she affects
the world around her.*

a powerful woman

owns her part.

10

~~~

Calling Your Future Forward

This chapter is designed to help you to experience your authenticity at deeper and deeper levels by releasing more of what might be in the way of your authenticity, and by creating new ways of being that will have you experience yourself as the powerful woman you are.

Who Am I?

What is important for people to know about you? Make a list.

Your list is probably a list of identities: "I am a daughter," "I am a nonconformist," "I am an introvert." We are always identifying ourselves to ourselves and to others, often without even noticing we are doing it. How often have you asked yourself the question, "Who am I?" The answers you come up with may range from "I am a neat person" to "I am an attractive woman" to "I am an American." You may say things like, "Oh, I would never camp out. I'm a luxury hotel person," or "I'm a West Coast person, not an East Coast person." Have you ever excused yourself by saying, "I can't help it—that's just the kind of person I am?" These are all identities. *They are not who you are.*

It is possible that the identities you have constructed contribute to what is holding you back from being your powerful self. By saying, "I'm a risk-taker," for example, you limit your choices about taking risks. If a risk-taker were "who you are," your first response would not be to weigh the situation carefully and act conservatively. If you find yourself in a situation that calls for cautious action, you might endanger yourself by not questioning your risk-taking self.

Charlene was a teacher and so she had three months off every summer. Her friends and acquaintances were firmly divided into two groups—"mountain people" and "beach people." Charlene identified herself as a "mountain person" and therefore would not consider taking a vacation at the beach. One summer, Charlene decided to buy herself a house outside of the city. Of course she knew it had to be in the mountains, so when her friend mentioned a lovely place for sale at the beach, Charlene said no without looking at it. Only later in her life did she realize how much she had limited herself by identifying herself as a "mountain person." When she finally went to the beach, she discovered that she really liked it and she regretted avoiding it for so long.

When you talk to your friends or when you are getting to know someone, how do you identify yourself to them?

You might be an antique collector, an opera aficionado, a vegetarian, and a cat lover. You have opinions, beliefs, likes and dislikes, thoughts, feelings, behavioral patterns, preferences, and roles that you play in life. What you may not realize is that instead of seeing that you *have* them, you may have *become* them. And *being* them might be limiting. If you *are* that you dislike cocktail parties, how can you go to one, even if you might meet someone there who would help you professionally? If you *are* that you believe you can never be as successful or charming as your mother, then how can you ever be yourself in her presence? If you *are* that you always follow other people's advice, how can you ever know what you want? If you *are* a career woman, how can you be a wife and mother?

Kathleen, a thirty-six-year-old photographer, is a liberal Democrat whose strong political beliefs dictated who she let into her life. At a postelection party she met Gabriel, a staunch Republican who entered into good-natured sparring with her. She enjoyed their conversation but was shocked when he asked her to have dinner with him the next night. How could she go out to dinner with a man who had voted for the opposition? She said no, but found herself thinking about Gabriel all week. When she ran into him at another gathering several months later, she found herself asking if the invitation was still open. It was—and today Kathleen and Gabriel are in a lively and loving relationship.

"I used to think that my friends or lovers had to vote my way," Kathleen admits. "Now I see that we can have a good relationship even if they don't agree with me." Letting go of the identity that she *is* her attachments and preferences has freed Kathleen to let peo-

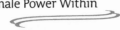

ple in who don't share her beliefs. She and Gabriel have found that it is not always easy to keep their views and their relationship separate, and Kathleen is now able to use their disagreements as opportunities to learn more about both of them. She can allow him to have his opinions and preferences without taking it personally.

In pursuing self-knowledge, the answer to "Who am I?" is often, "You are not *that*." If you can identify the ways you have been defining yourself, you will begin to see that they might describe something *about* yourself, but they are not really *who you are*. The identities you have constructed form your concept of yourself. They also may keep you stuck in certain patterns of behavior. To come into your own power it is essential to begin peeling away the layers of identities you have constructed for yourself. And to peel away the layers, it is necessary to see them. If you can see your identities as definitions of yourself that you have constructed, you can begin to free yourself from them and get to the core of you—your authentic self.

The following uncoverings list some identities you may use to define yourself. It would be powerful to go through the list and recognize that while you may *have* these identities they are not who you are. Please elaborate on the identities that resonate with you, and if you can think of other ways you identify yourself, please add them to your list.

See how you identify yourself through these categories. Examples are provided. Use the beliefs listed below. Answer "Description" and "Identity" for yourself.

Belief	Description	"Identity"
I am the body I live in	I'm too short	"I never look the way I want to"
I am what I like	I like the arts	"I am cultured"
I am what I dislike	I hate the beach	"I'm not a beach person"
I am the patterns I live out	I have only one good friend at a time	"I'm unpopular"
I am the success and failures I lived through	I didn't finish college	"I am a dropout"
I am the roles that I play	I am married	"I am a wife"

How identified am I by each of the above?

How does that limit me?

What is important to know about me…

Thoughts I have about myself are…

Feelings I have about myself are…

How do these limit my actions?

How do these limit the results I can have?

Your Essential Self

Who knows me and has known me for who I am?

The people who love you see that you are much more than the sum of your identities. Why would someone love you just because

you were a neat person or a vegetarian? People who love you are responding to something much deeper and more elemental than that. Your good friends love the essence of who you are. They can see past your identities even though you might not be able to.

In the past, perhaps you had a teacher or adult friend who saw the *you* behind the sulky child or rebellious teenager. That person gave you the gift of knowing something about your authenticity and responding to that rather than to the ways you were behaving at the time. There are people today who see the deepest part of you. They can see your essence, and this seeing acknowledges something about your authentic self.

Much of our Natural Power Work involves uncovering who you really are beneath the constructs you have built to survive, fit in, and be comfortable in the world. As we work to gently uncover your authentic self, it would help to keep in mind the people who have recognized your authenticity, including people who have passed away. We all need a few people in our lives who really *know* us. It helps us validate who we really are and aids us in freeing our authenticity. By looking to see the people you really know and by being open to more deeply knowing others, you will begin to see their inner power and experience the power of acknowledging authenticity.

Uncoverings

Who has known me and knows me for who I am?
What did they each see in me?
Who do I know for who she is?
What do I see in her?

Creating New Scorecards

What are the scorecards that would help me be open to the experiences life is offering?

You'll recall that back in chapter two, we talked about scorecards—those personal measures we all use to evaluate how we are doing in our lives. We talked about how our scorecards tend to limit us by defining our successes narrowly. Now, as you peel off the layers of identity you have constructed, you can create new scorecards that are more aligned with your essential self. Earlier, you identified scorecards that were disempowering and limiting for you. Now that you know yourself better, you can embrace the interesting challenge of setting authentic standards for how your life should look. Changing your scorecards gives *you* the power to decide what you want in your life.

What if instead of asking, "How am I doing compared to others?" you asked a question such as, "Am I available to have the experiences that life is offering?" This is a nonjudgmental question that allows you to notice whether or not you are open to what is already going on in your life. It doesn't imply that your experiences in life aren't good enough, or that somehow you haven't lived up to them. It simply begins to look at life as a process rather than as a series of results. This attitude toward life can expand and empower you, rather than limiting and discouraging you as your former scorecards may have done.

The questions you used to ask may have had you running around the game board of life, trying to get all your pieces around first. It would be powerfully female to let go of "Am I getting there fastest?" and instead ask, "Am I enjoying and learning from the process?" You could burn "Do I have all the newest gadgets?" and replace it with "Am I magnetizing what I want into my life?" It is powerful to let yourself feel okay about the choices you have made.

Your old scorecards may have prevented you from seeing what is really going on in your life. By measuring yourself against others, against a time frame, or against family expectations, it is possible you did not allow yourself to see that you are doing great work in many aspects of your life. Changing the lens you look through might allow you to see that you are doing a fantastic job of exploring who you are, working to become more of who you are, and being concerned with your own happiness and the happiness of others.

Bonnie, a sixty-four-year-old counselor and mother, had a scorecard that asked, "Is everyone around me happy?" This scorecard held her responsible if everything wasn't running smoothly around her. If a grandchild got into trouble at school or a client had a crisis, she would immediately rush to the rescue. She spent a lot of time and energy trying to make her friends, children, and clients happy—because if they weren't, it meant she wasn't a good enough counselor, friend, mother, and grandmother.

Bonnie's years at Life Works have helped her set up more supportive scorecards. A question she often asks herself today is, "Am I being a good listener?" When she is counseling a client or having a conversation with a friend, she concentrates on being present and available to hear them. Asking herself if she is listening well allows her to see if she is leaning back and quieting her thoughts so she can really hear what others are saying. And because she's quieted her inner voices enough to listen well, she doesn't have to run around trying to fix everyone's lives. She's discovered that often all they really want is a sympathetic ear.

What would life be like if...
you could use your energy for yourself instead of against yourself?

Wouldn't it be a relief to change "Am I doing it perfectly?" to "Am I learning from my mistakes?" Having a scorecard that actually reflects what is happening in your life can help you see your life in a way that will support your growth. You have probably been using up a lot of your energy on the scorecards that keep you limited. A scorecard that is healthy for you is one that supports what you are experiencing and what is satisfying and contentment-making on a deep level. It asks questions that attend to what is really important to you, not to what your family thinks is important or what women's magazines tell you is important.

A scorecard worth having would be, "Am I doing what is meaningful to me?" If you ask yourself that question and find that the answer is no, you do not have to go immediately to self-blame. You can see it merely as a tap on the shoulder, an opportunity to notice whether or not what you are doing is meaningful to you.

Another powerful question you could create as a scorecard would be, "Am I available to learn from what's going on in my life?" Like the first question, this one encourages you to look at your life as a process, and encourages you to be engaged in that process. Experiences keep showing up until you can be there and learn from them. If something challenging is going on in your life, you can see it as a learning opportunity instead of an opportunity to beat yourself up for not having handled it earlier or better. This is a powerfully female approach to life.

If gratitude is something you want to cultivate, one of your scorecard questions might be, "Am I grateful?" The question would serve as an opening to be alert for opportunities to be grateful. It doesn't mean you've failed somehow by not being grateful. It is simply a noticing that you haven't been, and that noticing allows you to do something about it if you choose to. Perhaps you would then take some time every morning to silently list everything you are grateful for, or you might write things you are grateful for in your notebook.

Scorecards can change as your focus in life changes. It would be powerful to make up a "Scorecard of the Week" based on what you have decided is important to you that week. Posting your "Scorecard of the Week" on the refrigerator or medicine cabinet will remind you every day of your focus for the week. It will allow you to look at life through a lens that lets your whole experience be there without being stifled.

Uncoverings

Following is a list of sample questions that would be empowering to have on a scorecard. As you read them, think about questions you would like to have on your personal scorecards that would allow you to expand your life. Then you can create your own scorecards that will work for you.

Am I available to have the experiences I'm having?

Am I available to learn from what is going on in my life?

Am I using myself well?

Am I grateful?

Am I contributing?

Am I doing my soul's work, becoming more authentic?

Am I using my power for myself and others?

What small steps am I taking?

Am I making the most of the situation I'm in?

Am I owning my part?

Am I having joy in my life?

Am I being tender with myself?

Am I trying something new?

Am I allowing support in?

Am I doing things for my greater health?

Am I making heartfelt choices?

Am I acknowledging myself?

Am I enjoying what already works in my life?

Am I letting go of what needs to be let go of?

Am I asking myself empowering questions?

Am I gentle with myself?

Am I having fun?

Am I self-loving?

Now make up a scorecard for yourself that supports what you want to focus on this week. You can change the scorecard every week if your focus shifts, or keep the same one if you want to focus on the same thing.

Your Effect Is Powerful

Think of a recent time...
when someone affected you by something they said or did.

You probably don't have to go back too far in time to find an example of someone affecting you because people are affecting you every day, all day. If your neighbor smiles and waves, it will probably influence how you feel, perhaps even change the tone of your entire day. If your neighbor walks past you with a scowl on her face, it will influence you differently. You may decide you must have done something wrong and begin the day with a chip on your shoulder. Your neighbor probably had no idea of the effect she was having on you or the power her effect had over you—and her smiling or scowling probably had nothing to do with you.

When you walk into a room, start noticing how you affect other people rather than concentrating on how they are affecting you.

You are extraordinarily powerful in relationship to your friends, your partner, your housemate, your parents, your siblings, and your coworkers. You have the power to soothe them, to excite them, or to make them happy—and you have the power to unnerve them, to anger them, or to challenge them. You have a dynamic effect on others, even if you are often unaware of it. Sometimes it may be in ways you want and sometimes it may be in ways you don't want. Becoming aware of your effect is the beginning of having power with it and knowing how powerful you are.

Imagine that you are constantly emitting an invisible vibration that other people can sense with their third eye chakra. That vibration affects the way people respond to you. If you are busy beating yourself up mentally all day, people will sense your negative force field and respond to you accordingly. If you are experiencing life fully and feeling comfortable with yourself, people will sense that too, and will probably respond to you more positively.

When you think you don't count, when you say self-deprecatingly, "Who me? Little old me?" you are denying knowledge of your effect on others. The act of making yourself small is the flip side of bragging. Bragging or false pride is speaking well of yourself from an insecure place, and humility is acting as if you are less than you are. If you get invited to a party and you don't go because you tell yourself, "It doesn't matter if I go or not, no one will notice anyway," you are depriving the people there of your company and depriving yourself of knowing you count. Your friend might be heartbroken that you didn't attend, and there might be someone at the party who would have liked to meet you but didn't get the chance because you didn't show up. Saying, "Who, me? I don't matter," is using your power in a negative way.

Swami Satchidananda says that if everyone had one loving thought a day it would change the world. The more we each are who we really are, the more we can reflect positively onto our portion of the world—and this gives us power to influence what happens to us. It is by changing our own inner vibration that we can change what happens to us and around us.

When you can begin to see the effect you have on others, you can begin to understand your own power. And you can use your power well by becoming in charge of the effect you have. What happens to you in life is not an accident. It happens because people are responding to you. If you wonder "Why does this keep happening to me?" it's partly because you keep putting out a silent message that stimulates others and that evokes a certain response in them. People respond to your way of being. It is the core of where your power is.

Diana ran a successful private violin program with thirty young students whose dedicated parents attended lessons with their children. Her students were fond of her and worked hard to improve. Often, at their lessons, Diana and their parents would get tears in their eyes listening to a practice piece evolve into beautiful music.

Diana had her students perform at two concerts during the school year. She built the concerts up to be a big deal so her students would work hard in preparation. Every time she planned a concert, Diana was sure it would be wonderful because her students were playing so well at their lessons. But as the date approached, she became more and more nervous, picking at each mistake her students made and assigning them longer and longer practices. Suddenly it seemed her students weren't playing as well as they had before. She became convinced the concert would be a disaster.

When the day arrived, Diana would be so nervous she could barely speak to introduce each student to the audience. She would sit in the front row clasping her hands, willing each student to do well. But she was always disappointed. Even Diana's best students almost always made mistakes, had to start over, or played out of tune. She often went home and cried to think that her hard work had not been rewarded.

One day Diana attended a concert given by the students of another violin teacher, Hannah. Diana was stunned at Hannah's happy-go-lucky attitude and the smiling way she led each student to the stage. She didn't seem nervous in the least, the parents in the audience seemed to be enjoying themselves, and above all, her students played freely and zestfully.

In awe, Diana approached Hannah after the concert. "How do you do it?" she asked. "My students always freeze up when it's their turn to play, the parents never seem satisfied, and we all dread the concerts. Everyone here seemed to be really enjoying themselves."

Hannah smiled. "Well, I just don't make it out to be a big deal," she said. "We think of it as a party and I have everyone bring something to eat for the reception afterward. I make sure they know if they make a mistake it's no big deal, and I have them practice playing in front of others ahead of time."

Diana realized that Hannah's sunny attitude about concerts had the effect that her students and their parents were relaxed and open to enjoying whatever happened, whereas Diana's nervousness and dread of concerts had created a building of nervous energy for everyone in the weeks leading up to the event. She realized that if she wanted her students to perform with joy in the music, she would have to change the effect she was having—and changing her effect started with the stories she was telling herself and her students about the concert. She started examining why concerts would affect her this way.

When Diana went into her history, she remembered her father supervising her practices when she was a young violin student. He would demand that she play pieces that were too hard for her, and then chastise her sternly when she made mistakes. When she played in a concert, he would sit in the front row, grimacing whenever he heard a note out of tune or a shaky bow stroke. Diana could feel her little girl getting tense and upset just thinking about her childhood practices and concerts, so she went through the Anatomy of an Upset with her. Freed of her past, Diana felt energized to develop a new approach for her students.

Taking Hannah's cue, Diana started making up positive stories about how the next concert would be a fun celebration of everyone's unique style. She assigned easy pieces she was sure her students could play and had them practice them in different places— in the bathroom, in the back yard, at their relatives' and friends' houses. If a student made a mistake in lesson, she smiled and said, "Great mistake!" which made them laugh. She enlisted the parents' help to come up with festive decorations for the recital room and to bring goodies for the children to eat afterward. If she noticed herself getting nervous, she breathed deeply and reassured herself it would be fun and it didn't matter what happened as long as everyone was having a good time. After two months, Diana realized she had changed her scorecard from "Is everyone doing it perfectly?" to "Is everyone enjoying the experience?"

The concert went brilliantly. Diana's students were more relaxed than they had ever been, and she realized she was really enjoying herself. Some students made mistakes, and when they automatically looked over at Diana, instead of frowning she would wink at them and mouth the words, "Great mistake!" The parents were thrilled with the cheerful tone of the event and showed their enthusiasm by clapping, hooting, and whistling enthusiastically after each performance. When everyone was eating cake and congratulating each other, Diana silently thanked Hannah, her mentor, for allowing her to see she could change the effect she was having, and therefore change the whole experience of the concert for herself, her students, and their parents.

Your effect creates an environment around you. When you criticize yourself, you create a negative force field. When you encourage yourself, hold your own hand through the hard parts, use empowering scorecards, do the activities that people naturally come to you for and what you always look forward to, have enough time in your life, and love yourself, you create a positive force field.

Uncoverings

Someone who had an effect on me today was…

What was the effect?

Someone who has a strong effect on me is…

A time recently when I did or said something that had an effect on someone else was…

What is the effect I have on people close to me? Think of three people and answer separately for each person.

What is the effect I have on people in a group?

What I notice about the effect I have is…

What effect do people say I have even if I don't really see it?

In the next weeks, I will stay aware to discover more about what my effect might be.

Shifting Your Effect

Now that you have taken the time to notice your effect, you might want to see if there are aspects of your effect that you would like to change. You might want to look at what is in your life that you wish were different and see if it has something to do with the effect you have. If you are lonely because people are not calling you, if you are always given more work than anyone else, if you are always chosen to take charge, if you seem to be taken from but not given back to—these situations might stem from the effect you have on others.

It is powerful to keep the ways you are affecting people that are good to have, and it is powerful to see the places where you might be having an effect you don't want to have. If you are not having the effect you want, it probably has something to do with your history and the identities you have constructed.

What effect do you want to have?

Jennifer achieved her childhood dream when she became head of nursing at a well-known hospital. Her efficiency, caring attitude, and attention to detail helped her move up quickly in the nursing ranks. Though Jennifer enjoyed her job, she sometimes felt used up by giving to others all day and not receiving anything in return. She couldn't understand why other people couldn't reciprocate her caring approach.

When Jennifer came to Life Works, she started to see the reasons why others only took from her and couldn't give her what she wanted in return. She looked at her history, her identity, and her beliefs that formed the effect she had. Once she saw what made up her effect, she saw that she had the power to change it.

Jennifer's identity was "Nurse Brown who gives and doesn't receive." Because she identified herself as the giver, she closed herself off to receiving what others offered her—and when they did offer something, it never seemed to be the right thing. Jennifer came to understand that she closed off people from doing anything but taking from her in two ways—by her expectation that they wouldn't give, and by being uncomfortable with receiving.

Jennifer looked into her history to see what might have formed her identity as giver. When she was a child, her mother was often ill and Jennifer helped take care of her. Her father praised her often for taking such good care of her mother, calling her "Daddy's little helper." Jennifer came to relish the role of caretaker, and when as a teenager her mother died, she continued her role by taking care of her father and helping her brother and sister through their grief. If anyone tried to help Jennifer or offer her sympathy, she brushed them aside, trying to fulfill her mother's role. After a time, being a support and caretaker was the only way Jennifer knew how to be appreciated. She naturally chose nursing as a profession that would keep her in that comfortable role.

Seeing that her identity and history formed the effect she had allowed Jennifer to begin shifting her effect. By owning her part in how people responded to her, she could work with her little girl to have it be okay for others to give to her. As she shifted her effect, she found with surprise that she actually became a better nurse because she could allow her patients to express their gratitude to her, which in turn warmed her interactions with them.

Once she owned her part in creating an environment where people didn't think to give to her, Jennifer was able to attract more people who gave to her life. Like Jennifer, you can own your part in the effect you have on those around you, seeing that your effect creates an environment that keeps people responding to you in certain ways. Once you own your part in your effect, you have the power to become in charge of it by shifting what doesn't bring you what you want. To shift your effect, you can find what you are wrong about, the identities you have, the historical beliefs you have, and do the Anatomy of an Upset (p. 176). Doing the Anatomy of an Upset on a regular basis will help you heal your history and shift what is not working for you.

Uncoverings

Think of three situations for each of the following two statements:

What happens when I walk into a room is…

What happens when I own the effect I'm having is…

What is the effect I want to have?

Your Magnetism

Imagine for a moment that you are a magnet that draws certain things toward you and repels other things away from you.

The effect you have creates a magnetism that draws toward you certain things and repels other things. Sometimes you magnetize things you want toward you, and sometimes you magnetize things you *don't* want. Sometimes you repel things you don't want away from you, and sometimes you repel things you *do* want. If you are always walking around expecting the best to happen, there is a better chance you will draw positive things toward you. If you are walking around expecting the worst to happen, there is a stronger chance that you will draw negative things toward you.

Jocelyn put her powers of magnetism to the test a few weeks before her birthday. The previous year her birthday was heartbreaking. Because it was her 40th, she had secretly built up a lot of expectations around it. She hoped for her friends and family to take her out for brunch, then throw her a huge party and celebrate all night with her. When all they did was send her gifts and call her to say "Happy Birthday," she was devastated.

This year Jocelyn decided to magnetize a good birthday to her by lightening up. She saw that what repelled a good time last year was the silent intensity of her expectations. If she were light-hearted and talked about her birthday, she might attract a joyful celebration. "Let's go skinny-dipping on my birthday," she joked to her friends. "Being forty-one gives me the privilege of not caring anymore."

Mentioning her birthday playfully made it clear to Jocelyn's friends that it was important to her, so they started asking her what she really wanted to do. When she said she'd like to go to an amusement park, they took her to Disneyland for the day. As the roller coaster plummeted from its peak Jocelyn screamed happily, thrilled that her magnetism had attracted exactly the birthday celebration she wanted.

Starting to see your magnetic powers gives you a way to change what you attract or repel. It may be difficult to see what you magnetize in your life, so looking at your friends' lives is a good place to start. Your friends may complain to you about what they attract or repel without realizing that they have power in it. If Barbara attracts men who go out with their buddies rather than spending time with her, she may complain to you that there aren't any good men out there. Meanwhile, her friend Sophie attracts men who love to spend time talking, cuddling, and watching movies together. It isn't that there aren't any good men out there, but something in Barbara's magnetism attracts the ones who will watch football or go to bars with their friends. If Barbara knew this, she could begin to explore why she attracts men who don't spend time with her.

Like Barbara, you magnetize what you expect from life. You may be uncomfortable where you are and wish it were different, but you may be magnetizing what keeps you comfortable in the discomfort. It may be that Barbara is not comfortable with intimacy, so she attracts men who won't give her too much attention. It may also be that Barbara is repelling men who would be able to offer her a deeper level of intimacy because she is not ready to have it yet. If she could see that she is magnetizing men who *cannot* be intimate and repelling men who *can* be intimate *because of her own discomfort,* she would be able to take steps to shift her magnetism.

Changing your magnetism involves healing what creates the expectations you have. First, you will want to see what is in your life today that you have magnetized and what is not in your life that you have repelled. You have probably magnetized things you want *and* things you don't want, and you have probably repelled things you don't want *and* things you want. Once you can see what you have magnetized or repelled, you can do the Anatomy of an Upset to see what might have happened in the past to have your little girl need to attract certain things and repel others, and then you can heal the part of you that was harmed and made a decision about what to attract and what to repel. Barbara, for example, might need to heal the little girl who experienced betrayal by her father when she was very young, in order to allow space to be comfortable with intimacy in the present.

When she attended the Life Works Mother Retreat, Nina got in touch with how angry she was at her mother. Doing her work at the Mother Retreat allowed Nina to release much of that anger and to discover underneath it a wealth of compassion for her mother. While she was going through the hard part, she felt in need of support and nurturing from her friends, but when she called that evening, not one of them gave her what she wanted.

At first Nina was furious at her friends for not giving her the support and nurturing she had asked for. In the midst of her fury, though, she had a revelation that the anger she was feeling was the same as the anger she felt toward her mother. In fact, as she looked further into her feeling, she realized she was angry with almost everyone in her life. Her constant anger had magnetized people who could not be nurturing and supportive, people she would have to be angry at.

In the course of the Mother Retreat, Nina continued to release her anger and access her compassion. She realized that she deserved to be nurtured lovingly and that the way to have it come into her life was to start treating herself lovingly. When she got home, she started doing things to care for herself. She took long, luxurious baths, shopped for exotic, flattering clothing, checked to see what she felt like doing instead of acting out of rote behavior, said "yes" when she meant yes and "no" when she meant no, let herself lean back and receive what was coming instead of struggling against it, assumed the best about people and situations, asked quietly for what she needed, and listened well to her friends.

After a period of treating herself well and compassionately, Nina noticed a shift in her magnetism. Some of her friends started offering her more support and encouragement, and she was starting to attract new people who treated her well and enjoyed nurturing her. She found herself accepting more dates and enjoying them more because she wasn't looking for something to be angry about. The men she attracted were kinder and more attentive. Somehow, nearly everyone in her life was being pulled to treat her well and lovingly. Nina realized her shift away from being angry and her decision to take loving care of herself had begun to magnetize what she wanted into her life.

When, like Nina, you have healed what needs healing in your history, you can start envisioning what you want. It may be that you need to widen your scope of vision because you might have had tunnel vision around the things you magnetize. You might not be able to imagine it another way, just as Barbara might not be able to imagine that there are men out there who can be with her lovingly. Envisioning what he would do, how he would approach her, and what he would say, would allow Barbara to begin shifting her expectations.

Finding a mentor can help you magnetize what you want and repel what you don't want. It is powerful to find someone who has what you want and watch how she attracts it. It would be powerful for Barbara to start observing Sophie and see how she is magnetizing men who are caring and attentive. Seeing how Sophie feels about herself and others can help Barbara change her own way of being.

It would work well to find a mentor and ask yourself questions such as, "What kinds of thoughts does she have? What kinds of feelings does she have? What does she expect? What might her childhood have been like that she is able to have this?" Hypothesizing will help you come to new ways of looking at how you use your magnetism. It will help you to see that it doesn't have to be the way it has always been, and that you can change things. Embracing the concept that there is no one way life is, and that you can change what is in your life by changing your expectations, has you see that you have the power to decide what is in your life.

Uncoverings

What do I attract into my life that I want?

What do I attract into my life that I don't want?

What do I repel from my life that I don't want?

What do I repel from my life that I want?

For those things that you want that you do not have, and for those things you have that you do not want, do the Anatomy of an Upset to clear the way to magnetizing what you want.

Owning Your Part

What would life be like if...
you knew how to become powerful in the situations
you feel powerless in?

It is human to look for blame when something challenging happens, yet placing blame only holds us back from having the power to change a situation. Taking responsibility is the cure for blame. Responsibility is a lens you look through that says, "Because something is happening in my life, it has to do with me." The minute you own your part, you can start seeing how you can change it. This gives you power to use your energy positively instead of beating yourself up for not doing it better.

Every time you blame something outside yourself, you are allowing yourself to be someone else's victim. Every time you blame an institution, you are allowing yourself to be the victim of the institution. Every time you blame yourself, you are being your own victim. The role of victim has no positive power and leaves you helpless to change your life. When you take responsibility, you have the power to change whatever is not working.

For example, let's say that you are desperate for a job because you have to pay the rent, so you accept a job that doesn't challenge or interest you. You may immediately want to start blaming your boss for keeping you in a role that is beneath you, when actually it is you who sold yourself short. You had good reasons for taking the job—fear of rejection, need to pay the rent, desperation. Your boss simply hired you because someone in human resources sent you over. Having an angry or resentful attitude at work will end up harming you and keep you in the cycle of selling yourself short. You may see that your only option is to leave the job, but it may actually be a job you could enjoy if you owned your part in getting it—because you could see that the job gives you what you need, which is why you took it in the first place. Owning your part will allow you to breathe more fully and to be in the moment, doing your best with a positive attitude. It may be that you need to find a different job, but taking responsibility for your part in getting this one will ensure you don't find yourself in a similar situation next time.

It may be that you haven't found the right man to be with, the career that best uses your talents, or the city to live in that offers what stimulates you. Until you find what is authentic for you, it is not unusual to find yourself in a situation that doesn't work. There are many ways to look at why you are in this uncomfortable situation—and the most empowering way is to see that it wakes you up to explore within and find what is authentic for you. When you can identify what is authentic, you can take better care of yourself and bring yourself what will make you happy. Taking away the blame can have you see what is in your life as positive learning opportunities.

The more you take your life on and have it be naturally and authentically expressed, the more you will know that you are responsible for what is in your life. When you are responsible, there is no one to blame—including yourself. You know it could be better, and if it's not it's because there is still something for you to explore. Knowing you are doing the best you can takes the blame off yourself, and owning what is in your life takes the blame off others.

To change what is in your life means taking ownership of what is already there and working to heal your past so you can attract what you want that isn't there yet. Identifying where your upsets are will help you see where owning your part would be powerful. The way to take back your power is to own what has happened and what is happening to you. If it is happening in your life, it has something to do with you. Owning what it has to do with you gives you power in it. As soon as you claim your part, you have power to deal with the situation.

You are the only one who can do anything about your life. When you see how you have gotten yourself somewhere, you can get yourself out of there and go somewhere else. This is the case even when it looks like it is the other person who is at fault.

Cassandra left her first husband after he was unfaithful to her with a colleague. Mesmerized by the pain of being wronged, she blamed her husband for the whole situation. Her friends all sympathized, encouraging her to find someone else. Two years later Cassandra met Bruce, the man she was convinced she would spend the rest of her life with. She moved in with him and lived in blissful domesticity—until she had an abrupt awakening. Bruce often worked late at the office and she respected his work ethic, so she rarely called him there. One night his mother was trying to get in touch with him, so Cassandra broke her unspoken agreement not to bother him and called his office. When no one answered, she realized he wasn't working late as he had told her he would be. When he arrived home at midnight, she confronted him and he admitted he was having an affair. Dazed by the shock and pain, she found the courage to look at the situation differently. She could see that a pattern was developing so she asked herself, "What is the same in both relationships?" The two men were as different as could be in looks, careers, hobbies, and background. What was the same in both relationships was Cassandra herself.

Painful as it was to have to own her part, it allowed Cassandra to see that she probably attracted men who cheated because her father had cheated on her mother. It was the only model she knew. Knowing this allowed her to begin healing her history, which helped her to attract a man who would be faithful to her.

When you see that you are the one who allows people to treat you badly, you can take your power back. You don't ever have to let them deal with you like that again. Owning the fact that they treated you badly because you let them puts you in the driver's seat. You may not have been able to do anything else because you were doing the best you could, but somewhere along the way consciously, unconsciously, or as a result of your history, you gave permission for the situation to happen. Now, by reflecting on it, you know you can work on finding a way to change what happens.

Grace had terrible luck with her bosses. She had quit three different jobs because the bosses had behaved unreasonably. One day, after her current boss, Mona, blew up at her for forgetting to deliver an important phone message, Grace broke down.

"I can't stand it anymore," she sobbed after her boss had stomped out. "Why does every boss I've ever had bully me?"

Fran, her coworker, patted her shoulder sympathetically. "Mona never yells at me that way, Grace. Maybe it's you."

Grace shrugged off Fran's support angrily, but she couldn't get Fran's words out of her head. Throughout the day she found herself reviewing her work situations and wondering whether she attracted being bullied. Lying in bed that night, she had a sudden memory of her mother standing over her and screaming, "I can't believe you broke that glass. Now I only have five left in the set. You'd better start saving your allowance to pay me back, young lady!"

Grace recalled feeling as powerless in front of her mother's anger as she had in front of her bosses. She remembered that at school she was always the one kids would pick on during recess. Bigger kids threatened her and would take her lunch away from her. Eventually she had become comfortable in the role of victim and had learned to feed on the sympathy she would get from others.

Once Grace nonjudgmentally owned her part in letting others bully her, she had power with it. She could work with herself lovingly to get out of the role of victim and take control of her work life. Before she had to go through being yelled at again, Grace decided to use the power of her vulnerability to sit down with Mona and talk about the situation.

Instead of complaining, Grace owned her part by saying, "I've discovered that I have something to do with why you yell at me. I've looked at my past and seen that I've spent a lot of my life as a victim because of things that happened in my childhood. I have often done things that will get me yelled at because I'm comfortable in the role of victim, but I'm really trying to change and I would like to enlist your help. I would really appreciate it if you could help me when I do something that makes you want to yell at me."

Mona was intrigued, but skeptical. "It's great that you want to change, Grace, and I would love it if I didn't have to get upset when you forget to give me an important phone message or when you come in to work late. But I don't really see how I can help. I don't know what else to do to get your attention."

"I think it would really help if you could just ask me, 'Grace, is this one of those times when you're being a victim?'" Grace replied. "Then I could see what I was doing and change it without having to react by crying."

Mona agreed to work with Grace. Neither of them got it perfect right away—Grace still did things to sabotage herself and Mona's first reaction was still to yell. But by coming from a place of owning her part, Grace was gradually able to change her behavior. As she changed, she helped Mona by not putting her in a situation where she felt compelled to yell. This allowed Mona to start changing her own pattern of abusive behavior.

The example of Grace and Mona is a best-case scenario, and not everyone may be open to help you own your part. Most people, though, will gladly support you in waking up because it not only makes your life better, but also as you change it helps their lives to shift. Ultimately, you are the only one in charge of the direction of your life.

Owning your part creates clarity, cleaning the window you see life through. When you combine it with tenderness, gentleness, and self-love, it helps you know you are doing the best you can and that you can't be where you want to be until you are there. Having a loving tone and texture in relationship to yourself will have owning your part take you where you want to go. It is a relief to own your part and stop blaming others and yourself. It untangles you from others and allows space for you to reestablish the relationship without the tangles.

Olivia had many friends and a busy social schedule. She was popular because she was always the life of the party—witty, charming, and happy-go-lucky. A bomb fell on her carefree approach just after her thirty-second birthday, when her mother was diagnosed with cancer. Olivia was devastated and didn't know how to handle it. She called some of her friends for support, but they all seemed too busy or too involved in their own lives to listen. They would offer sympathy, then change the subject or come up with an excuse to get off the phone.

Olivia felt betrayed and angry. What was wrong with these people? She had listened to them complain about their boyfriends, husbands, and parents, and had helped them move, attended their parties, and babysat their children—yet they couldn't take ten minutes to have a real conversation with her when she was in need. She stopped reaching out and vowed to deal with this on her own.

When her mother went into remission, Olivia had the opportunity to sit back and examine what had happened with her friends. At first she couldn't see why they had acted the way they did. Then she recognized that because all six of the friends she had called had responded in exactly the same way, there must have been something in her behavior to call forth their response.

She realized she had never tried to talk to any of them about serious personal matters before. She had been comfortable in the role of the good-time girl, the one people could count on to spice up a party or listen to their problems after they'd had a few too many drinks. Her sudden shift to the one who needed support had caught her friends off guard because they were people who were used to receiving support, not giving it. Olivia had chosen her friends based on their ability to have fun—not on their ability to be nurturing.

Olivia remembered that in her childhood her parents had entertained often. When they had cocktail parties, they would dress up Olivia and her brothers and let them serve snacks to the guests. Olivia loved to do this because she got so much attention from the adults. One day she dropped a tray of cheese and crackers and started to cry. Her mother took her firmly by the arm, led her to her room, and said sternly, "You will not cry in front of my guests. If something bad happens, you just smile and clean it up." Remembering this scenario made it clear to Olivia that she had absorbed her mother's lesson all too well. She had always acted as if she didn't need help from anyone, so she had attracted friends who just wanted to have fun. Realizing this helped her see that if she wanted more in-depth friendships, she was going to have to allow herself to be more authentic, which meant letting herself be more open and vulnerable.

Owning your part helps you be more authentic because it allows you to stop using your precious energy by being a victim or by having something keep happening to you that you don't understand. You have probably used up an extraordinary amount of energy in replaying circumstances over and over again, fulfilling your identities over and over again, and magnetizing people who will fulfill your expectations over and over again.

Owning your part is a powerful way to quickly disappear what doesn't work in your life so you can use your energy for what it is that will have you be content, satisfied, happy, and fulfilled. It is hardest at first because the tennis balls will be flying at you very fast and it will be stimulating—and it will get easier as you practice. Observing people around you and seeing the part they play in what happens to them is a good way to start. Remember, owning your part has nothing to do with blame.

It is powerful to know that you can change the texture of your life and the relationships you have. It may seem daunting at first to practice taking responsibility, yet once you start doing it you will develop a knack for it. Once you see how quickly things can improve, you will want to continue, because owning your part will bring you more satisfaction, authenticity, grace, and ease. Change becomes its own reward as you start to get positive feedback, a quieter mind, deeper breath, more relaxation, more time for what is important and less time taken up by things you complained about. Soon you'll have a life you want to wake up to every morning so you can make the contribution you are here to make.

Uncoverings

Respond to these questions without blame or judgment:

What situations keep happening that are uncomfortable for me?

Notice that I am in each of these circumstances.

What is my part based on my behavior?

What is my part based on my expectations from my history?

What new outcomes do I want in these circumstances?

a powerful woman

*is confident that life will continually
offer learning experiences,
and welcomes them.*

a powerful woman

*interacts with her life, expecting it
to turn out well.*

11

Creating the Future You Want

Creating a Future That Is Different From Your Past

Think of a time...
  you kept trying to change your life, only to end up
  repeating your past.

Coming into your natural power has you healing your past, returning your energy to yourself in the present, and beginning to create a future you want. It allows an opening for your future to be different from your past. Rather than doing the same thing over and over again and expecting different results, you are moving toward an authentic life that will have you be happy, content, fulfilled, and satisfied. Opening your chakras and creating a relationship with your little girl has you healing the past so your essential energy can return to you, the higher self, which allows you to experience and express your power in the present. When you are present in the moment, you are available to receive what comes your way, use it well for yourself, intend what you want to happen next, and envision the future from a leaning-back position.

You have already begun to change your future by altering your perception of your present and your past. You know that if you keep making the same decisions from the same places you always have, you will continue to get the same results in your life. Your little girl will keep repeating her past because she is making decisions out of her history in the solar plexus and her survival reaction in the anal chakra. The committee members who are frightened or frozen in time will continue to run the meetings and make decisions based on vows made long ago that may no longer serve you. You will continue to have the same effect you have always had and to magnetize what you have always magnetized into your life, strengthening your belief that "life is just like that and there's nothing I can do about it." Your scorecards will tell you that you aren't measuring up. And you will expend a lot of energy wondering why all this keeps happening to you because you haven't yet owned your part in what has happened.

Now that you have begun to explore and heal your history, build a practice of the chakra meditation, develop a relationship with your little girl, help yourself through your upsets, see yourself as the light, create new scorecards, be in charge of your effect and your magnetism, and own your part—you have the tools to create a future that you will look forward to. In this chapter we will explore further some of the ways you can help yourself have the future you want.

What You Think Matters

Think of a time...
your circumstances changed when you started thinking differently about them.

Notice that what you think about a circumstance influences your experience of it.

As you change in the present you are already transforming the thoughts you have about your future. Freeing yourself from the identities you have constructed, your family way, cultural expectations, committee members based on your history, and your old scorecards allows you to have different thoughts about yourself. If you have always thought, "I can't work for myself because I'm undisciplined," "I have to stay single because I'm an independent career woman," "I have to stay in low-paying jobs because it's honorable to be poor," "I can't have children because I don't want my life to look like my mother's life," you are limiting how your future could be.

Now you have the tools to change the way you see yourself and this allows you to have new thoughts. Thinking differently produces different feelings, and having different feelings allows you to take different action. Taking action in a way you never have before will probably produce a result you have never experienced before. That's how change happens.

How often have you had a conversation with yourself in which you say things such as, "It can't happen because it doesn't happen like that," or "It's bound to happen that way because that's how it happened before"? Thinking that life must be a certain way usually happens because one or more of your committee members is holding onto an old belief. She has magnetized certain things into her life that prove her belief, so she now holds it as a truth. That belief keeps you in a cycle that doesn't hold the possibility for change. Your committee member who feels safe where you are right now may be holding you back from change because she is frightened. She has you experiencing it just the way you expected because you behave as if it's going to happen. As you work to heal your little girl and your frightened committee members, you will be able to have different thoughts about your future, which will then allow your future to be different.

Jesse has a history of messing up important job interviews. Every time she has an interview her little girl tells her, "It will be no different from all the others. I'm sure to flub my presentation and say something stupid or inappropriate. I always act like a simpering bimbo, even though I'm an intelligent woman." Because she believes this thought that originated when she was a frightened little girl, she can't possibly act like the intelligent woman she is. Her interview becomes a self-fulfilling prophecy.

What you think about something comes true because you take an action to fit the thought you are having. Jesse can stop the cycle of disastrous job interviews by changing the thoughts she is having about it. She can change her thoughts by going through the Anatomy of an Upset with her little girl and healing the original situation that had her believing she would always say the wrong thing. She can hold a committee meeting and listen to what all her committee members have to say, then put her hand on her heart and her throat to ask her empowering committee members, "What is good for me?" and "What is right for me?" Once she is centered and grounded, knowing she is her higher self and able to access the power of her chakras, she can be calm enough to help herself have her thoughts be different.

It would work well for Jesse to *act as if* she were someone who is good at interviewing. She could ask herself, "What would I do differently if I were a person who interviewed gracefully?" Maybe her answer would be to get a good night's sleep before the interview instead of lying awake obsessing about past mistakes. Maybe she would discover she needed to think carefully about her answers to probable questions and prepare herself by researching the company that was interviewing her.

Jesse could further support herself by finding a mentor to help her rehearse for the interview. Rehearsing would help her have a thought such as, "I've done my best to prepare for this interview." By thinking differently about the interview, Jesse could behave differently and would probably get a different result. By thinking of herself as well prepared, well rested, and graceful, she would present an entirely different picture to the interviewer.

You always have the option of replacing your negative thoughts with thoughts that will be empowering for you. Start by grounding and centering yourself, know you are your higher self, work with your little girl, hold committee meetings, and consult your higher chakras, and you have the possibility to be in charge of what thoughts you are having. Practice having these thoughts: "It's all coming to me, it's just a matter of time," "I am worth the time it takes," "I am the fulfillment of a boss's / lover's / friend's / parent's dream," "All it takes is one," "Why *not* me?", "The universe is on my side," and "What can I learn from this?"

Uncoverings

A circumstance that has me talk negatively to myself is...

What influence does that negativity have on how I experience the situation?

What influence does that negativity have on the possible outcome?

What else can I say about this circumstance that would empower me and support me to have the result I want?

Words Matter

What changes when what you have always called "overwhelming" you now call "stimulating"?

The words we use matter. When you change the thoughts you are having about something, you will often change what you call it—which allows you to have power with it instead of letting it frighten you. At Life Works, we use the word "stimulating" instead of "hard," "scary," "painful," "confronting," "overwhelming," or other descriptions that set up a negative vibration and have you look at life through a filter that will influence your experience. If you call something "bad" it becomes bad because you interact with it that way. If you use a more neutral word such as "stimulating," you open space for an experience to be different.

If you are driving to your annual family reunion, you might be feeling a combination of things that has you dreading the party. If you identified the body sensations you were having as "stimulating" rather than "nerve wracking," you might have a different attitude about what you are facing. You might even realize that you are more excited than nervous and that the stimulation you are feeling gives you the energy to deal with your extended family.

If you've just had an argument with your partner, your body might be charged with energy from the confrontation. The adrenaline released from the anal chakra during the upset might have you wanting to take an action. If you call what you are feeling "angry" or "devastated," you might take an action that would be damaging for you. If you instead call what you're experiencing "stimulating," you might be able to stop yourself from picking up the phone and leaving a nasty message that you'll regret later. You can then ground yourself in your chakras and ask yourself "What is good for me?" or "What is right for me?" to do in that moment, rather than taking actions that might be damaging for you. Instead, you might be able to let yourself use your stimulation to do something creative or empowering.

Saying "I'm feeling very stimulated right now" can have you acknowledge what you're feeling without letting it have power over you. If you say, "Going to that reunion scares me," you are likely to start making up negative stories about it, and then take action based on your stories. If you say, "Going to that reunion has me stimulated," you will have more space to calm yourself and create a positive scenario—and then you will experience the reunion differently.

If you are going through a traumatic time such as a divorce, getting fired from your job, the death of someone you love, or any major life change, your first tendency might be to describe what you are going through as heartbreaking, difficult, devastating, horrendous, or unbearable. Changing how you describe your experience might not change the feelings you are having, but it could allow you to move up out of your upset in the anal chakras and the solar plexus into a larger experience of what is happening. You could allow yourself to be in the crown chakra point of view, which would have you understand that you can use whatever comes your way for more understanding.

Using empowering words to describe what you are going through will have you see the possibility for growth and change that is the undercurrent of your suffering. It would be powerful to describe a difficult time as broadening, rich, enormous, full-bodied, and strong. Seeing that you are being strengthened and broadened by your grief or suffering can allow you to use your experience well for yourself as you move into the future. When you can speak to yourself in a positive way, you will start having a more heartfelt relationship with yourself. If you are not constantly punishing yourself with negative self-talk, you will be more available to help yourself go through what you have to go through in a loving way.

Alice had a good job at a major accounting firm, but she was starting to feel overwhelmed by her workload. When she attended her weekly Gathering, she would often complain that she wasn't satisfied. She was given far too much work to do, and she never seemed able to get ahead enough to take time off for a vacation—much less have a personal life.

When her firm merged with another company, Alice was stunned to discover she was being laid off. She was offered a generous severance package that included eighteen months' salary, medical benefits, and vacation she had acquired in her overworked career. Despite the severance package, Alice felt devastated to be let go and shared how terrible she felt at the Gathering.

The women in the Gathering encouraged Alice to see her situation as the opportunity she had been asking for. She could now take the trip to Asia she had been wanting, having a chance to recoup while she looked for the next career opportunity. Instead of describing her situation as "devastating" and "terrible," Alice could see it as "stimulating," "broadening," and "enriching." Using positive language could help her see that her prayers had been answered and that she had actually gotten what she wanted.

You can be in charge of what you call yourself and your experiences. If you call yourself a "victim of circumstance," it doesn't leave you much power to change what is happening to you. If you instead call yourself an "active participant in life," you give yourself the power rather than giving it to people, institutions, or forces outside you—and describing yourself differently will have you magnetize different things into your life. Saying "Whatever is coming my way is good if I use it well" gives you the opportunity to create your own future because you know that whatever comes toward you is what needs to be coming toward you, and you can shape it into something wonderful. Living in the crown chakra point of view that everything coming your way is for the good has you be grounded in the present and engaged in the flow of life—and when you are present and engaged, you are not living from your history, so your future will be different than your past.

Uncoverings

Play with using neutral words to describe what you are experiencing when you are in a stimulating situation.

Notice how you and other people use words that color their experience and see if you can turn them neutral.

Examples:

> *problem = challenge*
> *difficult = I'm having a strong learning experience*
> *inevitable = I don't know how it can be different*
> > *I'm not sure it could change*
> *confusing = not enough information yet*
> > *not enough time to mull it over yet*
> *discouraging = I don't know what will fix it…yet*
> *overwhelming = stimulating, large*

Going Outside Your Comfort Zone

Think of something…
you want to change in your life.

Being in the flow of life means that change will happen. You know that change is necessary and often good if you don't want to stagnate—and at the same time you may resist it because changing can be uncomfortable. Sometimes being where you are, no matter how uncomfortable it is, is preferable to stepping into an unknown. The nature of change means that you have to take a leap into the unknown—and even if you want to do it, your human nature may stop you in all the ways it knows how.

Think about how difficult it is to change even the smallest part of your daily routine. You can want change and your mind can envision change, but having it manifest physically in the world takes patience, acceptance, and repetition. If you want to start exercising more because you don't feel as energetic as you know you can be, you might get the process going by joining the local gym. Perhaps you go to aerobics class a few times, but soon the enthusiasm wears off and you find yourself back on the sofa in front of the television. You might attribute the failure to the fact that you don't have willpower or you are lazy—but really all that has happened is that you have acted like a human being.

Because you are human, you are more comfortable where you are—even if it is uncomfortable—than making a shift toward something new. Who knows where that one change you want to make could lead you? It may be that if you really got in shape, you would want to start going out more because you would look better and you would have more energy. Going out more would mean you might meet someone interesting and stimulating. Meeting someone interesting and stimulating might lead to developing a relationship with them, and that might involve being vulnerable to rejection. Being vulnerable to rejection might mean that you could get hurt. Of course, it might also be that you would meet someone you would have a successful relationship with. But the not knowing might keep you from ever experiencing it because it is so uncomfortable not to know what to expect.

If you stay at home on the couch, you know exactly what to expect, and there is a feeling of safety and control in that. Being in the unknown means being out of control for a period of time—and we all hate being out of control. When you are in your known discomfort, you already know what the outcome will be, so you keep doing it the same way over and over. Of course, this means you have the same results over and over, too. Being in the unknown means taking a risk, not knowing how something will turn out, and being willing to give up some control.

Wanting to be in control may have you hold back from change by saying, "I want to change this, but it's not a good time. I'll do it when I feel better (or when the stars are aligned correctly, or when the economic situation cools down a bit, or when I get my new outfit)." Because change is uncomfortable, you may tend to wait—for the right time, for the right situation, for the right partner, for the right weather, for your hair to look the right way, or for a thousand other "rights." Your mind might think that if only you wait until everything is perfect for the transition, it will feel good. Somehow, though, the right time never seems to arrive.

It would be good for you to know that there probably won't be a time when change feels terrific, that it is human to resist change in many creative ways, and that you don't have to let your resistance stop you. When you want change, it will help if you simply expect resistance. A group of people wanting to change their rights and privileges in society will meet with great resistance, and any civil rights movement or revolution plans for opposition carefully. It would be supportive to grant yourself the same advantage, rather than thinking that if you want change it should just be able to happen. Once you know to expect resistance you can notice it nonjudgmentally by saying, "Oh, here is the resistance I was told to expect. I guess I'm on the journey of changing."

Change involves a level of trial and error because doing something a new way means it may not work out the way you want it to the first time. As a human being, you are probably uncomfortable going through a process of trial and error because you don't want to risk humiliation, disappointment, criticism, or regrets. It will be helpful to keep reminding yourself that this is a trial-and-error universe, and that nothing great ever was accomplished without risk.

Risking a change means not knowing what the outcome will be because you are doing something differently. You might start telling yourself a lot of negative stories about how it will turn out. Knowing that you are in charge of the stories you tell yourself can give you power in the process. You can tell yourself a positive story rather than a negative one. After all, isn't it just as possible the outcome will be positive as it is that it might be negative? Going to the gym, having more energy, and getting out to meet people could just as easily lead to exciting new relationships as to rejection and loneliness.

You might want change to happen faster than it can really happen. When you are working to change your future, it is helpful to realize that your mind may be way ahead of your body. Change takes time to manifest, even though your mind might be able to envision it in a millisecond. Think about how long it takes for a rock to turn into sand or for a tree to grow to maturity. Your changes won't take nearly that long, but it would be kind to yourself to allow the time you need. Letting yourself believe that "it will happen, it's just a matter of time" will have you living from an optimistic viewpoint and will allow you to disregard the negative voices that try to stop you from moving forward. Having a positive conversation with yourself will allow you to hold your own hand through it and will encourage you rather than discourage you. It would be helpful to reflect on a time when you went through a change successfully and bring forward what it was that had it work for you.

So how can you help yourself get through the process of change without stopping where you have stopped before? You can remind yourself that you are worth going through the hard part. You can remember that you are human, reassure yourself that the feelings you are having are fine to have, and know that they don't have to stop you from moving forward. You can access the power of your chakras so you can have a grounded, creative, willing, loving, authentic, knowing, and connected relationship with yourself. You can know yourself as the light, and as your higher self you can soothe your little girl who is afraid she won't do it right. You can hold committee meetings and heal the committee members who are holding you back from changing. You can look at the effect and magnetism you have and see what needs to shift for change to happen. You can lean back, open your arms, breathe into the experience, and allow yourself to let it happen.

Uncoverings

Think of a time I wanted something to change and I waited for it to feel like the right time—and it never happened.

Think of a time I felt uncomfortable and did it anyway.

Think of something I want to change. Take the first step.

Envisioning Change

Think of a time...
you had a vision of something you wanted and it happened.

As you grow into an authentic life, it will be important to envision what you want so you can have your life shift in that direction. To know what you want, it would be powerful to be in touch with your yearnings. What you long for is often what you want in your life that isn't here yet, so your yearnings can be a powerful indication of what you want your future to look like. As you connect with your yearnings, you can allow your natural powers of envisioning to unfold a picture of your future in your mind. It would be good to have your picture be somewhat flexible, because it may be that something similar could fit in even if it's not exactly what you envisioned.

What you envision has a way of coming to you. Once you have envisioned your future, you will want to be present in the moment so you can see what is coming your way that you can use. It would be supportive of change for you to be awake to what life is sending you, and willing to take what it is and use it well for yourself, even if it doesn't look exactly the way you thought it would.

Brie had been alone for ten years since her divorce, and her solitary life in the country was beginning to wear on her. She was almost always on the go, commuting half an hour to work and involved in activities that kept her away from home in the evenings so she wouldn't have to face being alone.

"I'm tired of being alone," Brie told her sister Wanda on the phone one evening. "I'm ready to have a man in my bed again, and I've even been thinking of getting a dog for company."

"Could you really have a dog?" Wanda asked. "You're away from home so much, I don't see how you could take care of it."

"I guess you're right," Brie sighed. "Same with a man, right?" They laughed.

Brie forgot about her conversation with Wanda and continued on with her life without doing much to search for either a man or a dog. One day a few weeks later she was taking a walk on a wooded road during a thunderstorm. She was enjoying the whipping wind and the driving rain, lost in her thoughts—when suddenly she heard what sounded like a howl from the bushes at the side of the road. Startled, Brie leaned down to look in the bushes. Cowering underneath a branch was a tiny gray kitten, soaked through and moaning piteously.

Brie wrapped the kitten in her damp sweater and carried it home underneath her jacket. She called all her neighbors, but no one knew anything about a lost gray male kitten. After a few days, it was clear no one would claim the cat, so Brie decided to keep him. She called Wanda to tell about her adventure.

"I found this adorable kitten in the bushes, Wanda, and I named him Moses," Brie enthused. "I never thought about having a cat, but he's a perfect companion because he can take care of himself all day while I'm gone, and he curls up on my pillow to keep me company at night."

Wanda laughed. "Well, Brie, I guess you got what you wished for, didn't you?"

"What do you mean?" Brie was puzzled. "I never wished for a cat."

"Well, you said you wanted a man and a dog to keep you company," Wanda explained. "And you got a four-legged male creature who sleeps in your bed." Amazed, Brie realized that what she had envisioned had come to pass, bringing her what she wanted in a different form. If she hadn't been awake, she may not have realized that Moses was what she wanted and she might have passed up the opportunity to have the love and companionship she craved. Being awake also allowed her to have the optimistic viewpoint that because she could create a pet that fulfills her desires, magnetizing a man into her life is probably on its way.

It is female to be flexible and receive what life offers, knowing you can use it well for yourself. If your picture of how you want your future to look is too rigid, you might not be open to receiving what comes your way. It is powerful to be open and awake because, as in Brie's case, you may not have thought of all the options when you created your picture. Things may come along that you hadn't even thought of, and being open and available will allow you to incorporate them into your future. Allowing what comes toward you to unfold can have you create a future that is even more magnificent than you imagined.

Uncoverings

Think of something that you yearn for.

Create two or three visions that would satisfy your yearning.

Mis-takes

Think of a time...
   you learned something important from making a mistake.

What would life be like if...
   it was okay for you to make mistakes?

Being human we are often terrified of making mistakes. Making a mistake means being vulnerable and risking humiliation and criticism, both from ourselves and others. We can be so terribly hard on ourselves when we don't do something perfectly that it is no wonder we don't want to take a risk. If you could let yourself see that making mistakes is a valuable part of the human experience, you would open yourself up for learning from the situations you find yourself in.

When a director is making a movie, she expects many mistakes before getting the final take of a scene. There may have to be ten, or twenty, or a hundred takes before she achieves the take that will become the final product. Sometimes the take will then be edited out anyway, and this is just what happens. The director does not expect the film to spin out effortlessly the first time without any mis-takes, revisions, or editing—yet she is confident that the final product will look smooth and beautiful.

It would be supportive for you to see your life as a movie that will involve many mis-takes and trust that the mis-takes can add to its richness and beauty. Knowing that you may not get it right the first (or second, or fifth) time allows space for you to forgive yourself and learn from the mis-takes—and to enjoy the process. When you know there is no way you can be master of a situation that you have never been in before, you can be compassionate and loving with yourself as you make changes.

Mistakes can be wonderful learning opportunities. Many a mistake has been transformed into a great discovery or a beautiful piece of artwork. Being matter-of-fact about mistakes and being willing to learn from them will free you from the confines of perfectionism and will open up possibilities you might never have dreamed of.

Accepting and learning from mistakes involves a willingness to be wrong, and we all hate to be wrong—especially women. Seeing that it is okay to be wrong and that it can lead you to something that is right is a powerful position to be in. If you are holding on tight to having to be right, you won't be able to be in the flow of life. The flow includes being willing to be wrong about what has gone on before. If what you want isn't happening, you must be wrong about something.

A question you might ask yourself is, "Do I want to be right, or do I want to have what is good for me?" Being willing to be wrong has you experience surrendering to life, and then you can point to what you were wrong about. The good news is that as soon as you can point to being wrong about something you can become right about it, because it is a learning spot. The place where you were wrong is a place where you have the opportunity to make a shift.

Uncoverings

Think of some things I didn't try this week because I didn't want to make a mistake.

Think of a time a mistake led me to something I really wanted.

Am I willing to be wrong?

Living Through Disappointment

What would life be like if...
you could find a way to live through disappointment?

Risking being wrong means you not only have to face humiliation and criticism, but you might have to experience disappointment. Fear of disappointment can powerfully keep you from taking risks and moving ahead in your life. If you know it is part of your total experience as a human being to be disappointed and that there is no way to avoid it, you can be more open to taking risks and to being softer with yourself if a risk doesn't work out the way you wanted it to.

Often the reason you might engage in negative self-talk is that when you are approaching a new situation, your little girl reaches back into her history and finds the times it didn't work. Remembering how and why it didn't work serves to protect her from the possibility for future disappointments. Saying "Well, it never worked when I did it before so why should it work now?" or "I don't want to get my hopes up" are ways your little girl shields herself from disappointment. Unfortunately, expecting disappointment doesn't really make the experience of disappointment any easier. What it does is stop you from taking risks that might have you move forward, learn something new, and gain new experience in life.

We think we shouldn't experience disappointment because perhaps it means we have failed at something. If you know it is

human to experience disappointment you can help yourself not be stopped by it. Being disappointed is part of living in a trial-and-error universe where nothing is perfect. Opening yourself up to the possibility of being disappointed will let you have that part of the human experience, which can bring you to the fulfillment of knowing your authentic self and your power.

Uncoverings

What historical disappointments color my experience of do-ing something today?

Go through the Anatomy of an Upset with your little girl to heal yourself.

Change Changes Things

Think of a time...
when you changed something and other people were affected.

It would be wonderful if once you have had the courage and grace to change, life became more comfortable and enjoyable—and it will, eventually. Part of what happens when you move forward is that you are turning your back on what doesn't work in your life. Turning your back on something in the past means you are facing something entirely new and different, which can be uncomfortable. If you can anticipate the discomfort of something new, you leave yourself the option of walking through it rather than running away from it or fighting it. Like breaking in a stiff new pair of shoes, change is uncomfortable at first and then molds itself to you as you live with it.

Jill worked for years to change her pattern of attracting destructive relationships with men who treated her badly. Finally she decided she needed time to herself without a man in her life. Immediately after swearing off men she met Scott, an artist who swept her off her feet. She tried to maintain distance, but found herself unable to stay away. Sure that this relationship would be different, she finally dove into it. Scott was artistic, sensitive, and treated her with incredible attention and love. Everything seemed perfect.

After two months, however, Jill found herself increasingly uncomfortable with the love and attention she was getting. She started asking, "What's wrong with him? He's too nice. He must be hiding something. Maybe he's a nerd." She took to running off and spending weekends away to get space from Scott, which bewildered and hurt him. Finally, Scott gave her an ultimatum—accept him and really be in the relationship, or leave. Suddenly Jill saw that the reason she was so uncomfortable was that Scott offered her the opportunity to have what she wanted. Now that she had it, she had no idea how to deal with it. Once she realized this, she was able to share her discomfort with Scott and work through it with him.

If Jill had known that it would be uncomfortable to get what she had always wanted, she might have been able to share it with Scott right away instead of jeopardizing their relationship. Having your future be different from your past means being willing to live through the discomfort of something new. If you anticipate that not only the process of change but also its result may be uncomfortable, you can help yourself get through it.

Jill's commitment to her relationship with Scott had some surprising effects on other people in her life. Her best friend got angry and lashed out at her, her mother gave Scott a hard time, and her boss teased her constantly. Jill couldn't understand why the people who cared about her weren't happy that she'd gotten what she wanted. Later, she saw that her relationship with Scott had also changed her interaction with the other people in her life and that those changes made them uncomfortable. Her best friend was envious of her relationship and expressed her envy through anger. Her mother was threatened at seeing Jill in a relationship that looked like it might lead to marriage, and felt the need to test Scott. Her boss was only comfortable joking about how awful men were, as she had always done, so she continued in the same style as before.

When you change and start getting what you want in life, other people around you will often be uncomfortable. You have traditionally played certain roles in your family and in your friendships that keep everyone feeling comfortable because they know what to expect. When you change, you're not taking up the same spot you did before, and it makes space for other things to shift around you. This may make others feel confused or threatened because they no longer know what to expect. After all, they're human and therefore they resist change as well.

Lucy was considered the "interesting" one in her family. At family get-togethers her aunts and cousins would listen enthralled as she related her latest adventures in Paris with a wealthy admirer or a disastrous meeting with an ex-boyfriend at a glamorous nightclub. After years of wild adventures Lucy felt it was no longer fulfilling for her to be committed to an adventurous lifestyle. She met a man who was steady and loving, and eventually married him. She no longer had exciting stories to relate. She enjoyed domestic life with her husband and they rarely traveled or stayed out late. Her family, however, still expected her to fill the role of the "interesting" one. They would ask her what had been going on lately, and she found she didn't have much to say. She was happy, she and her husband made dinner together and watched videos. Her lack of stories left an uncomfortable gap in her family gatherings.

You can probably think of some people who will be threatened or challenged as you make changes in your life. People are often disquieted by others' changes because it means they may have to take a look at their own lives. You may find that there are friends and family members who will not support you in changing. "Why do that? What you've been doing is perfectly fine. You'll never be able to make a go of it."

When others are living out of their own defenses, they will project their fears onto your situation. They may not tell you directly that they are uncomfortable, but their actions will show you that they are. When Jill's mother met Scott, she grilled him ceaselessly on his career and income prospects, alienating him and angering Jill. When Jill's best friend realized she was no longer first on Jill's social list, she made cutting remarks to Jill, Scott, and Jill's other friends. It is not uncommon for people close to you to feel threatened by your moving ahead in your life because it arouses their fear or envy.

Uncoverings

Who will be uncomfortable when I change or my life changes?

Who will be happy when I change or my life changes?

How will I be uncomfortable with others when I change or my life changes?

How can I help myself through the discomfort when I change or my life changes?

People Will Want What You Have

What happens when you see envy as an indication of wanting something that is authentic?

As you grow into yourself, you will become more successful and happy in your life. This may cause others to regard you with envy or competitiveness and even to try to sabotage your success with whatever tools they have. Knowing that they are acting the way they are because they are threatened in some way by your success will help you understand their behavior, not be stopped by it, and have compassion for it.

Envy is part of the human experience for everyone, so as you have more of what you want, your success may spark the unfulfilled desire of others. Because they may not be able to see that envy can help them find out what they want, they may experience envy in a way that makes them want to sabotage what you have. You have probably been the object of another's envy at some point, and it is an uncomfortable place to be. You might want to push it away because when others are envious they can be cruel, either intentionally or unintentionally. You may have a resistance to doing things or having things that might allow others to envy you.

Another aspect of envy is that when you have more in your life, it can make others unhappy. Watching others be unhappy when you have more is also uncomfortable. If things are going well for you and they are not going well for a friend of yours, how much of what's going well for you can you share with her? It is probably much easier to share in the energy of what is not going well for her than to share in what is wonderful for you. You may feel shy and unwilling to be great because the discomfort with your friend's envy keeps you there. Envy can be a deterrent to moving forward because it is a hidden conversation, something that stops you in a way that may not be obvious.

You can help yourself not be stopped by this hidden conversation by understanding that people experience envy in part because they are afraid there isn't enough to go around. Knowing that it is an abundant universe where there is plenty for everyone can help you be comfortable with your own success. Coming into your own power is not taking away from anyone else's success—in fact, as you become more yourself you add to the positive vibration of being a woman on the planet, which opens the way for more women to live authentic lives.

Another way to help yourself not be stopped by envy is to understand your own envy differently. You can look at envy as a way of waking you up to what it is you desire. People envy different things because they have different desires that are authentic. Noticing what you envy can help you identify what is authentic for you. If you envy someone's relationship with her partner, it could be that you want a relationship like that for yourself. If you envy someone's expensive clothes, it could be that you desire more income so you can also buy yourself beautiful clothing. Seeing envy as a clue to your desires can take the barb out of it and allow you to experience it as part of your process of growth and stretching.

Uncoverings

What do I envy?

How can I best handle those who try to keep me from changing?

Who can I trust to support me as I change?

What are things I can do to support myself as I change?

Welcoming the Support You Need

Think of a time...
someone supported you through a challenge or a change.

Having the strength and grace to change means acknowledging that you need support. It is not weak to need support—in fact, it takes great strength to acknowledge that you need it, and then to ask for it. Your answers to the questions in the uncoverings above can help you build your own support system as you become more powerful in life. Asking for support from people who can give it will ease the way for you as you reveal your authenticity and uncover your power.

It would be helpful to look at the support system you have now, and in doing so you may notice that some people in your life may be unhealthy for you. It may be that you need to find some new peers who will support and encourage you in your growth. There may be adjustments needed in relationships that already exist, and you may attract new people who share something different with you. Finding new peers can mean you might go through a period of loneliness. If you expect that you may experience loneliness, you can move through it by reassuring yourself you will come through it with new companions who support you. You can also know that changing doesn't mean you will suddenly be on your own. If you have people in your life now, you will still have people in your life later.

The more you are yourself, the more you will magnetize people who are healthy for you into your life. You can use your new powers of magnetism to get support from others who may be going through their own changes or who are already somewhere that you want to be. If you want to be happily married, you can find someone who is happily married and get support from her. If you want to make more money, you can find someone who has a successful career and ask her for advice. Finding a mentor who can offer you wise advice will be powerful both for you and for her. You don't necessarily need to find a mentor who has exactly the thing you want, but one whose life is one of grace and ease in that arena. If you want a graceful life, you can find someone whose life is graceful and learn from her—even if you don't have or want exactly the same lifestyle.

Getting support from a group of people doing the Natural Power Work is a powerful way to support yourself. The Natural Power Gatherings powerfully help women get support from each other as they learn, stretch, grow, and change. It is empowering to see a strong, powerful woman go through the hard parts because you can see that her being stuck in her history and wrestling with issues doesn't make her less powerful. In fact, her struggle can powerfully help you as you go through your own changes. It is powerful to see that not everyone gets stuck in the same places and that a place where another woman is stuck may be easy for you. Seeing this can allow you to have more compassion for others and for yourself when you are upset.

Being engaged in a group of women, each going through her own unique experience, lets you do the Work and see yourself in

ways you might not be able to when you are caught up in it. You can be grateful for each woman's process because you are learning by watching her make mistakes, go through the hard part, and be engaged in her own life. That doesn't mean you have to get involved in her life or try to solve her problems. You are supporting her by being there with her just as she is supporting you by being there with you.

Seeing each woman courageously going through her process of learning and growth can powerfully support and bolster your own experience of change. If you don't have access to the Gatherings, you can receive some of the same benefits of support by magnetizing toward you women who are committed to growth and change. As you each work through what you need to work through, you can be strengthened by each other's willingness, courage, vulnerability, openness, and heartfelt engagement with life.

Uncoverings

Am I available to be supported?

How can I make myself more available for support?

What kind of support works for me?

Where can I get that support?

In what areas of my life would a mentor be helpful?

Who would be a good mentor?

a powerful woman

knows she is responsible for
creating her world.

a powerful woman

bathes herself in womanliness.

12

Reinventing Your Power

A New Paradigm

What is it to be a powerful woman?

As we come into our natural power, we can see that the way we used to think about being powerful no longer serves us. As we become powerful females, we can understand that in powerfully using our male side we often came from a place of anger at being sidelined or overlooked, and fear that we would not be acknowledged. We had to express our power in a male way because we didn't know any other way to be powerful. Now we can finally relax into what is natural for each of us. We no longer have to be forceful, loud, or fierce in order to feel powerful. We can take a fresh look at what it is to be a powerful woman.

A powerful woman accesses her natural balance of male and female—and since she is at least fifty-one percent female, her biology is female, so she naturally accesses her female qualities—tenderness, intuition, communication, cooperation, optimism and empowerment—more than her male qualities. Now that you are in the process of being authentic, you may feel released, energized, relieved, known, loved, playful, alive, adventurous, and curious. There could also be some awkwardness in experiencing yourself differently than you have before. You may spend more time thinking about yourself because you don't want to rely on your knee-jerk reactions or patterns of past behavior when you find yourself in challenging circumstances. Part of the awkwardness might come from not knowing what being powerfully female looks like. We don't have many models for it yet, or if we do, we may not have recognized them as powerful.

Allie, a thirty-three-year-old executive, always saw herself as a powerful woman. In fact, she used to be so focused on being powerful and independent that she pushed people away. She carried her strength with her like a badge, using it to prove she was worthwhile and to keep at bay anyone who might disagree with what she wanted. What she didn't recognize was that it took strength to allow herself to be disagreed with, to be wrong in someone else's eyes.

Allie was so fierce that she intimidated her coworkers, her friends, and the men she went out with. She often complained about being lonely and not having support while simultaneously bullying her way through life.

"Now I can love myself enough to be with someone who might not want to do everything my way," Allie says. "I used to always want things my own way, and I couldn't see others' opinions as valid. Now I can lean back and have it be easier. I don't have to be ruthless in trying to get what I want. I can be softer and more open, keeping my view from the crown chakra that everything is happening for the best. And this female viewpoint allows me to see that what I perceived as strength before was actually fierceness stemming from a fear of being ridiculed or ignored. I see now that it is actually stronger to lean back and receive what life is offering me than to strain forward and shout to make myself heard—and I actually get what I want more now than I ever did before."

Allowing herself to lean back and be softer opened up the possibility for a committed relationship, and to her surprise, Allie is now married—something she never believed could happen. Like Allie, you may have areas in your life where you felt you had to be strong in ways that you can now see were actually sapping your essential energy by keeping you living from anger or fear. Now you can understand that you are being strong when you return your power to yourself, when you are being tender with yourself and available to help yourself through the hard parts, when you have a heartfelt relationship with yourself, when you can ask for the support you need, and when you can lean back and embrace life in the knowingness that you can transform what comes your way into something that you can use to learn more about yourself. That strength feels different from the strength of making yourself known by being forceful and aggressive. It is the strength that emanates from you when you are experiencing the Female Power Within.

A Powerful Woman Allows Herself to Be Tender and Vulnerable

A powerful woman is not afraid to open herself to others or to share her humanity with them. She knows that allowing herself to be tender and vulnerable is being strong, and that hardness is often a defense. You are being a powerful woman when you are able to let someone know you are hurt rather than reacting in anger, or when you are able to admit you are afraid rather than putting up a defense. Responding to someone with a gentle caress or speaking softly is being strong because tenderness is far more powerful than defensiveness.

If someone is feeling afraid, or hurt, or caught in their history and they share this with you, they are being powerful. And it is powerful for you to share those feelings with someone else when you are experiencing them. When you open yourself to being truly known, you will be able to see that you are often hurt rather than angry, and rather than acting this out, you can let yourself be with the experience. It takes strength for you to share what is difficult for you. It is powerful to allow yourself to share your feelings because vulnerability has openness in it, and openness lets you be available to experience. If you are closed off, you may miss out on many things life has to offer.

Tina didn't know how to deal with feeling hurt. She was afraid that expressing her hurt would make her appear weak, so when her husband Wesley said something that hurt her, Tina didn't let him know. Her unexpressed hurts accumulated and she often found herself angry and resentful. After a while it got comfortable for Tina to be in a place of frustration and annoyance because she never had to open herself to the possibility of hurt. Sometimes she saw that how she was acting was damaging, but she was too afraid to acknowledge it. It would have meant opening up in a way that would risk humiliation.

One night at a restaurant, Tina was nagging Wesley in the way that had become familiar to them. Suddenly she found herself looking deep into his eyes and she saw the hurt that was there—the desire in him to be with the Tina he had met and asked to marry him, the Tina who wasn't constantly on the offensive. With a wave of horror, Tina realized that she had become like her mother, who didn't know any way of communicating with her husband besides nagging and complaining.

Gulping, Tina said, "I'm sorry. I'm acting like my mother, and I just realized it doesn't work for me." Her husband, relieved, took her hand. They pledged to be more tender with each other and stay in touch with each other in a deeper way. In that moment, Tina felt tender, frightened, and vulnerable—and powerful. She realized that thinking about acknowledging her behavior was more painful than actually doing it, and that her fear of humiliation had been holding her back.

By being willing to be soft, Tina had changed the dynamic between herself and her husband. If she wasn't on the offensive, then he didn't have to defend himself. Letting herself be vulnerable allowed her to take responsibility for the situation, and opened up the possibility for change. Later, as Tina looked back on that dinner, she realized it was a turning point in both her relationship with her husband and her relationship with herself.

A Powerful Woman Knows She Is an Environment

When Lesley, a marketing manager, moved from a home office to an office in a large corporate building, she felt uncomfortable with the cold starkness of her surroundings. Gradually, she began to bring in items from home that made her feel comfortable. She brought plants, an African carving, her favorite tea and teapot, comfortable chairs, and pictures for the walls. Some of her staff shook their heads and asked her why she was bothering to bring in decorations and furniture from home. "We like to leave home behind us when we come to work," the men said. "Why go to all that trouble?"

Lesley explained that it helped her work better if she had treasured objects around. They shrugged their shoulders and went about their business. But soon, Lesley noticed a change in the attitude of her coworkers. The smell of her jasmine tea would drift down the hall and entice them into her office. They would come in and sit on her comfortable chairs and chat. Soon, it became habitual for Lesley's staff to seek comfort and solve particularly thorny problems in the homey environment of her office. They felt free to express themselves and they often remarked on how they came up with their best creative strategies there. Drinking a cup of the herbal tea Lesley always kept on hand, they would talk in a more productive way than they did in their own stark white cubicles.

When Lesley moved to another firm several years later, her staff was devastated. "We'll miss our creative meetings in your office," they confessed. "It always felt like being an honored guest in your home." Lesley smiled, recalling the resistance she had encountered when she first started hauling in furniture from home. She was touched by their sadness and realized that by being herself and sharing some of herself with her staff, she had created a safe, comfortable, productive environment for them to express themselves.

A powerful woman knows the powerful effect she has on others. In chapter ten we talked about how the effect you have creates an environment around you. When you are caught up in your upsets or criticizing yourself in your mind, you create a negative or critical environment around yourself. Think of Pigpen in the *Peanuts* cartoons, with the cloud of dust all around him. When you are in your upsets, your environment is like that cloud of dust, repelling people from you.

When you are in a handholding, heartfelt relationship with yourself and when you are present for others, you create a very different atmosphere. If Lesley had not created a comfortable universe around her through expressing herself naturally, she would never have had the opportunity to provide a supportive space for her staff, and they may not have created the award-winning marketing campaigns. Similarly, what you create in the physical and psychic space around you affects what is drawn into your universe.

Certain things are attracted into or repelled from your environment based on the identities you hold, the history you have, decisions you make, your acceptance of yourself, your ability to be compassionate, and many other factors. What you repel might go unnoticed because it doesn't happen, but you may be repelling things you want. If you identify yourself as a "New Yorker," that will repel some people and attract others. If your family style doesn't allow space for you to be friends with someone of another race or religion, you will attract people who are similar to you and repel people who are different from you. If you believe that there are no good men left, chances are you will repel men who are good and attract men who are not good for you.

Megan is always getting free gifts, winning lottery tickets, and receiving unexpected windfalls. It could be that her belief in the abundance of the universe attracts wealth into her life. Kate, on the other hand, may be constantly stressed out about money and pinching every penny, and she never seems able to get a financial break. It could be that she creates an environment of deprivation around her, so she repels expressions of abundance.

Carla may create an environment of respectful distance around her. No one ever acts disrespectfully to her because they wouldn't think of it in her presence. By creating an environment of distance, she repels people or situations that would be free and easy. Perhaps Esther is always frantically busy, rushing around trying to get things done, so she attracts a quality of chaos in those around her. If you go over to her house, you instantly feel the vibration of frantic activity, so it is almost impossible for you to relax. Esther creates a harried environment in part by magnetizing frantic energy toward her.

Looking around at the environments your friends create around them can help you understand the environment you create around yourself. Seeing yourself as an environment is a powerful position to take. If you take responsibility for what you attract into your environment, you begin to see that there is no such thing as an accident. Certain things happen around you because you attract them into your life, and certain things happen around other people because they attract them into their lives. Looking at your life from this perspective gives you the ability to take your life in your hands. It gives you the opportunity to mold and create it in a way that will reflect who you are and what you want your life to be like. This is a nonjudgmental, nonblaming noticing of yourself and the environment you create.

The more your essence shines through, the more good things happen in your environment. The more good or bad things happen to you, the more you learn about your essence and the quality of your female power. As you gently uncover the layers that obscure your essence, you will begin to attract things you want that you used to repel. You will come to know your female power when you are creating an environment around yourself that allows it to shine.

A Powerful Woman Is Open to What Comes Her Way

A powerful woman owns her part. When she is centered and grounded in herself, a powerful woman knows she has an effect

and a magnetism that create an environment for certain things to happen or not happen around her. She stands firmly in the center of her life nonjudgmentally, taking responsibility for what is there and for what is missing. She doesn't need to be defensive about taking responsibility because she doesn't blame herself or others for her situation. She doesn't need to be frightened of what is in her life or what is coming because she knows she can use it well for herself. She knows that she is worth going through the hard part and that she can hold her own hand through it—and that sometimes she needs to go through the hard part to get where she wants to be.

A powerful woman embraces the hard part. When a massage therapist starts deeply manipulating your muscles, it often hurts. The tendency is to automatically tense the muscles and press up against the therapist's fingers. But if you relax, breathe, and let her in, it doesn't hurt anymore. By relaxing into the experience, you have eliminated the struggle involved. The massage therapist is still deeply manipulating your muscles, but your experience is easier and more pleasant. So it is with any difficult situation. You can tense up and fight against it or you can choose to embrace it.

Things don't always go the way you want them to go, and your reality may not measure up to the picture you have of how your life should be. When you don't like your feelings, when you feel impatient, when you are not known or understood, you may be convinced that life is one struggle after another. You know now that you can reduce your struggle by accepting your feelings, putting your thoughts in their place, and dealing with your upsets differently. You have better ways for dealing with life's difficulties, but that doesn't mean difficult situations won't come up. There will be struggles in life because that's part of being human. If you can accept that struggle is a part of life, it will make your life a little easier. Struggling against a struggle, like pulling against a tangled knot in a string, only increases the difficulty. If instead you could choose to embrace all that life has to offer, including struggle, you could reduce the effort you expend and smooth the edges of your life.

It is powerful to allow the struggle that is in your life to be there because the most important lessons can often come from the most difficult situations. If you fight against them, they may come back at you with all the energy that you are expending pushing them away. Fighting something is an extraordinary waste of your precious energy. Embracing struggle doesn't mean loving it. Embracing struggle means opening your arms and saying simply, "Okay, here it is!" Leaning back and opening your arms to what is coming toward you is a female way of being.

Perhaps one day you notice that you have a toothache. It hurts a lot, but it goes away after an hour. "Ah, it's gone," you say with relief, and promptly forget all about it. The following week, however, the toothache comes back. This time it lasts for two hours before it goes away. Again you think, "Ah, it's gone," and forget about it. But the next week it comes back, and this time it lasts five hours. "Hmm," you think. "Perhaps this really is something serious. Maybe I should do something about it." But when the toothache goes away after five hours, you sigh with relief and forget about it again. Eventually, the toothache will get so painful and so long-lasting that you will no longer be able to ignore it. You will have to say to yourself, "I have a toothache and it's not going away." Finally, you have embraced the situation. At this point you are ready to make an appointment with your dentist so the situation can change today. In hindsight, you can see it would have been more self-loving to pay attention to your tooth at the first or second signal.

A powerful woman embraces life the way it shows up. The sooner you can embrace a situation, the less time and energy you will spend struggling against it. In Montessori schools, teachers watch for points where a child is struggling with a subject. Each child has a chart to monitor their progress. The teacher draws a circle around the point in a subject that causes the child to struggle. This is called a "learning spot." It is a place for extra learning to take place. Similarly, when we are struggling we are at a learning spot. It is an opportunity to learn something new about ourselves. If you look at your past, you will probably see that the most difficult times in your life were also the turning points. Any day that you took a risk was probably difficult, but you remember that day because it changed the course of your life.

Embracing a situation doesn't mean surrendering to it. It is not succumbing and giving in. It is simply a statement of fact: "Okay, here it is!" If you add, "And I want it to be different," you are acknowledging that you want change. This frees up your energy so you can use it for the natural, creative expression of yourself.

A powerful woman feels gratitude for her life, even if what she is experiencing is difficult or challenging. Allowing yourself to feel grate-

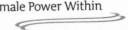

ful for what is in your life energizes the heart because it has you see life as a gift and all its offerings as precious.

Gratitude involves noticing, and noticing means being in the moment and really experiencing what is making your life what it is. Sometimes what is in the moment isn't pleasant, and it may be difficult to feel grateful for it. If your car breaks down on the freeway as you're commuting to work, it may be difficult to see that situation as a gift. But as you look back on it, you may see that you learned something from that situation, or that it was in some way a valuable part of your life experience. The person who stopped to help you might have been there not just to assist you with your car, but also to have you see that people want to help and that you sometimes have trouble taking in support. The breakdown may also have forced you to slow down that day and allowed some unexpected time into your life. The break in the routine of your hectic commute may have been a wake-up call for you to make a change in your life, or it may simply have given you an hour to read the newspaper as you waited for your car to be fixed.

It would be powerful to be able to feel gratitude for difficult situations not only in hindsight, but also in the present moment. This happened to Tess one morning as she was waiting in a long line at the airline ticket counter. Just as she reached the front of the line, it was announced that her flight had been delayed and that anyone on the next flight should go to the front of the line. Immediately, twenty people rushed in front of Tess waving their tickets. Tess felt the stress building in her chest and the urge to scream became almost intolerable. Something told her to take a few deep breaths, and as she did, her Natural Power practice inspired her. Suddenly she felt a deep sense of gratitude for simply being alive and having the opportunity to stand in line at the ticket counter. She was so relieved that she couldn't help laughing out loud. She waited another half hour in line with a smile, grateful for the hustle and bustle of life around her.

You will recall that when Nancy was waiting for the ferry in Bari, she was definitely not feeling grateful for the opportunity to sit quietly and observe real Italian life. However, as we suggested in chapter two, if she had changed her scorecard from "How much am I accomplishing?" to "Am I enjoying myself in the moment?" she would have opened up the possibility for gratitude. Instead of sitting on her bench fuming, she might have been able to appreciate the opportunity to experience another culture. Feeling grateful for that opportunity might even have had her smiling as she sat on the bench, and her smile might have attracted friendly exchanges from some of the Italian families waiting on the dock with her. Being in touch with gratitude might have brought her some new friends and a wonderful experience to remember the rest of her life.

Gratitude may not change what is happening, but it can change your experience of what is happening. Recognizing that difficult or challenging circumstances are here to help you learn can allow it to be a little easier. Embracing the hard parts allows room for gratitude, and gratitude allows you to enjoy your life more. Seeing life as a gift and its offerings as precious helps you use your power productively rather than use it up fighting against circumstances you can't control.

A Powerful Woman Is in the Flow of Life

A powerful woman is present with what is happening in her life because she knows that the only moment she can have power in is the present moment. Being in the present moment allows space for the feminine qualities of power. How can you be nurturing if you are worried about what just happened? How can you be tender if your mind is going over a recent upset? How can you be receiving what life has coming your way if worrying about the future is keeping you unavailable to what is happening in the present?

Worrying about the past and trying to control the future are disempowering for you because they use up your essential energy. Being in the flow of life means being able to tell yourself, "Everything I want is coming to me; it's just a matter of time." It allows you to be more available in the present moment. When you are in the flow, you can envision a positive future for yourself because you are in the perspective of the crown chakra that everything that is coming your way is ultimately for the good. Feeling a sense of yearning, then, no longer feels bad; it simply means that what you yearn for is on its way, and you can start making room for it physically, psychologically, and psychically.

A powerful woman sees the universe as abundant. Receiving what is coming your way and working with it is very female. Leaning back and opening your arms to what is coming toward you gives you a wider, gentler perspective than straining forward toward a goal. If you take the approach of leaning back and inviting life in, you will have an entirely different experience of attaining what you desire. It is female to examine your desires rather than to set arbitrary goals and march straight toward them. If you believe that the universe is abundant and that what you desire is out there, you can take a different view about how to attract it.

A powerful woman allows things to take the time they take. Think of something you desire—then ask yourself if that is really what is important to you. You may think you want something, but it may be that what is really important to you is something deeper. Stephanie may think that what she desires above all else is to move away from her small town and live somewhere more exciting. If she takes time to examine her desire, though, she may find that what she really wants is for something to change. Stephanie could start the process of change by doing a forgiveness retreat, going to a Natural Power weekend, or enrolling in a Gathering. Doing work on herself might allow her to see that she wants some shifts to happen. She might decide to make space to have children by cutting down to a four-day workweek, using the extra day to create a child's room in her house. She might start exploring ways to work from home or create her own business, and she might work on enhancing her relationship with her partner.

By examining her desires, Stephanie can come to learn something about herself and make a real change in how she is living her life. If she had instead focused only on attaining what she thought she desired, moving, she may have ended up keeping herself miserable by being unhappy with the small-town life. If she had acted on her desire and moved to a larger city, she may well have found that things weren't that different for her and that her innate dissatisfaction had not shifted, because she hadn't addressed the real source of her desire.

Identifying what is important to you takes time. If you are busy marching toward your goals, you may not have the time to lean back and contemplate your desires. By taking the time now to lean back and examine what it is you really desire, though, you may actually give yourself a gift of time. After all, isn't it a waste of time to march toward a goal that may not really be what you desire in the first place? Keeping your eyes on the carrot may get you the carrot, but if what you want is deeper satisfaction with your life, you will benefit more from contemplating what the carrot really means to you. As you examine it, you may find that what you want is not a carrot after all, but an apple, or the apple tree.

For example, perhaps your goal is to have a relationship. If you take time to examine the reasons you want a relationship, you may find that one of them is so you will feel good about yourself. To have a good relationship you need to love yourself more. Perhaps, then, what you also desire is a better relationship with yourself. If you know you desire this, you can put your time and attention into working on your relationship with yourself as part of moving yourself toward a relationship with someone else. You can drop your eyes from the carrot, take a deep breath, and focus on what you need to do *now.*

What you need to do now may mean focusing on healing the past so you can function more fully in the present, building your relationship with your little girl, and accessing the power in each of your chakras. Gradually, you might start eating healthier, getting enough sleep, and exercising. Because you have more energy, you have time to nurture your creativity. Maybe you sign up for a pottery class, something you've always wanted to do. You might enjoy your pottery class so much that you get there forty-five minutes early and go to the corner coffee shop to go over your notes from last week. There you might notice a man you've seen there before. He notices how you're glowing from the new relationship you're having with yourself. Eventually, you get to know each other and in your new confidence you have a different interaction than you've ever experienced. One day you realize that letting go of your goal to meet a man led you to improve the texture of your daily life, which led you to meet a man.

A powerful woman knows that the texture of her life is just as important as her achievements. Rather than straining forward toward a goal, she allows herself to lean back and open to what life is sending her way. It is not a passive receiving, but a dynamic receiving. She is there and present in the moment, working with and learning from it. It may not even be the big things in life that change its texture, but the little things that happen during the course of each day. Allowing a leaning-back view of the myriad of little things that happen can smooth the texture of daily life. Life is a buffet.

Imagine that you are driving around looking for a Spanish restaurant that you really want to try out, and you are growing more and more frustrated because you can't find it. It may be that you pass another restaurant that looks enticing, but you are so focused on finding the Spanish restaurant that you don't even see the one you just passed. What if you leaned back and said, "What is life sending me? There must be a reason I can't find the restaurant. Hmm, maybe I'll look around and see what else is in the area." You might find a wonderful place to eat that you never would have had the chance to experience otherwise.

Knowing that if everything you want is coming to you and it's just a matter of time leaves you free to appreciate what life is offering you right now. Because what you want sometimes arrives in a different form than you envisioned, it is important to be available to notice what is happening. Rather than straining forward and rushing toward something, having the life you want means leaning back and seeing what life is sending your way. Having a good relationship with yourself is central to all this. Believing that what you want is already out there and will come to you when you are ready frees you from chasing goals. It allows you to take time to enjoy your life as it is happening and to become active in your own growth.

A Powerful Woman Takes Care of Herself

A powerful woman is able to maintain a heartfelt, handholding relationship with herself while going through something that is challenging, confronting, difficult, or painful. She has compassion for herself when she is going through the hard part.

A powerful woman is resilient. She knows that rather than getting caught in her upsets, she can put her hand on her heart and ask, "What is good for me?" or she can put her hand on her throat and ask, "What is right for me?"

A powerful woman can stay in a space that is disturbing for her rather than reacting to it or running away from it. Beryl, a forty-two-year-old movement instructor, explains, "If a powerful woman does react, she catches it quickly. It is really strong to be able to back away from something and to be able to get some perspective on it." Beryl recalls a recent situation when her boyfriend disagreed with her about abortion, an issue that is very important to her. "I was strong enough to let him talk and have his opinions instead of blasting him with my arguments. And yet I had to also be strong enough to set boundaries with him, to let him know that harping on views he knew were disturbing for me was ultimately harmful for the relationship."

A powerful woman communicates her needs to others and sets boundaries that are healthy for her. Within the boundaries she sets, she allows herself to remain soft and tender because she knows there is strength in her tenderness. She recognizes the power in her ability to be compassionate, to forgive, to be grateful, to be generous, and to be moved and inspired.

A powerful woman is expressive in speaking her mind and is also available to listen fully to others. She doesn't always charge ahead trying to make things happen, because she has the ability to receive what is coming her way and make something beautiful out of it.

A powerful woman can give up needing to be in control. Heather, a single woman in her forties, used to be afraid that if she didn't appear to be in control of a situation, she would not be able to handle it. Gradually, as she did her own work, she realized that having to be in control kept her from expressing her female power. "If you can own who you are and own your feelings, giving up controlling behavior and allowing yourself to be vulnerable is actually being incredibly authentic," she says. "If you could hold it that way, it would be the highest way you could possibly be."

A powerful woman stands in the middle of her life and receives what is being sent to her. She is not wasting her precious energy struggling against what *is,* and she is not striving toward what she thinks ought to be. She knows that her power is in being awake and in the moment, and that practicing the Natural Power Work will bring her into the moment more often. She is allowing in what life sends and working it into her own tapestry, weaving the texture of her own life. She knows that having a handholding, heartfelt relationship with herself is what will allow her to express her female power.

A powerful woman is actively engaged in creating a life that is authentic for her. She has the courage to take ownership of her life with all its difficulties, its challenges, and the incredible opportunities it provides. She acknowledges her own strengths without ego and in a matter-of-fact way. She lives in a way that is authentic for her, and knows that in her authenticity lies her power.

More Qualities of Female Power

A powerful woman
accepts her humanity and the humanity of others.
A powerful woman
accepts herself.
A powerful woman
accesses her natural balance of female and male.
A powerful woman
allows herself to make mistakes.
A powerful woman
allows things to take the time they take.
A powerful woman
asks for support.
A powerful woman
bathes herself in womanliness.
A powerful woman
becomes in charge of what she thinks.
A powerful woman
blossoms in the company of others.
A powerful woman
can be disagreed with.
A powerful woman
can be uncomfortable and still do what is best.
A powerful woman
can give up needing to be in control.
A powerful woman
can separate people's psychology from their essences.
A powerful woman
can wait to express herself.
A powerful woman
communicates her needs to others and sets boundaries that are healthy for her.
A powerful woman
creates an environment of tenderness.
A powerful woman
does not clutter her life with drama.
A powerful woman
does not compare herself to others.
A powerful woman
does not have to speak.
A powerful woman
does not take things personally.
A powerful woman
embraces life the way it shows up.
A powerful woman
embraces the hard part.

A powerful woman
> empowers what is good for herself and others and ignores what
> is not.

A powerful woman
> encourages authenticity in herself and others.

A powerful woman
> enjoys cooking while she experiences being independent.

A powerful woman
> enjoys exploring.

A powerful woman
> enjoys her feelings and observes her thoughts.

A powerful woman
> enjoys her natural self-expression.

A powerful woman
> enjoys herself in the moment.

A powerful woman
> enjoys leaning back and receiving what comes her way.

A powerful woman
> enjoys others' successes.

A powerful woman
> enjoys the process while moving toward a desired outcome.

A powerful woman
> expects things to go well.

A powerful woman
> expects to go through trial and error while walking toward her
> desired future.

A powerful woman
> experiences softness and tenderness as strength.

A powerful woman
> expresses her needs and wishes in a way others can help her
> have what she wants.

A powerful woman
> feels gratitude for her life, even if what she is experiencing is
> difficult or challenging.

A powerful woman
> gives herself the benefit of the doubt.

A powerful woman
> gives others the benefit of the doubt while able to observe and
> take care of herself.

A powerful woman
> has a life of ease and grace.

A powerful woman
> has compassion for herself when going through an experience
> that is difficult, painful, challenging, or confronting.

A powerful woman
> has the ability to be in the company of most people
> comfortably.

A powerful woman
> interacts with her life, expecting it to turn out well.

A powerful woman
   is a fun playmate.
A powerful woman
   is a generous giver.
A powerful woman
   is a generous receiver.
A powerful woman
   is a natural healer.
A powerful woman
   is a peacemaker.
A powerful woman
   is able to be vulnerable instead of angry.
A powerful woman
   is able to be wrong.
A powerful woman
   is able to maintain a heartfelt, handholding relationship with
   herself.
A powerful woman
   is able to move away from situations and people who are not
   good for her.
A powerful woman
   is able to own her part in what happens in her life.
A powerful woman
   is actively engaged in creating a life that is authentic for her.
A powerful woman
   is awake, alive, and in the moment.
A powerful woman
   is aware of her strengths and talents and lives with them as a
   matter of fact.
A powerful woman
   is aware of when she is repeating an historical experience and
   uses it to heal her past.
A powerful woman
   is confident that life will continually offer learning experiences,
   and welcomes them.
A powerful woman
   is expressive in speaking her mind and is also available to listen
   fully to others.
A powerful woman
   is gentle with herself.
A powerful woman
   is gracious.
A powerful woman
   is grateful.
A powerful woman
   is in the flow of her life.
A powerful woman
   is living in the magnificence of her femaleness.
A powerful woman
   is many faceted.

A powerful woman
   is not stopped by her feelings when going toward what is
   authentic.

A powerful woman
   is open to be moved and inspired.

A powerful woman
   is present with what is happening in her life because she knows
   that the only moment she can have power in is the present
   moment.

A powerful woman
   is resilient.

A powerful woman
   is sensual and receptive.

A powerful woman
   is strong enough to be forgiving of herself.

A powerful woman
   is strong enough to be forgiving of others.

A powerful woman
   keeps knowing what is authentic for herself and supports others
   in knowing the same for themselves.

A powerful woman
   knows everything is coming to her—it's just a matter of time.

A powerful woman
   knows herself as an environment where certain things can
   occur and certain things cannot.

A powerful woman
   knows herself as magnificent.

A powerful woman
   knows herself as the higher self, always available to the little girl.

A powerful woman
   knows how far to let someone in and when.

A powerful woman
   knows how powerful her effect is.

A powerful woman
   knows how to enjoy and savor life's experiences.

A powerful woman
   knows how to keep her commitments and when to change
   them.

A powerful woman
   knows if you can do it once you can do it again.

A powerful woman
   knows just because she feels bad, it doesn't mean a bad thing is
   happening, and just because she feels good, it doesn't mean a
   good thing is happening.

A powerful woman
   knows she contributes by being herself.

A powerful woman
   knows she influences the world around her.

A powerful woman
   knows she is already as powerful as she will ever be.

A powerful woman
  knows she is complicated.
A powerful woman
  knows she is powerful when she empowers others.
A powerful woman
  knows she is responsible for creating her world.
A powerful woman
  knows she is the light and sees others as the light.
A powerful woman
  knows she is worth going through the hard part.
A powerful woman
  knows that it is powerful to be vulnerable.
A powerful woman
  knows that no one is like her and knows she is a unique
  contribution.
A powerful woman
  knows that she is powerful when she is tender, nurturing, and
  empowering.
A powerful woman
  knows that she makes a difference.
A powerful woman
  knows that tenderness is more powerful than defensiveness.
A powerful woman
  knows that the resources she needs are available to her.
A powerful woman
  knows that the texture of her life is just as important as her
  achievements.
A powerful woman
  knows the effect she has and has power modulating that effect
  for her benefit and the benefit of others.
A powerful woman
  knows the point of power is in the moment.
A powerful woman
  knows the power of tenderness.
A powerful woman
  knows there is abundance in the universe.
A powerful woman
  leads a considered life.
A powerful woman
  lets herself take time to discover an authentic solution.
A powerful woman
  lets people be with her vulnerability.
A powerful woman
  listens fully to others.
A powerful woman
  lives a luscious life.
A powerful woman
  loves herself.

A powerful woman
  notices when she is using her energy against herself.

A powerful woman
  opens her arms and embraces what is coming toward her.

A powerful woman
  owns her part.

A powerful woman
  receives what is coming her way gracefully.

A powerful woman
  revels in her creative energy.

A powerful woman
  says "no" when she means no.

A powerful woman
  says "yes" when she means yes.

A powerful woman
  sees anger as a defense rather than an offense.

A powerful woman
  sees herself as the light.

A powerful woman
  sees others as the light.

A powerful woman
  sees others' vulnerability as strength.

A powerful woman
  sees situations as opportunities for growth, healing, and stretching.

A powerful woman
  sees the universe as abundant.

A powerful woman
  separates herself from the influences of her past so she can be
  her true self.

A powerful woman
  stands in the middle of her life and receives what is being sent
  to her.

A powerful woman
  stays in the light of optimism through discouraging experiences.

A powerful woman
  steps into others' shoes to see what it is like for them without
  losing herself.

A powerful woman
  takes in compliments graciously.

A powerful woman
  uses all her experiences for her well-being.

A powerful woman
  uses her intuition well.

A powerful woman
  works to be peaceful.

A powerful woman
  works to fulfill her desires.

A powerful woman
  works with what is happening to get where she is going.

Uncoverings

Reread the list of qualities of Female Power, slowly this time. Consider each of the qualities one at a time. Please add to the list if you think of qualities. As you read, notice:

Which qualities you respond to

Which qualities you feel empowered by

Which qualities you know you are already practicing

Which qualities you know you want more of

Which qualities you find confusing

Which qualities you want but don't know where to begin

Which qualities you need to give more time, attention, and focus to

Pick a quality you want more of to focus on.

Envisioning What Is Coming Toward You

If the future is not a march toward goals, it can be a wonderful exploration of your desires and a productive use of what is already on its way toward you. Women are natural visionaries, and all we need to do is nurture our natural ability by paying attention to it. A wonderful way to make this envisioning of the future more concrete is to create a collage out of pictures and words from magazines, cards, or anything else that you feel called to include. Gather picture magazines, glue, scissors, and construction paper in colors that you like. Give yourself the chakra meditation. Bring your little girl into the room. Open your third eye.

Some people use lots of paper to make a large sheet, or a number of small sheets. See what seems right to you and find your way. As you make your collage, have the intention that it will help you manifest what you want in your future. Allow you, the higher self, to select pictures or words for your collage that you are drawn to. It may be something that you know your little girl would automatically reach for. Try not to analyze what you are selecting, but simply let it happen. Once your collage is finished, put it up on the wall.

Once every few weeks or every few months, take some time to look at your collage. Has anything on your collage manifested in your life? You may be pleasantly surprised, as many of our participants have been, to find that what you envisioned has actually manifested.

a powerful woman
creates an environment of tenderness.

a powerful woman
blossoms in the company of others.

13

Visions of the Future

Blossoming Womanhood

We are in the process of uncovering a new model for womanhood. The new model has each of us living a considered, authentic life—one that allows us to blossom into our own unique magnificence. As each of us comes into our own power we will change the face of womanhood. We will be able to function from a place of collective gentleness rather than from the collective noncommunication and fear that can come to a head in war.

The future of womanhood is not about gaining power, wielding power, or getting more power. The future of womanhood is about coming to the power that is already inside us, and letting it shine out into the world. This female way is exactly what is needed for a softer, more communicative, nurturing, and tender world in which each person matters. One woman at a time, we will transform the planet.

Laying the Groundwork

What do you want the future to look like for your daughter, granddaughter, niece, and great-niece?

Natasha, a forty-year-old project manager, has a vision of what she wants the future to look like for her daughter. "I want her to have a peaceful awareness of self, a wholeness, and a knowing that who she is and what she contributes is valuable. I want her to have the intention to create an environment that is conducive to self-expression and creativity. I don't want her to have to spend years lost in harmful relationships or looking for recognition from external sources. I want her to be free to have important thoughts, not spend her energy wondering why someone else got it and she didn't." Natasha sees that women can create a safe and peaceful environment by doing their own work and by working together, by being aware, and by not looking into someone else's life to see how hers should be.

Amber, a thirty-one-year-old professor, says, "As we come into our power, it is possible that men will return to being the main breadwinners—not because women can't do it, but because we would be better used in another way. Nurturing our children, helping others, and spreading the light of our unique talents may become our focus. If someone else is working to pay the bills, it frees us up to use our powerful female energy to save our hurting and needy planet."

Amber sees the fact that two incomes are needed today to support a household as no accident. "The need for a dual income today provides women with the experience of earning money," she explains. "We have to know that we are capable of being financially independent, so if we choose to have men support us it won't have anything to do with our experience of dependence or independence. We will know that at any moment we can earn a living if we need to, but we won't feel as if we must. We can be free to appreciate that our men are making a living for us, and men can be free to appreciate that we are feeding the hungry, nurturing the children, and negotiating between nations. Women will not have to barter their talents anymore because we will know we can take care of ourselves."

In her 1992 book, *Revolution from Within*, Gloria Steinem observes that we still think our success is a fluke. Because we don't have an historical model for female success in the world, we doubt our abilities, thinking that if it happened all over again we wouldn't be successful. But as we come into our own power, we will no longer doubt that we are each capable of great accomplishment. Our successful careers today will shape the future of what it is to be a woman because they will provide models for our daughters, granddaughters, nieces, and great-nieces. They will be able to look to our example to know what they are capable of, and they won't have to prove it all themselves one by one.

Uncoverings

What do I want the future to be like for women on the planet?

Choosing Your Future

Right now, you have your own future to form. As you come into your natural power, the way your future looks will shift. The future we all face is an intermediate future—a future in which women are still coming to understand our own power, doing the work to come into ourselves, and supporting each other. Once we have all blossomed into ourselves, possibilities open up for the longer term. Our work today is focused on moving our lives up out of the survival reaction in the anal chakra and out of the history in the solar plexus. We can then come from a place of making decisions from the empowering aspects of the anal and solar plexus chakras as well as from the sexual, heart, throat, psychic, and crown chakras. Living from a place of authenticity means being grounded in the anal chakra and experiencing your female power in the creative center of the sexual chakra. It means expressing your will and willingness in the solar plexus. Living authentically means knowing to ask the heart chakra, "What is good for me?" and the throat chakra, "What is right for me?" The third eye is where we can experience the future in a way that has us trust the unknown. When we can use the psychic chakra more fully, we will be able to psychically look at what is happening in our lives and make higher, more effective choices for ourselves. The crown chakra will have us look at the future as an experience of connection. We will be able to see what is the greatest good for everyone, and we will be able to help others experience joy, dance freely in life, and see themselves as the light.

Right now, what will work for the future is for each woman to be present in the present. The Natural Power Work is preparing you for that. Part of being in the present is acknowledging that you and others are in the process of manifesting female power, and that it doesn't look ideal yet. Being in the moment is the only place of power you have. Every moment that you are present creates the possibility for a future moment in which you are present—and that is powerful.

Collective Tenderness

There is a common theme to positive visions of the future, and that theme is the unspoken belief that moving toward a tender, enlightened future means that people will live in peaceful connectedness. Today in Western society most people are far from living that way. In fact, most of us are at the opposite end of the spectrum. Imagine a clock where the twelve at the top represents living a fully authentic life and the six at the bottom represents living a wholly material life. Our society is about at the seven—we have been living wholly material lives, but we are now beginning to explore our place in the world.

Imagine people living together cooperatively, honoring the Earth and each other as each develops her own unique talents. Alicia, a city professional, sees women having a community that supports them in choosing what's good for them. "Where I live, success is measured by the scorecards that ask which plastic surgeon you use, what kind of car you drive, where you eat out, where you live, and how many diamonds you wear," she says. "Success in the future can be measured by each individual's satisfaction, fulfillment, and creativity." Alicia also believes that in order for the world to work better, women need to allow men to be by their side. As women do their Natural Power Work, they will be able to allow men into their lives without feeling threatened by their power.

Georgia, a sixty-two-year-old healer, sees people interacting differently in the future. "People will be able to process in the moment," she says. "They will know that their upsets are not who they are and that they may feel awful in that moment, but there is a higher self they can tune into. If everyone is doing it, the environment will support it. We'll be interacting with each other, not with each other's history." Like Alicia's vision of the future, Georgia's is based on every woman doing her work. As each woman shifts, others around her will shift. Like a grassroots movement, the future is created one person at a time, perhaps not in a sweeping universal change.

"In the future, I see everyone being able to access the power of the chakras," says Julie, a thirty-two-year-old businesswoman. "If we could all access the incredible power we have, we wouldn't have to be afraid. If we all knew we were the light that moves through the chakras, we would be able to see people for who they really are instead of reacting to their defenses. Wouldn't it be incredible for everyone to see each other as the light of their essence? There's a lot of work to do in order for that to happen, and the work starts in the heart of each person."

Ancient civilizations have been more spiritually advanced than we are in that they were living their lives at one with their spirituality. In Bali, people still live in a way that is close to the twelve on the peaceful connectedness clock. They are moving down toward the material ways of the West, but they still live more communal, spiritually oriented, art-filled lives. They leave food outside their doors for spirits to stop and partake of as they pass, and when you enter a Balinese house you must turn many corners because evil spirits can only walk in a straight line.

In *The Kin of Ata Are Waiting for You,* Dorothy Bryant presents a vision of a female culture where dreams are more real than "real life." The people of Ata live together in total harmony on an island removed from the rest of the world. Their work, their art, and their relationships are created from their dreams. There is no such thing as material wealth or success, because the only aim of Atans is to dream higher dreams. The path to higher dreams is different for everyone, and every person must find their path on their own. They must work hard physically and eat lightly in order to prepare their bodies for their dreams. There is no written language, and their stories are passed down in the form of dances in which everyone participates.

A large gathering hut is surrounded by circular paths around which the other huts are placed. In the gathering hut, the Atans share stories of their dreams, dance, and eat. Because food is often scarce, they do not feed themselves, but everyone feeds others to ensure everyone gets enough. The Atans are in their huts only to sleep, and they sleep with their feet together and heads facing outward like spokes of a wheel. When they awake in the morning, they tell each other their dreams.

Atans are nonhierarchical and old age is respected. There is no government, because each person takes responsibility for his or her own actions. If someone does something violent or nasty, they won't dream good dreams, and the thought of this is punishment enough. If someone is going through something difficult, they retreat to a small dark hut that is like a Native American sweat lodge, and they stay there alone, asking for guidance from their dreams until they receive it.

The narrator, a lost soul who had a car accident in the real world and ended up in Ata, describes the life there: "Every act had become ritualized to serve the dramas of their dream life, which in turn dictated their waking life. The very plan of the village had occurred in a dream of someone long ago, no one could remember when. I pointed out... that everyone walked at least an extra mile getting to the la-ka [meeting hut] because of the circular paths, but he said that is how the dream said it should be done, and it would remain that way unless superseded by another very strong dream." Dreams are the highest law in Ata, where everyone is deeply attuned to the psychic and spiritual. The land of Ata is a manifestation of a society that is living at the twelve on the peaceful connectedness clock— one in which the feminine principle of "at-one-ment" and connectedness is lived and acted on as a matter of course.

As you come into your own power you can develop and enhance your vision of what the future can hold. As you play with your visions of the future you may want to read other women's futuristic visions to stimulate your ideas. Women have written their versions of the future in the form of essays, science fiction, and novels. When enough of us can envision a cooperative future, it will be able to happen.

Uncoverings

What is my vision of a cooperative future?
How would I participate?

The Gathering

Think of a time...
you received support and it made all the difference in the world to you.

If we are going to change the world one woman at a time, we will need support and acknowledgment. We can't do it alone, and our future lies in working together as a community. There is a lot of support out there for gaining male power, but how often do we acknowledge each other for owning our part, for being nurturing, for empowering someone else, for cooperating with someone, for communicating?

It will support change in yourself and in others for you to acknowledge when someone is being tender and powerfully female. If you see someone struggling with how to balance a career and children, what would it be like to say to her, "I'm so inspired by the fact that you are working on making considered choices in your life and I recognize that you are being powerful"? Or you might notice someone nurturing her friends and say to her, "My heart opens when I see that you are being powerful by encouraging and caring for others." Or at a business meeting you might see a woman make a contribution that is perhaps overlooked because of the subtlety of female power. What would it be like to say to her, "You made the difference in how the meeting turned out"? In our culture's way of being today, it is up to us to acknowledge each other.

Because coming into our power is a relatively new process, and because it is not necessarily supported by the culture, it can be very grounding and healing to have a support group. Women function best in cooperative units rather than trying to struggle through it alone. Left to ourselves, though, it is easy to create fears that have us avoid change. Finding others who are going through their own changes can help us see that moving toward being ourselves is not so impossible as it may seem when we are alone.

Some women of the baby boom generation have a complicated relationship with support because we went to support groups during the women's movement, but we went to be angry. We were not only angry at men, but also at other women. After a while, we began to feel that we should be able to do it all on our own, and that it was weak to ask for support. Asking for support now can make us feel we've failed somehow, but it is powerful to recognize that asking for support is a sign of strength.

We need each other as we go through the incredible transformation of becoming ourselves. Natural Power Work is not work that is done once and then it is finished. It is an ongoing, lifelong process of each woman coming into her own power. Having support in that process is the easiest way to ensure that it will continue, and that you can continue to grow and expand into yourself.

In our Natural Power Gatherings in New York we experience firsthand the power of supporting each other. Many of the women in the Gatherings have participated in the Natural Power of Being a Woman Workshop, and most of them have attended other workshops we offer as well. The Workshops allow women to see a new personal vision, and the weekly Gatherings support them as they shift their perspectives and therefore themselves.

The Natural Power Gatherings are designed to uplift women as they go through the everyday of life. Every Gathering has a meditation, a discussion topic that is designed to help women further their investigation, and a time for sharing. Women sit in a circle, which is female, and on the floor, which grounds us. There is one chair placed prominently at the edge of the circle, and this is what we call the Magnificence Chair. The chair is thronelike with ornate carved arms and plush cushions. At the end of the Gathering, everyone who wants to do so has a chance to sit in the Magnificence Chair to communicate about herself and receive the unconditional support of everyone in the room. It is her opportunity to be magnificent and to be listened to as magnificent. In the Magnificence Chair women share their small shifts, which are actually enormous because it is the small shifts that transform their lives. As the women move on in their lives they will have more and more opportunities to be magnificent in the world.

The tone of the Gatherings is empowering and safe. We have simple but firm rules that ensure confidentiality and help everyone's little girls to feel safe. The rules help the women in the Gatherings to support each other and give them the opportunity to enjoy cooperation and practice openhearted compassion. We hold the belief that if you've done it once you can do it again, and if you're near someone who has what you want, you are close to it yourself. Some women enter the Gatherings with a Cinderella view of a limited universe where there aren't enough men, jobs, apartments, or whatever they need. When they start seeing the power of women going through their processes, they begin to see that there is enough to go around and that the success of one woman actually opens more space for the success of another woman. There is no competition because we are all going toward becoming the best individual we can be, and there is infinite room for everyone to be their best. Women who gather together in this atmosphere can experience each other's essence and can see each other becoming the most they can be. The Gatherings are a vision of what the future of womanhood can look like when we are all engaged in our lives and supporting each other.

In the Gathering women are free to lean back and learn about how others stretch. They are free to see that there is no one way to do life. It may be that Myra figured it out one way and Rose figured the same thing out a different way entirely. In the Gathering they can watch and learn from each other's learning, and a cross-pollination occurs from this deep kind of sharing that speaks to the essence of each woman's experience and does not require storytelling. Watching someone else allows each woman to look at her own life in a slightly different light, rather than feeling she must emulate someone else's way of doing it.

The women in the Gathering can speak the best about the impact the Natural Power Work has on their lives. Most of the women

quoted here have been attending Gatherings for several years, and its importance in their lives is evident in all their testimonies. It is the ongoing support for their inner work that they receive in the Gatherings that allows them to continue the process of growth.

Rochelle, a forty-seven-year-old financial advisor, has been doing work on herself for twelve years, but until she came to Life Works she had never had the support she needed for deep change. "In other places they talk about support, but I truly experience support here for the first time in my life. I've been able to go places because I haven't had to go there by myself.... In this group, there is a way in which I'm allowed—and even expected—to be all that I am, and that is very good for me. I've made friends here that are lifetime friends, absolutely there for the long haul no matter what happens. There is a foundation I can depend on, whether I'm nice or not—an incredible acceptance. And that's not a small thing."

For Vanessa, a thirty-eight-year-old educator, the work she has done has allowed her to see her life from a different, healthier perspective. "In Jewish mysticism there's a concept that God contracted Himself in order to create the universe, but there is a corollary that God fills all the world. Supposedly you can't understand both things because they're inherently contradictory—but they're not, actually. And that's how I feel about this work. You have to be in your life to have your life, but you have to be able to pull back and see what you're doing." In the process of pulling back, Vanessa has discovered the value of having the support of other women. "It's so unbelievable to have a place where you can do it, and you can make the mistakes and talk about it. You can have it pointed out to you, and there's nothing like it. It's taken years to learn this, and I'm so incredibly grateful that I have faith in the process. I'm just grateful to have a place to come, because there's no other place like it."

Elle is a sixty-five-year-old professional musician, artist, and mother of three. She says that the consciousness-raising groups she's been working with for over twenty years were all helpful in certain ways, but that she would always end up leaving when the work got too deep. "When something really got me I'd be gone—but the point is to catch yourself at that moment. Now since I've been doing this work, I've somehow found the courage to be with my feelings. I've been able to be objective and observe myself having them, and this allows me to have a richer, happier life."

Fortuna, an artist and healer of forty-two, has found the work deeply helpful in her relationship with her family and in partic-

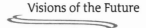

ular with her two nieces. "I used to have the belief that I had to change everyone, or I would die. I believed there was something wrong with me if I couldn't get my family members to behave. With this work comes the ability to lean back and let them be whatever they have to be, and go through whatever they have to go through. Also, I've learned that there's nothing wrong with me, which is big for me because I used to tell myself the story that if something went wrong, it was because I was the problem." As a healer, Fortuna has incorporated her own Natural Power Work into the work she does with her clients. It has given her a language to use with them that isn't clinical or technical, but tender and human. "It's very powerful," she concludes.

Annette, a twenty-nine-year-old teacher, finds that the work has helped her in her professional life too. "I use the work very successfully at school. I have a lot more compassion for the students, and I find I don't have to be arrogant because I know things they don't know. It's changed everything at school. It used to be that there was a group of students that loved me, and the rest hated me and saw me as a real ego-cracker. Now it's so much softer."

Women supporting women is powerful. "I never knew that I could have women as best friends," says Beth, a thirty-five-year-old movie executive. Growing up in the South, she experienced the jealousy and competition that ruled so many female relationships. Being in the Gathering has changed her perception about female relationships. "I'm looking around now and realizing that women *are* my best friends. They're important to me in ways that were never safe for me before."

Forming support groups for ourselves is a key to coming into our power and moving into the future differently. When we can really be there for each other, each doing our own work of discovering ourselves, emerging from being trapped in our own sculptures, then we can begin to change the future of womanhood. When we can really root for each other, acknowledge each other, and see when we are being tender, we can change the texture of what it is to be powerful in our culture.

Uncoverings

What are my experiences working with women?

What is my experience of women working in groups cooperatively?

What needs to be healed for me to work with groups of women cooperatively (if there is healing needed)?

Acknowledge female manifestations of power in others and in yourself.

See You in Our Dreams

Doing the work of coming to your female power has you at the front of the line with all of us who face the exhilarating unknown without a road map. Not knowing exactly where the work will take us is thrilling when we allow ourselves the female posture of leaning back and trusting that we are going in a direction that will be good for us.

You are already transforming your life because you are giving yourself the gift of discovering your authenticity, and being your authentic self allows your expression to shine in the world.

When you are living authentically, you can make a difference in a multitude of ways—including forgiving someone who needs forgiveness, empowering someone to do something she didn't believe she could do, expressing your creativity, changing your magnetism, owning your part, and having a loving, heartfelt relationship with yourself. Isn't it wonderful to know that you can make a difference simply by having your heart be open, by being tender with someone, by listening well, or by doing something that comes easily and naturally to you?

Some people will make a difference in a way that looks obvious to us, by being a political leader or a social activist. Others will make their contribution in a quieter way—by being a nurturing and loving mother, by volunteering at the local library, by meditating every day, or by creating beautiful artwork. Everything we do that is a true and positive expression of our selves has an effect on those around us, and they will affect those around them, so that our contributions ripple outward into the larger context of the world. As each of us comes into our own power, we begin to have an effect that can spread beyond our own particular world. Then, perhaps, some of us will join together and help people in other places have tenderness, communication, and cooperation. In this way female energy can spread over the whole planet.

It is our sincere intention that our offering will inspire further thought and the creation of more tools for women's development. We hope that it will spark more women to look at what is true for us and what works for us as we come into our rightful place of power, self-expression, heartfelt gratitude, openness, and good feeling about how fortunate we are to be standing at this moment in history with enormous possibility opening before us.

Revealing the full magnificence of women's power is something that happens on two dynamic levels. As we become authentic and come into our *own* power, we contribute to a fuller manifestation of female power. As each of us does the work to uncover her power, we will discover more about the nature of female power—and this discovery will add to the tender, compassionate, openhearted vibration of being female on the planet. It is exciting to know that each reader, and therefore this book, contributes to our transformation.

When we are awake and aware in each moment, we can trust that in each moment we will make a decision that will be authentic for us. The more we can make authentic decisions, the more we can express ourselves magnificently. As we each release our completed sculptures from their stone prisons of history, identities, and defenses, we will share with the world the unique, fully expressed, authentic, tender female light of our powerful selves. As each of us releases our light, we will illuminate the world.

Closing Meditation

Merger Poem

And then all that has divided us will merge
And then compassion will be wedded to power
And then softness will come to a world that is harsh and unkind
And then both men and women will be gentle
And then both men and women will be strong
And then no person will be subject to another's will
And then all will be rich and free and varied
And then the greed of some will give way to the needs of many
And then all will share equally in the Earth's abundance
And then all will care for the sick and the weak and the old
And then all will nourish the young
And then all will live in harmony with each other and the Earth
And then everywhere will be called Eden once again

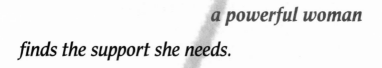

a powerful woman

finds the support she needs.

a powerful woman

is grateful.

Afterword

Our experience of being women has gone through enormous transformation in a relatively short amount of time. If the changes sometimes left us feeling confused and uncertain, imagine how the men around us must have felt as they watched us and interacted with us. Men have changed in response to our changes, yet their process may still be in the beginning stages. They still may have to go through a transformation of their own, and we do not know what their metamorphosis will be like.

As we come into our fully realized, authentic selves, we open up space for men to come into themselves in whatever way they need to. We are already on our path to fullness, and we thank the men who are supporting us as we make our journey. As our female power emerges more fully, we can be ever more available to return that support as men take the further steps on their path. We cannot know what their path holds, only that we will give them the space to grow into themselves as we have begun to do.

Now that we have let go of the anger we no longer need, we can open our hearts to men. Our female nature allows us to be optimistic, trusting that they will find their way and that they too can blossom into the best version of themselves they can be. We can let go of any preconceived notions we have about how men should be, just as we let go of our own history, identities, and defenses that held us back from being fully ourselves. Having been through our own process, we can have infinite compassion, forgiveness, tenderness, and generosity as men proceed on their own exciting journey.

We wish them well and look forward to the adventure.

Starting Your Own Gathering

Part of the Life Works mission is to help women have the incredible experience of being in a Gathering no matter where they live. The Gatherings are highly specific events, with a well-trained leader and emphasis on safety and confidentiality. We are developing a distilled training program for women interested in leading Gatherings. If you feel that leading a Gathering is authentic work for you and are interested in starting Gatherings in your area, please contact the Life Works office.

We will also be happy to help you find someone in your area who is trained in the Female Power Work and may have a Gathering you can join. Please contact us at:

Life Works, Inc.
55 Fifth Avenue—Penthouse
New York, NY 10003
212-741-8787 or toll-free at 877-741-8787
fax 212-741-9242
www.lifeworksgroup.com

Acknowledgments

We gratefully thank

Swami Satchidananda who first tapped us on the shoulder with his teaching, "The rose is itself and the bee comes."

To our husbands, the late Vishnu Lee Jayson, Bill Speers, and Tod DiCecco for their loving and patient help and support.

The Life Works Guidesses in New York: Barbara Blair, Debra Cox, Carole Forman, Lisa Gilpin, Paula Kramer Weiss, Sue Krevlin, Sara Lustigman, Sylvia Moss, Miriam Nelson-Gillett, Anne Prather, Nancy Schreiber, Gloria Waldman-Schwartz, Peg Warren, and Marion Yuen. And those in Dallas: Susan Lockard, Chris Shull-Caldara, and Carolyn Greco.

The women who have contributed their wisdom to this endeavor: Patti Accarino, Liz Bard, Emily Baerga, Savitri Bess, Christine Casati, Mercedes Sackett, Debbie Goldstein, Penny Dragonetti, Cathy Ellich-Owen, Linda Ercole-Musso, Robin Felberbaum, Beth Greer, Judy Hoy, Arlene Kaplan, Elizabeth Law, Joanne Levitan, Gisela Mandl, Cheryl Marks, Carol Maryan, Linda Mello, Jeanne Moore, Cathy Petter, Barbara Pettijohn, Nell Robinson, Carol Tarshis, Annie Lincoln Tilden, Susan Vancil, Susan Wallace, Patricia Walsh-Haluska, Susan Walsh, Melissa Weisstuch, Liz Wolfe, Ruth Anne Wolfe, and Marsha Wolkoff.

Supporters Beth Weiner, Joseph Russo, Kenneth Robins, and Gilbert Hemsley.

Heartfelt thanks to the team who helped birth this book: the wise Paul Kelly, our book midwife Caroline Pincus, our word nurse Naomi Lucks, the clarifying proofreaders Nancy Newlin, Jeff Braucher, and Tom O'Leary, the faithful, accurate, and lovely Mary Lee Kellerman, designmeisters John Buse and Jason Gray, Ellen Kleiner for unfailingly good advice and moral support.

To all the guides and teachers who have asked the questions and provided the wisdom that makes this work possible.

Finally, to our parents Frances and Maxwell Graman, Michael and Rosemary Walsh, and Catherine Todd and Walter Erston who taught us it was possible to be powerful women before we knew what those words meant.

Additional Reading and Viewing

Following is a list of books, movies, and Web sites you can use to expand and stimulate your exploration of female power.

Books

Angelo, Bonnie, *First Mothers: The Women Who Shaped the Presidents*. New York: HarperCollins, 2000.

Baker, Christina Looper, and Christina Baker Kline, *The Conversation Begins: Mothers and Daughters Talk About Living Feminism*. New York: Bantam Books, 1996.
> Personal and enlightening mother-daughter sharing about how feminism has affected their lives.

Bess, Savitri L., *The Path of the Mother: Female Versions of God*. New York: Ballantine Wellspring, 2000.
> A six-stage journey to union with the Great Mother. Bess's journey from aloneness to love contains spiritual practices for every day.

Bolen, Jean Shinoda, *Goddesses in Everywoman: A New Psychology of Women*. San Francisco: Harper and Row, 1984.

Bryant, Dorothy, *The Kin of Ata Are Waiting For You*. New York: Moon Books/Random House, 1971.
> Vision of a female society in which people live for and through their dreams.

Dass, Ram, *The Only Dance There Is*. Garden City, NY: Anchor Press, 1974.
> Based on a series of talks by the inspirational guru, this book is a useful guide for understanding the nature of consciousness.

Freeman, Jo, ed. *Women: A Feminist Perspective*. Mountain View, CA: Mayfield Publishing Co., 1995.
> Comprised of essays by feminists and feminist scholars, this book provides a good overview of feminist issues and history.

Friedan, Betty, *The Feminine Mystique*. New York: W. W. Norton and Co., 1963. *The book that started a revolution!*

Friedan, Betty, *Life So Far*. New York: Simon and Schuster, 2000.
> Friedan's autobiography contains new insights into the feminist movement and her personal life.

Lenz, Elinor, and Barbara Myerhoff, *The Feminization of America: How Women's Values Are Changing Our Public and Private Lives*. Los Angeles: Jeremy P. Tarcher, Inc., 1985.

An interesting look at how women had begun to change the male culture of the mid-1980s.

Steinem, Gloria, *Revolution From Within: A Book of Self-Esteem*. Boston: Little, Brown & Company, 1992.

Steinem's personal investigation into self-worth is woven together with research and case studies.

Films

In some of the work we do we use films to inspire and illuminate. These films provide experiences of the female dilemma, female power, and the process of change. If you have any films to add to this list, please email us with your suggestions to be reviewed for future editions.

Antonia's Line	*First Wives' Club*
Baby Boom	*The Kid*
Chocolat	*Norma Rae*
The Contender	*Ruby in Paradise*
Dangerous Beauty	*Places in the Heart*
Enchanted April	*Steel Magnolias*
Erin Brockovitch	*Welcome to the Dollhouse*
Ever After	*Working Girl*

Web Sites

www.lifeworksgroup.com

www.femina.com — Provides women with a comprehensive, searchable directory of links to female-friendly sites and information on the World Wide Web.

www.DistinguishedWomen.com — Biographies of women through history, quotes.

www.ldresources.com/etext/quotes/women.txt — 2000 quotes by women

www.refdesk.com/factquote.html — Quotes

www.leadershipforwomen.com — The concept of the glass ceiling originated in 1991 when the Glass Ceiling Commission was formed as part of the American Civil Rights Act of 1991. It was used to describe the "artificial, subtle, and invisible barriers that operate to prevent women and minorities from being promoted to executive posts."

Your are invited to spend a weekend with us

The Female Power Within
Weekend Workshop

Currently offered regularly in New York City the Workshop is an intense and experiential investigation into our natural, female power and is the inspiration of ***The Female Power Within—A Guide to Living a Gentler, More Meaningful Life***.

The Weekend will focus on what is between us and the highest natural expression of ourselves. In the weekend we will discover:

> *The value of contacting our authentic female power*
> *When we lost our sense of deserving, our sense of value*
> *How we chronically conceal our power*
> *How we use our power for ourselves and against ourselves*
> *Where we learned our style of expressing our power*

Through these discoveries, we reveal how to authentically express our power, how to use it for our own well-being and the well-being of others. Results reported by women who have completed the Weekend are:

> *Finding right work that is a natural expression of who they are*
> *Increased authentic self-expression*
> *New ease in relationships*
> *Experiencing more ease and pleasure in everyday life*
> *Learning how to quiet the mind*
> *How to find the resources needed within themselves*
> *Feeling more in control*
> *Having opportunities and openings come toward them*
> *Happier with themselves and more contentment with their lives*

Graduates report increased ease and satisfaction in many areas of their lives as a result of this work. The course is open to women of all ages and levels of experience. We'll begin on Saturday and be together from 10am to 9pm. Sunday hours are 9am to 6pm. There is homework to be contemplated, gathered, and researched before the Weekend. Participation is limited. Call Life Works at 877-741-8787 for schedules and further information.